ADVANCE PRAISE FOR
FINDING HAPPY

"Peter Samuelson is one of those rare living angels who rove the earth, who never forget to treat every human being with respect, who always try to help make others better beings and better off, and daily, constantly innovating to fight suffering. Peter's profession is as a film producer, but he is also a formidable social entrepreneur. He created the Starlight Foundation to grant special wishes to terminally ill children, and the Starbright Foundation to use entertainment and technology to advance the needs of terminally ill children. Among his other innovations, most recently he conceived EDAR ('Everyone Deserves a Roof') which is a mobile mini-bed/home for the homeless. At night it turns into a bed, and during the day it allows them to keep and transport their possessions."

—**Daniel Lubetzky**, founder, OneVoice, Kind Bars

"A remarkable story! Lessons to be learned by both young and old that should be required reading for Americans ages fourteen to twenty-two as a practical and workable philosophy for life. 'A chapter a day makes fear and ignorance go away!'"

—**Judge Charles Gill**, Connecticut Superior Court, leading advocate for children's rights

"Most self-help books merely tell readers how to achieve their goals. But in *Finding Happy*, Peter Samuelson illustrates how to go about weathering the challenges of that quest by recounting the circuitous paths he personally took. This inspiring book is a must for everyone about to embark on that journey."

—**Alan Zweibel**, original *SNL* writer, playwright, screenwriter, Thurber Prize–winning author of *The Other Shulman*

"Peter Samuelson made some great films, but that isn't nearly as important as the five innovative and effective charities he invented. They serve seriously ill children, teenage patients cut off from friends and family, foster kids, the homeless, and college students who need narrative film-making skills to create good in the world. He is the rare leader not in pursuit of money, but saving young lives."

—**Morton H. Meyerson**, computer services pioneer at Electronic Data Systems, Perot Systems, and General Motors

"Peter has fulfilled his purpose for being on this earth by dedicating his life to improving outcomes for seriously ill children and bringing smiles to their faces. Full of wisdom, life learnings, and moments of pure joy, this book will bring tears to your eyes and a smile to your face as you accompany him through his story, learn how you can make the world a better place, and develop your own purpose."

—**Dawn Wilcox**, vice president, Children's Hospital Los Angeles, board member, Starlight Children's Foundation

"A master storyteller, Peter Samuelson engages our sense of wonder and awe while finding humor in life's journey. His is a world of limitless potential and jaw-dropping adventures, where anything is possible—it's a magic carpet ride behind the scenes of the entertainment industry through the eyes of a young, British-American David coming of age in an entrenched world of Goliaths. Peter's optimism, hard work, and ingenuity often delivers what seems impossible. Intended as mentorship for young adults, this is a truly fun and inspirational read for everyone. It touched the part of me that longs for adventure and success. It gives us all practical tools to manifest something wonderful waiting just around the corner!"

—**Sheryl Stamps Leach**, creator of Barney the Purple Dinosaur, philanthropist

"Peter's journey should be an inspiration to anyone seeking to help make the world a better place for others."

—**John Rosenberg**, chairman, Starlight Children's Foundation USA

"Peter Samuelson has worked tirelessly over forty years to make the world a better place for youngsters, whether seriously ill or abused and neglected. Peter masterfully weaves together stories from his life as a filmmaker and philanthropist to share the blueprint of how to create a meaningful life that is full of purpose. While written as a guidebook for young adults without a mentor, it is a fantastic read for anyone. Peter's stories are entertaining and, at times, poignant. Peter has helped millions of children have a brighter future through his work with the Starlight Children's Foundation and First Star charities. This book has the potential of helping millions more find the path to success and happiness."

—**Dr. Brandon Lane Phillips**, Starlight Wish Child, later board member, and now MD in pediatric cardiology

"Peter is suggesting clues to finding meaning in all our lives through his extensive work with foster youth, continually trying to give them practical hope. Along the way, he curates wisdom from his own 'hero's journey' into this heartening collection."

—**Mark Goulston, MD**, author of *Just Listen: Discover the Secret to Getting Through to Absolutely Anyone*

"Peter Samuelson weaves essential life lessons throughout this series of hair-raising stories from his remarkable life as a movie maker, entrepreneur, and inspired philanthropist. In these endeavors, he perseveres against incredible, often hilarious, odds and emerges from every trial and tribulation more determined than before and asking, what next? It is a fun, funny, thought-provoking, meaningful, and moving read that will inspire readers toward greater good for themselves and the world (to Samuelson's point, they are the same thing!). Upon finishing the book, one cannot help but ask: What more can I be doing to reach my goals and to make a contribution? What am I afraid of? Samuelson has a wonderful way of convincing the reader that if he can do it, so can they. His guidance through example is a potential life-changer for young people. Luckily, it is also a fantastically entertaining read!"

—**Shari Goldstein, PhD**, clinical psychologist

"My exposure to Peter is multi-dimensional, in person and now through his wonderful book. If you are not fortunate enough to know him firsthand, the book captures his extraordinarily giving essence. You will be a better person for the experience of reading it. Peter's book is an amazing primer!"

—**Fred Klein**, founder of Gotham City Networking, counsel to Tarter, Krinsky & Drogin LLP, a New York multi-dimensional law firm

FINDING HAPPY

A USER'S GUIDE TO YOUR LIFE, WITH LESSONS FROM MINE

PETER SAMUELSON

A REGALO PRESS BOOK

Finding Happy:
A User's Guide to Your Life, with Lessons from Mine
© 2025 by Peter Samuelson
All Rights Reserved

ISBN: 979-8-88845-871-6
ISBN (eBook): 979-8-88845-872-3

Cover design by Conroy Accord
Interior design and composition by Greg Johnson, Textbook Perfect

PUBLISHING TEAM
Founder and Publisher: Gretchen Young
Editorial Assistant: Caitlyn Limbaugh
Managing Editor: Madeline Sturgeon
Production Manager: Kate Harris
Production Editor: Rachel Paul

As part of the mission of Regalo Press, a donation is being made to charities founded by the author.

Some names have been changed.

This book, as well as any other Regalo Press publications, may be purchased in bulk quantities at a special discounted rate. Contact orders@regalopress.com for more information.

No part of this book may be reproduced, stored in a retrieval system, or transmitted by any means without the written permission of the author and publisher.

Regalo Press
New York • Nashville
regalopress.com

Published in the United States of America
1 2 3 4 5 6 7 8 9 10

*For every young person who shared
their secrets and dreams with me,
and those who asked for help.
I see you.*

For Saryl

*Thank you for making my life a pleasure
and a privilege.*

Contents

Prologue 1

Chapter 1: Why This Book? You and These Times 3

Chapter 2: How to Read This Book: Takeaways and Reflection Questions 8

Chapter 3: Why Tell Your Story with Empathy: The Girl Who Froze 13

Chapter 4: What Is the Meaning of Life? Part One. 17

Chapter 5: What I Learned from My Dad. 22

Chapter 6: What Is Luck? Early Days. 26

Chapter 7: When Can Apologizing Be a Life Hack?. 29

Chapter 8: Why Do Bullies Bully? What Can You Do About It? 32

Chapter 9: How Do You Find Your Mentor? Mr. Lund, Who Lifted My Self-Expectations 35

Chapter 10: What Is Love For, Actually? And Where Can You Find It? 41

Chapter 11: First Love, Eloping, and the Telegram 46

Chapter 12: Get Your Foot in the Door, and Then Don't Blow it. *Le Mans* 51

Chapter 13: What Is University For? Cambridge 62

Chapter 14: When Should You Take Risks? How to Survive Your Risk-Taking Years 72

Chapter 15: How Can You Dare to Do? Marrakech to Monte Carlo. 79

Chapter 16: How Can You Seize the Day? *The Return of the Pink Panther*. 88

Chapter 17: Travel as Education. Filming in the Philippines 98

Chapter 18: Value Your Own American Dream. Coming to Hollywood. 104

Chapter 19: Is Citizenship a Responsibility as Well as a Right? 108

Chapter 20: Stand Up for Your Rights. Children Are Not Property 112

Chapter 21: Which American Lives Are Most Different from Yours?
Thank You, Navajo Nation 116

Chapter 22: Should You Pursue a Long Shot? Crazy Luck: *A Man, a Woman, and a Bank* . . 124

Chapter 23: Is Failure a Matter of Opinion? What Is Success? Revenge of This Nerd 131

Chapter 24: What Is an Entrepreneur? What Is Leadership? Starlight 135

Chapter 25: What Are Your Priorities? Why? The Robin Hood Effect 143

Chapter 26: What Is Genius? Hello, Mr. Spielberg 148

Chapter 27: What Is Leadership? What General Schwarzkopf Taught Me 153

Chapter 28: How Can You Use Technology, and Not Let It Use You?
GPT-4, AI, VR, EIEIO, LOL 157

Chapter 29: How Do You Craft a New Solution to an Old Problem? First Star 163

Chapter 30: What Will Be Your Cause? Welcome to the Circus, Kids!. 173

Chapter 31: What Is the Answer to Everything, at Least in Producing Films? 178

Chapter 32: How Can You Be in the Arena? *Arlington Road* 182

Chapter 33: Why Stick Up for Each Other? Oscar Wilde and Me. 188

Chapter 34: When Should You Give Up, When Not? What If You Can't? *The Gathering* . . . 194

Chapter 35: How Can You Get Arrested without Being Killed?. 203

Chapter 36: What Does Eccentric Mean? Is It Good, Bad, or Neither? 215

Chapter 37: What Must You Do When People You Love Lose Their Compass? 222

Chapter 38: How to Leverage to Achieve Your Goals. ASPIRE and the Medici 228

Chapter 39: Why Don't Human Beings Think Ahead? Lessons of Hurricane Katrina. 232

Chapter 40: When Is Perfection the Enemy of the Good?
EDAR and the Old Lady in a Box 238

Chapter 41: How to Empower a Team? First, Stay Away from Helicopters. *Stormbreaker*. . 246

Chapter 42: When Is Impossible, Not? Surviving a Producer's Crisis 251

Chapter 43: What Makes a Good Friend? How Can We Choose Them Wisely?. 255

Chapter 44: How Can You Live Your Passion? *Foster Boy*: Carpe Diem 265

Chapter 45: How Can You Extrovert Yourself? Public Speaking:
Stand-up, with Fewer Jokes 273

Chapter 46: How Can You Fight Tribalism in Your Own Heart?. 278

Chapter 47: Are Humans Lost? A Story: Aliens, Viruses, and Planet Earth. 282

Chapter 48: How Can We Walk in the Shoes of Others? First, Take Off the Mask 288

Chapter 49: Why Care about Democracy? Why Should We All Fight for It? 293

Chapter 50: How Can You Make a Difference? The Meaning of Life, Part Two 300

Chapter 51: How Can You Bend the Arc of History? How Can You Contribute? 306

Chapter 52: What Will Be Your Place in the Universe? The Meaning of Life, Part Three . . . 310

Acknowledgments 313

About the Author 317

Prologue

There will never be anything in your life as fulfilling as making a difference in somebody else's. Everybody here wants to see you take your integrity, your curiosity, your creativity, your guts, and this newfound education of yours and use it to make a difference. Everybody always thinks you got to go do something big and grand. I'll tell you where you start. You start by being good to at least one other person, every single day. Just start there. That's how you begin to change the world.

—**Oprah Winfrey**, Tennessee State University, 2023

Man is eminently a storyteller. His search for a purpose, a cause, an ideal, a mission and the like is largely a search for a plot and a pattern in the development of his life story—a story that is basically without meaning or pattern.

—**Eric Hoffer**

It's like everyone tells a story about themselves inside their own head. Always. All the time. That story makes you what you are. We build ourselves out of that story.

—**Patrick Rothfuss**, *The Name of the Wind*

With First Star students on the roof of the Capitol Records Building in Hollywood.

Where is that elusive key to the Meaning of Life? It's not under the mat. All of us spend our whole life dealing with our inner child, who, like it or not, is still a work in progress. You are not alone. I can't see you, but I feel you.

I'm the kid who was first in his family to college, on a Cambridge academic scholarship. The immigrant who came to America alone. The career producer of twenty-seven films, who started decades ago making coffee for the crew. The founder and entrepreneur of five major charities that have raised well over $1 billion for those less fortunate, in four countries over forty years.

A really happy guy who can explain how he got here.

The career producer who got the star who refused to work to get back out of his trailer. A storyteller with a good memory for mad events and crazy people. The man who hid machine guns under his bed in Marrakech.

The guy who nearly died rescuing a kitten.

CHAPTER 1

Why This Book? You and These Times

I realize that I know some stuff. Perhaps a lot of stuff. I've got many things wrong, many things right, and I've learned from all of them. It seems to me that one of the challenges of being a young adult is that you simply don't know as many helpful life skills until you grow older. But sometimes by then, it's too late to use those skills. So the intergenerational hand-me-down ought to be that those who have lived more life should share whatever they have picked up along the way with the younger people they care about, so that they don't have to make the same mistakes.

This applies for sure to every young adult, but especially those with no parents, or with dysfunctional parents carrying so much abuse of their own. Or mentally ill, or drug-addicted parents, unavailable or ill-equipped, whose advice may be wrong or at least unhelpful. Nobody is a lost cause; but what if you need help immediately, or a second opinion? What about teenagers who have been removed from their parents and placed in foster homes with strangers? If you have perfect mentoring in your life, then you may not need this book. Or it might be icing on the cake. You can live a long and happy life by taking onboard helpful experiences and lessons from your parents, grandparents, uncles, aunts, teachers, professors, coaches—from those with insights and wisdom in the art and the science of life. If you have them, do ask!

The most viral video I have ever produced happened on a whim. There is an extraordinary British polymath, raconteur, actor, writer, philosopher, and all-around high-IQ genius named Stephen Fry. I got to know him well when we made the film *Wilde* together, where he starred as Oscar Wilde, opposite Jude Law and Vanessa Redgrave. Several years ago, when Stephen was living in a rented house above Hollywood, we had lunch, and I asked if I could interview him on video. He said yes. My daughter Pamela set up a camera on a tripod, and I proceeded to ask him only one question: "What do you know now, Stephen, that you wish you knew when you were eighteen?" Then I just sat back and Stephen talked for thirty minutes. I then broke down his very smart and often funny replies into six five-minute videos. I put them up on the internet and forgot about them, only to realize much later that millions of people had watched them, downloaded them, learned from them, and made them part of their knowledge base. And I even got fan mail! https://vimeo.com/11414505

This book is my attempt to share the benefit of some rather extraordinary experiences in show business and in life. I am not as smart as Stephen Fry, but I've definitely had some huge adventures, and I'm foolhardy enough to share the ones where I completely screwed up, as well as those where I occasionally had a victory to enjoy. I would love to hear from you: peter@mentorproject.org. If there are dozens, I'll answer each one. If hundreds, I'll read every one. If thousands, I promise to do my best.

These Times

Feng Menglong wrote in 1627, "Better to be a dog in times of tranquility than a human in times of chaos," and there is also the old curse, "May you live in interesting times." You, dear reader, will have noticed and reacted to recent changes for the worse in the world around you. Let us call these external circumstances Macro: You had to cope with the disruptions of COVID. You see climate change destroying the predictability of weather systems and creating more storms and extreme

Why This Book? You and These Times

temperatures. You see autocracy, the top-down form of authoritarian government, trying to push back on personal freedoms, and the truth of science and the scientific process under attack. You hear those in power talking about expelling people who have lived here for years and sometimes decades. You are probably worried about the effect on you of all these things. When you read your online news, you see wars where young people are sent off to kill each other on behalf of their countries. When you apply critical thinking to what is going on, you may well be upset, frightened, and wondering what it means for your future.

There are many aspects of the Macro for all of us that are potentially bad, but the first thing to realize is that these Macro outcomes are far from being certain to affect your life. For example, things said in the heat of battle during an election period, the fighting words, very often do not come to pass. It is much more difficult to implement massive and threatening changes than it is to yell them as a politician trying to get elected. Politicians try to give out easy solutions, and targets for their loathing and hatred, because blaming a group feels more comfortable than being scared or confused. But for those scorned and criticized, these frightening concepts suggest an uncertain future. Remember that these people's bark is frequently worse than their bite. Cruelty, discrimination, and othering are going on, but your personal future is far from bleak, even amid these Macro disturbances. The dread and fear you may feel while half asleep as you begin your day or end it in bed do not seem so disturbing awake, walking around and going about your business.

Reinhold Niebuhr wrote a really smart prayer: "Give me grace to accept with serenity the things I cannot change, the courage to change the things I can, and the wisdom to know the difference." I sincerely hope you do your level best to improve the world around you. That instinct should certainly be a core part of your life and happiness. The purpose of this book is to help you chart your path to finding happiness, fulfillment, tranquility, and success for yourself and those of your friends and family who travel through life with you.

Our system of government has many checks and balances. The executive branch has to persuade Congress to go along with anything

FINDING HAPPY

that requires a budget. The president and Congress can face opposition in our court system, which has shown itself in this decade to often win verdicts against those government actions opposed to the best interests of our country. That is one large reason why we have a judiciary!

If you work really hard to read the press outside the rabbit hole of your social media, you will see that there is a vibrant, brave effort to push back on untruths by applying research and the megaphone of publication. It is important that you don't just read the work of journalists with whom you already agree. Read those from the other side of the fence as well, then take your own view. Talk to your friends, talk to your mentors, and do not let anyone tell you what is right. Carefully form your own opinion.

You need mentors. We all do! A mentor is someone with more life experience than you who helps you find your best personal path. The other function of a mentor is to share their views with you, the views of someone you respect, so that you can bear them in mind, informing your own opinion. If you do not have a mentor, this book aims to help you find one.

When the world around looks bleak, go Micro. You have a limited ability, but some for sure, to influence the Macro world, but you are the author of the rest of your life, of your Micro path, and that is where this book will help you focus. Think about threatened changes in your Macro environment in terms of how they may affect you. You can use the techniques in this book to run an analysis of the likelihood of changes affecting your personal life and the lives of those you care about. You can think about steps you can take to prepare for the worst, while yet keeping an optimistic view of what may well turn out to have no effect at all on you.

Remember that our country and our world have faced much worse and yet survived! Life as we value it carries on through great adversity, and so does our democracy. We must engage and be part of the town square of opinion, while pushing back on aspects that are wrong, inhumane, cruel, opposed to scientific process, and untruthful. But please live your life as a cup half full rather than half empty! This will not only feel better, but is most productive as you chart your path to do well by doing good.

Why This Book? You and These Times

You may have grown up with more than your share of hard knocks in your younger life. From that come many things, some positive and some negative. One large positive is that you have had to be resilient to reach this point. That same resilience will allow you to plan ahead, to play the chess game of life many moves in advance, and to make the best of all your circumstances. Dare to dream, take both the baby steps and those that lead to your best long-term destination. Study, learn, volunteer, be a good friend, stand up to bullies, exert kindness, earn your academic qualifications, build your life and career. Build your family, and pass on your best thoughts to the next generation. My goal, as your author, mentor, and friend, is to help you make something splendid of your future, and through that to achieve real happiness.

CHAPTER 2

How to Read This Book:
Takeaways and Reflection Questions

You don't need to start on page one and read the whole book. Use the Table of Contents and read what you find helpful or interesting. This book is not homework. You can dip into it by keeping it on the table next to your bed. Or next to your toilet.

We all have challenges that are our priorities. I've tried to shine light by using as examples the relevant snippets of my history that I found scary, hilarious, frustrating, or just plain confusing. At the end of each chapter, I have suggested *"Chapter Takeaways and Reflection Questions for You"*—some possible directions to think into, where you can seek to apply anything you learned from the chapter. If you happen to write down your thoughts, I'd love to read them: your response, your action plan. Go for it! It's always easier to understand things when you write them down.

I am sometimes asked, during the Q&A after I lecture, how best to establish a personal path. What are the first steps? I tell my students that you won't know what direction to walk unless you first look on the horizon for a destination. There is great merit in reverse engineering individual solutions to individual problems. First, think about the goals and purposes of the arc of your *whole life*. I hope you will live a fulfilled, happy, satisfied, worthwhile, and contributing hundred years, during which you are part of the life force, united with other intelligent souls around you, who love you and show you their unconditional love, just as you show it to them. To get there, first decide on your goal or goals. Make a list! It is fine to change your mind later.

Who do you want to be in five years, in fifteen, in twenty-five?

When I periodically have felt overwhelmed, I have found it helpful to break down the challenges into bite-sized chunks. I use a piece of paper and a pen. I create a thing called a spider graph. It is based on a radar graph, which is usually a way to chart statistics "in the round," like a radar scan. I use it to get my head around challenges: Whom do I need to deal with to solve them? How does the big challenge break down into less scary steps? I cartoon my face in the middle, and then I draw a first line that radiates out in any direction to something that bothers me, a challenge. I then shoot out two or more lines from that challenge to its parts. I move around the paper with lines arcing out from the face in the middle, like a family tree of challenges in the round...until I have in front of me a map of everything going on that needs sorting out. That needs a plan. Immediately, it is much less scary.

I stare at it. I let the ideas, concepts, and challenges run around my head several times, in the few minutes before I fall asleep and after I wake up. In that time, our subconscious is more to the front of our thinking. It is possible to free-associate and come up with solutions that were always there, but our conscious self couldn't see. As I come up with a plan of attack for each of the spokes on my wheel in its outer area, I add the bullet points of those steps; and finally, outside the whole circular wheel, I write down the short-term, medium-term, and long-term goal for each spoke.

If you do this, you may well find, like me, that it is incredibly helpful to see your life laid out before you on a piece of paper. Sometimes, you can see the ground easier when you go up to thirty-five thousand feet, rather than being down there among the weeds, where you can only see what is closest to your face. Try it. Does it work for you?

Date it. And do keep it safe. It is amazing to look at an old one and realize how well you did in addressing most of the challenges, and how others just fell away, all by themselves. As I look back on plans I drew decades ago, I see that some were spot on, others dead wrong. But the spider graph was helpful even if my initial path turned out to be wrong. The fact that I had a plan made me move forward one step at a time. Taking action in a thoughtful way was the key. When the plan didn't work, by moving forward one step at a time, something better developed. Having the plan in front of me was important.... I did not just blow around in the wind.

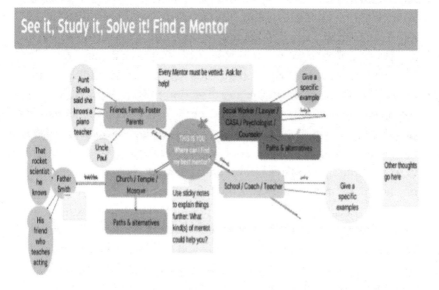

Chapter headings in this book frame the questions addressed by the chapter that follows: the Who, What, When, Why, and How of what we look into. Being organized is one of our greatest gifts to ourselves, and an important key to a less stressful, more productive life. Stressed students do their homework on the bus on the way to hand it in. Calm students did it several days ago.

It is not relevant that looking at a spider graph helps *me* to lay out problems and solutions. What counts is the best way for *your* *brain* to see the path forward. Ask yourself what method works best for you—let's say in a class, or in learning from a book? Do you find yourself copying the whiteboard into your notebook or computer? Or does it help you to say it out loud in private, pretending you are teaching it yourself? Or do you learn best from discussing it with a trusted person, with a friend perhaps? Does it help you understand if you write out bullet points, or a whole script on the issues? What if you pretend you are a famous influencer and are laying out the subject on TikTok or Instagram? Not everyone can be well organized, but we can all improve. And I've seen the spider graph work often and well for those who often hide behind complaining, "I just can't get organized." You can and you will. Try it!

I don't know if we each have one life, or if we have many. If we come back, I'm unsure whether it will be as an insect, a plant, an animal, or a human being. So, I suggest it is prudent to make the most of the life we each definitely have right now. This one. You are the author of your life story...and you should write it to maximize your happiness and make the most of it!

I've discovered that the solution to happiness is not money, although having some is certainly helpful. Happiness instead has a great deal to do with three things: creating what matters, helping other people, and being smart about using this glorious life. Happiness lies in creating as much good for ourselves and others as we possibly can. It is the best recipe for the cake of a life. And you can't just ignore an ingredient because you don't have it in the fridge. And if you don't have the missing ingredient, ask yourself how and where to go and get it.

It is a strange thing that what we care about when we're young is not necessarily what we look back and feel was most important when we are older. So, in sharing some things that have happened to me, both good and bad, I'm trying to answer the question I posed to Stephen Fry: "What do you know now that you wish you knew when you were eighteen?"

FINDING HAPPY

Peter with an EDAR, the single-user homeless shelter on wheels.

CHAPTER 3

Why Tell Your Story with Empathy: The Girl Who Froze

In First Star, the charity I founded, we operate eighteen Academies in partnership with big universities across the United States and the United Kingdom. We house, educate, and encourage high-school-aged foster youth in grades nine through twelve at the universities, with the goal of encouraging as many of them as possible onwards to a university education when they graduate from our Academies.

So it was that I found myself at UCLA, where we have a terrific partnership and run a vibrant Academy. I sat in the Northwest Campus Auditorium, in the audience with perhaps two hundred other adults. We watched the First Star student talent show unfold. One by one, our Scholars came down onto the stage and sang, danced, or performed their spoken-word poem. A wondrous opportunity for self-expression.

It was all going well until a tenth grader I'll call Catalina came down onto the stage to sing her song. Up came the playback music. But Catalina stood there, frozen like a deer in the headlights, unable to get the first note out of her mouth. And now, even worse, the music had left her behind. We were all horrified. She was clearly embarrassed. I could feel

13

FINDING HAPPY

the director of the Academy getting ready to go down onto the stage to usher her off. I thought to myself, what we have accidentally done here is incredibly bad. Her self-esteem was already burdened with PTSD from abuse and neglect. We were making progress in taking a shy young lady and giving her back her voice, her agency. And now we had inadvertently crushed her. We had made things much worse.

And then an amazing, shocking, magnificent thing came to pass. A young man in her cohort of thirty students, the size of a linebacker, came down onto the stage and planted himself with his back to the audience, completely blocking our view of Catalina. There was some whispering that we couldn't make out. And suddenly there were two other students, girls from her cohort, also in the whispering session; and then there were eight and then fifteen and then twenty, and then the entire cohort of thirty students were in a scrum on the stage. Completely hiding Catalina.

We held our breath. A hand on the outside of the scrum, palm up, made an upwards gesture, to say, "Start the music." As the music began again, out of the middle of this little group of fifteen-year-old foster kids came Catalina's voice, at first faint and hesitant, but with growing strength as the song went on. By the end of it, she sounded like Beyoncé on a good day. The audience went nuts. We stood up, we applauded, and there were a lot of tears. On the stage, when Catalina finished, the students came down with their arms around each other. It was epic.

I was so moved that I had to go for a little walk. I thought to myself, *We didn't do this. It's magnificent because the kids did it themselves. They have made a family, and family is unconditional love.*

On that stage, something wonderful took place. Our First Star program created the environment for these young adults to each find family, community, and encouragement, to give Catalina back her voice, and to pick her back up when she fell. Her peers exerted the power of family, and in that, the greatest value of our First Star program; I was proud and I was emotional. The real deal. I hope you feel it too.

Why Tell Your Story with Empathy: The Girl Who Froze

Recent offers to First Star graduates from twelfth grade.

Chapter Takeaways and Reflection Questions for You

- Everyone needs unconditional love to thrive. If someone loves us, we can soar.
- Who loves you unconditionally? Whom do you love unconditionally?
- If the answer to either is "nobody," think about a goal to correct that vacuum. How might it be possible? Use a spider graph to break it down into parts.
- After you make your spider graph, date it. Ponder it, keep it somewhere safe. Try the bathroom mirror or inside your phone case.
- The core evil of child abuse and neglect is that they kill the love every child needs. That we all need.
- Family and love are where you find them. You don't have to be born there.
- We all need someone to love, someone who loves us, and we need to laugh.
- Receiving and giving one random act of kindness every day is incredibly helpful.

FINDING HAPPY

- When we tell a story, like the story of Catalina, we can move the hearts of our audience. We can bond with them and create empathy, find our common humanity. And in that space, we can accomplish great things. Emotional understanding makes change.
- Apply this to yourself, now. What are your thoughts? Write them down.

CHAPTER 4

What Is the Meaning of Life? Part One

I apologize in advance for the possibility you will find this maudlin or overblown. But isn't one of the defining features of an alert life to look back, to look forward, and to ask, "*What is this all for?*" I have, and I continue to do so.

In our First Star Academies on university campuses for high-school-aged foster youth across the US and the UK, I designed a two-class empathy curriculum. Other than film-making, it is the only class I feel qualified to teach. "Random Acts of Kindness and Pay It Forwards" is for our Scholars, foster kids aged fourteen to eighteen—youth and young adults to whom life has dealt a raw deal. This course encourages emotion often, and deeply. I tell our Scholars—street-hardened though most are, through abuse and neglect—that it is OK for men to cry, and that from time to time they should allow life to give them the excuse. I teach them that giving is the highest and noblest instinct of a human being—that it lifts us up, and that beyond anything else, it makes the world revolve every day. It is counter-intuitive to the Scholars at first, that they should consider being generous, when they themselves are so deprived. But by the end it creates magic in their hearts, and they love it. See what you think.

first star
putting students first

I start by asking the class why, if Darwin was right, and if the world is a ruthless jungle where only the fittest survive, would anyone ever be kind? Why ever would a person passing a homeless man or woman sleeping on the sidewalk quietly slip a five-dollar bill under their arm? Why do we feel moved to help those less fortunate, often anonymously and with zero personal benefit? We go on to define and discuss the Golden Rule, the sense of equity, of balance, of social and personal justice, that exists in the scriptures of every single religion of the 170 in the world. And we ask, "But is it only religious?" and we parse the Second Law of Thermodynamics, which tells us that in any closed system—whether it is an engine, a garden, a family, a city, or a planet—if energy is not applied, entropy drives the system, over time, to random chaos: the engine seizes up if you don't oil it, the garden grows full of weeds, the family implodes, the city is overrun with crime, and life on the planet dies out.

Generosity, I discover, is not initially intuitive for every fourteen-year-old foster youth. If any human is raped, beaten, starved, and ignored, their thoughts understandably do not automatically go to "How can I help others around me?" But the instinct is invariably still there, and in the second class, we go from theory to practice, as the students compete to help others. It gets to the point where nobody can do anything for themselves.... It becomes a funny, happy, shared, humane experience in communal self-support. These young adults are my heroes.

We tell each student that one of our donors, my friend Mort in Texas, has anonymously put up some money, and thus each of them now has

What Is the Meaning of Life? Part One

the ability to give away $200. There are rules: you can't give it to yourself; A cannot give it to B and then B gives it back to A. That would be cheating. It is supervised, tight, and the ethics are clear. We start with a written proposal by each student. Many are remarkable explorations of what really matters in a life. Jimmy wrote, "I am adding ten dollars of my own, because that makes $210. It takes $70 at the humane shelter to stop them killing a stray dog. So I can save three dogs. Because the last time I was there, I looked into the eyes of a puppy that had been badly beaten and I saw my own eyes, because I was badly beaten too."

And our stubborn, wonderful Karl wrote, "I'm giving $200 to this Academy, because after I was expelled, I was given a second chance and let back in, and nobody ever gave me a second chance before that." And we said no, that Karl had personal benefit from his proposal. It did not meet the rules. And so he rewrote it and said, "The rules will not allow me to give the $200 to the UCLA First Star Academy. So I am giving it to the First Star Rowan University Academy." And we sent the check to New Jersey, and the sixty students there each wrote Karl a thank-you note. And by the way, Karl became our male class president, and his ambition after earning his bachelor's degree was to become an officer in the Marines, and teach Kinesiology and Athletic Conditioning. Karl's mom has been in a coma since she gave birth to him seventeen years ago. That is why he went into foster care.

We had a Christmas party on Westwood Boulevard in a swanky, donated restaurant. Afterwards, our fifty teenage Scholars, their Youth Coaches, and the rest of us stood on the sidewalk and waited for the vans (we always seem to wait for the vans) to return the students to their placements. The head waiter came out and asked me, "What do you want us to do with all the cupcakes left over?" And I said, "Put them in boxes and give them to the kids to take home." And he did.

Five minutes later, out of the corner of my eye, I saw Sam, one of our most troubled students, walking away from the group. I was getting ready to act: Was he running away? But all on his own, he walked up to a homeless woman, prone and fast asleep a hundred yards away on the sidewalk. He put his muffin box under her arm without waking her up. He walked back to our group, and never said a word to anyone. I was so overcome by emotion that I had to take another little walk of my own.

FINDING HAPPY

And that, my dears, is the closest I can get to telling you The Meaning of Life. And if not every life, then for sure mine. You raise your kids, by a miracle they turn out fine despite all your mistakes, you love your wife and friends, you do random acts of kindness, and then you die. That's the best deal we can get, and it's pretty wonderful.

There! Now you know the secret too. Pass it on!

Family is where you find it!

Chapter Takeaways and Reflection Questions for You

- Do you agree or disagree on the Meaning of Life? Why?
- What is the meaning of *your* life? (Clue: Fine to be still seeking it.)
- Do you make a place and a time in your life to think about really big issues like these?
- Have you tried generosity and kindness, to do good, and to feel good about yourself and your place in the Universe?
- Is there someone, or some people, in your life so far with whom you feel a real bond? Some magic?
- What have you done together?
- Do you volunteer?

What Is the Meaning of Life? Part One

- What is God, and how do you touch Their face?
- If you want to achieve much of anything, you have to first tell your story, to create empathy so that people want to help you. That is what I just tried to do for you. Did you feel it?
- How will you tell your own story, concisely, compellingly, movingly, with your goal in mind?
- Practice, practice, practice. I'll help!

CHAPTER 5

What I Learned from My Dad

My father died in December 2022, exactly a week after his ninety-seventh birthday. Perhaps he hung on until then because he liked milestones, especially birthdays. His passing was overwhelmingly sad, and yet it was a celebration of his long life. In writing his eulogy, I tried to explain the enormous values he taught me:

I have been my Dad's son for 71 years. For 71 years, I've had the benefit of the world's best father, coach, mentor, encourager, a man who saw one of his primary tasks as helping his three sons, and then his grandchildren and great grandchildren to be the very best that they could be. A man who showed me the high value of a good marriage, a love affair of 76 years. A man whose every waking moment was an example to me, of everything that is good, high achieving, and humane. My father who showed me what a man should be.

My father understood poverty, because he had experienced it. He left school on his 14th birthday, not through any lack of intelligence, but because quite simply, his mom, my grandmother, Marjorie, Grandma Sammy, needed his pay packet every Friday

What I Learned from My Dad

to help feed four hungry teenagers. My Dad did a lion's share of raising his two younger brothers, Michael and Tony. And as he made a wildly successful career for himself, he never forgot how difficult life frequently is for those less fortunate.

My father had, and we still have, what must be one of the largest Rolodexes in the world. This thing has the strength of an industrial machine. It is silver and almost the size of the wheel on a car. It contains 1000s of index cards. From long before anyone dreamed up computers, my Dad had a system to keep track of pretty much everyone he ever met. But the really remarkable thing about Sydney Samuelson is what he did with that Rolodex. You see, my father believed strongly that he was put on earth to help other people. The British film industry has 1000s, literally 1000s of people in it, who he gave their first break, that free loan of equipment, that helped them start a career. The introduction that led to a job. My Dad believed that if he could help anyone to get a foothold in an industry that is frequently insular, hierarchical and nepotistic then he jolly well should do that. And he always did. But it went beyond the industry.

My Dad talked to everyone. His favorite thing was sitting on a bus or the London Tube and striking up a conversation. So that by the time his stop was reached, he already knew where the person had grown up, everything about their parents, their siblings, what they did for a living, what their dreams and hopes were. And in every single case, if my Dad thought he could be helpful, he would give them his card. They would get in touch, and he would do his level best to lift them up. I remember once getting on the Tube train at Golders Green with my father to go into town. It was crowded. He sat on one side and I sat opposite. I watched in amazement, as he struck up a conversation with the random lady sitting next to him, which became quite animated. When we got off the London Tube eight stops later, my father handed me a business card, and said "Here, take this. That lady is the executive director of a grant-making charity. I told her you would be in touch about First Star and looked after children." I was in touch. From that 15 minutes on a Tube train grew a set of meetings and a collaboration.

FINDING HAPPY

I believe that all humans have two lives. We have the one with a beginning, a middle, and unfortunately, an end. But then we have the potential of a second, equally real life which consists of our effect in lifting up those around us and making their lives better. And the brilliant thing about that second life is that, as they then forge careers, families and friendships and achieve things, we go with them. We are in them. And that knock-on effect, the passing of the baton, is like ripples on a pond, ever widening. And so it is that my father is in the life and the spirit of every person here today. He is part of us. He inspires us. We carry his flag, we lift his torch. And by following his example of exerting ourselves to leave the world better than when we found it, we do as he did for 97 years, we rise above the mundane and the mortal, we soar and touch the face of God. My life is ripples on my Dad's pond.

Sir Sydney Samuelson,
7 December 1925–14 December 2022

Chapter Takeaways and Reflection Questions for You

- If you don't have someone you can look up to in your family, where can you find a coach, a mentor, a reliable grown-up to help you?
- How do you persuade someone to help you? (Clue: First, make sure they are safe to be around. Are they properly vetted? Then, be brave. Tell them your story and try to move their heart.)
- What types of help do you ask for easily?
- What types of help are harder to ask for, and why?
- Are you persuasive?
- Do you have any fears or concerns about asking someone to help you?
- Where is the line between sensible risk, and dangerous risk?
- How can we think through the Law of Unintended Consequences (Google it!) before we risk our lives, our happiness, and our safety?
- What is your best future, and how can you experiment and explore it before you make a commitment? (Clue: College or university: limited risk, guaranteed housing, many paths to try!)

Opening of new First Star University of Utah Academy.

CHAPTER 6

What Is Luck? Early Days

I should never have existed. The fact that my parents met, married, and that I was born must constitute one of the greatest flukes, and I suppose I literally owe it my life.

In 1946, my father was a sergeant in the Royal Air Force, stationed at the RAF airfield in Stanmore, Middlesex, north of London. In early December, his friend Bernard Lewis said to him, "What are you doing for your twenty-first birthday on December 7?" My father said, "I don't know. I guess I'll be here at the RAF station." Bernard said, "No, no, no. You get on your bicycle and you come and meet me. I've joined a youth group in Wembley; there's a film show of *Pride and Prejudice*, and we should go. There will be women. And it's your birthday."

When they got there, the rickety 16mm projector was set up on one table on top of another table, pointing over the heads of the audience at a sheet hanging on the wall. The lady who would become my mother, then Doris Magen, age eighteen, was making the sandwiches. Halfway through the film, the celluloid got bunched up in the projector, and the film melted and broke. My father, who had trained before the war as an assistant projectionist, climbed up on the table to fix the projector. Somewhere in the audience, Doris raised her eyebrow, thinking that

What Is Luck? Early Days

he was not only a handsome young man in a uniform, but also pretty handy mechanically.

They arranged to meet again, and then again, and those dates went well. And then for the third date, they arranged to meet at Baker Street Tube Station. My father thought they agreed to meet outside the Left Luggage Office. Vivacious young Doris was quite sure they agreed to meet outside the Lost Property Office...a completely different place. And there, separately, they each stood for the better part of an hour before giving up and going home, never having found each other, and both really angry. When Sydney called, Doris refused to speak to him.

Some days later, an acquaintance of my late grandmother, Doris's mother Ann, mentioned to her over a cup of tea that she had seen that handsome young Air Force man who was dating Doris pacing around, frustrated, outside the Left Luggage Office at Baker Street Station. Doris phoned him, they each apologized for thinking the worst of the other...and the rest is history. They were married in 1948, and I came along in 1951. Ponder that for a moment...without successful apologies, there would have been no me! (Our next chapter suggests the value of a forthright apology in converting those angry or critical of you into allies. A life hack, indeed.)

What are the odds against that fluke in a London station? The acquaintance had to have a cup of tea with my grandmother. She had to be able to recognize Sydney. She had to have been in the Tube station when he was there, and to walk past him. She had to mention it to my grandmother. For the whole of my life, since it dawned on me how very long the odds were, I've thought that my being born was a complete fluke. It would be presumptuous to say that it was meant to be. I prefer to think that I benefited from the most extraordinary long odds, hundreds of thousands to one against, but nevertheless, here I am.

What can we learn from this shockingly unlikely stroke of luck? We cannot make luck, but we can try to be in the arena where it might happen. You can't get lucky in finding a job unless you apply for it! And make the most of luck when lightning strikes. Keep an open mind. If Doris found enough good in Sydney to date him twice, why did she immediately assume he did a bad thing and refuse to speak to him? Give people the benefit of the doubt. Don't jump to conclusions. I was

FINDING HAPPY

once angry someone didn't turn up for a meeting, and then found out his child was in the hospital after a car crash that morning.

Chapter Takeaways and Reflection Questions for You

- Nobody can use magic to make luck, but how do we create the best chance for luck?
- Is it being in the right place at the right time, enough times?
- Have you been really angry with someone, who then turned out to not have done what made you angry?
- How can we keep our minds open and not jump to conclusions?
- How can we give others the benefit of the doubt?
- Apologies are free. Why is it so difficult for us to say, "I'm very sorry?"
- Why are second chances important? How do they work?

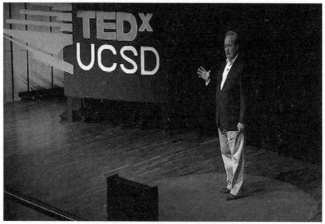

TEDx. I spoke at two. Both scared the heck out of me, but sometimes you Just. Do. It.

CHAPTER 7

When Can Apologizing Be a Life Hack?

It takes many years to realize that the uncomfortable act of apologizing can actually be an incredibly powerful tool to improve a situation. There is an art and a science to successful apologies. None of us really want to apologize, because we are humbled, we feel small when we admit out loud to somebody else that we did wrong and behaved poorly, that we should have done better! None of us want to hang out a banner saying, "I screwed up." But if we think medium term and long term, there can be wonderful benefits from taking responsibility for something we have done, and saying it out loud.

Think it through: By apologizing, you almost completely remove the other person's ability to blame you more. It is often a really smart move. In fact, if you apologize carefully, you can encourage the other person into *helping* you on the path forward in ways that are personally useful to you, as well as strengthening the relationship. And there may be benefits from the rebuilt relationship going forward. I would not exist if my parents had not apologized to each other for an epic misunderstanding. So, what is a good apology? Or rather, first, what is a bad apology?

FINDING HAPPY

A bad apology, a failed apology, is usually a half-hearted one, a self-praising one, a defensive one. The first great rule is to phrase your apology in the way that will completely sell the idea persuasively to the other person. Don't say it weakly. Don't say, "This is unfortunate." Say, "I'm sorry for what I did." Don't say, "I want to apologize." Start just by saying openly, "I apologize." Take responsibility: "I got this wrong, and I'm so sorry." Don't make excuses in the apology. You may know that you did what you did for some rather good reasons, but those don't belong in your apology. Don't say, "I wasn't feeling well," or, "I had great stress in my life." Nor "I was having a bad day." And don't blame the other person. Just say, forthrightly, "I apologize." And say that it will not happen again, if you possibly can achieve that. Amazingly powerful. Now the conversation can go your way! Apologies are most effective when they are brief, and there is less to argue with.

After receiving an apology, almost every human soul changes sides and will help you move forward. The adversary simply cannot continue to bang away with criticism. You cut the legs off that criticism by acknowledging that you did wrong. In the rules of life and by the rules of human interaction, they invariably have to join *your* team in moving forward in a productive way. And the rare one who does not accept the apology condemns themselves.

In the Bible, in other scriptures, in great works of philosophy, and in common sense, the theory of redemption involves more than the apology that begins the process. People who apologize have to make good—they have to do their best to perform good deeds, to lift up the life force and the nature of the relationship in positive directions. In my life, I have handled apologies both well and badly. I look back on my behavior, especially as a young man, and realize that I often had a kind of unhelpful self-righteousness that made apologies challenging. A strong personality, the force of will, was very helpful in driving me forward and keeping me afloat through the choppy waters I successfully navigated, one entrepreneurial process after another. But sometimes that robust ego, though an overall major asset, has also stopped me from seeing the world through the eyes of those around me. In middle age, I realized more that pausing, listening, deducing what others were thinking—and replaying the tape through their voices, and not

When Can Apologizing Be a Life Hack?

just mine—was incredibly helpful in charting my own path forward as a team leader. There is a concept called servant leadership that is taught in business schools. It involves active listening, understanding, and harnessing those whom one leads to become a part of leadership itself. In reality, being an effective leader is being first among equals, the specialist whose own specialty *is* leadership. And, helpfully, this is fully compatible with making those who are led feel proud to be team members: though they may not be the quarterback or team captain, the team feels like *their* team, and they are proud to wear its shirt.

When you have a conflict with someone else, think carefully, medium term and long term, whether a forthright apology will move you on from the problem, diminish it greatly, or make it go away completely. Will it allow you to address things more productively? It is often your choice as well as your responsibility to fix a relationship by apologizing. It can be your greatest friend, and that is why it is a life hack.

Chapter Takeaways and Reflection Questions for You

- Which three relationships are most challenging for you at this moment?
- For each of them, thinking medium term and long term, how can you make them much better? Spider graph perhaps?
- Are those relationships important enough to work further and try to make them good? (Clue: Some relationships are just awful, and the best thing can be to move on without them. Walking away is a choice, and it can sometimes be the best.)
- What are the principal rules for an effective apology?
- Address challenges one at a time...the easiest one first.
- Learn lessons from that and your subsequent experiences in fixing relationships.
- You have the technology: think hard, apply critical thinking, and use it. Good luck!

CHAPTER 8

Why Do Bullies Bully?
What Can You Do About It?

My first experience of being bullied was the summer before my sixteenth birthday. I interviewed for, and got a job at, Religious Films. They were making a series of short films at Bushey Studios north of London, each with a moral message designed to encourage people to live good Christian lives. Religious Films was owned by J. Arthur Rank, who believed that film could not only entertain but also persuade. Unfortunately, his crew at Bushey Studios must not have taken those scripts to heart.

In 1966, Britain still followed the apprenticeship system, which had grown up to handle entry-level employment in medieval times in the various guilds: the tanners, the iron workers, the engineers, the architects, and the rest. And so in the film industry there was also a very strict hierarchy, enforced by custom and practice, as well as by the unions. You started off making tea and saying, "Yes, sir!" to those more senior, which was everyone else who asked you for a cup of tea. You ran and never walked. You did everything that was asked of you. There was widespread cruelty, bullying where every level of the hierarchy considered it their right and duty to bully those who were more junior. No, it's not only a British thing. It goes on at almost every school in the world. Especially boarding schools.

On one occasion, someone shouted at me to go and fetch something across the studio stage. I went to run off, only to fall flat on my face, twisting my ankle. While I had been standing there on the wooden floor, one of the grips had crawled up behind me and put a nail through the welt of my shoe so that it was firmly rooted to the floor. It's a miracle I was not more badly hurt. As I took off my shoe and got up off the floor, I looked around and realized that the entire crew were laughing at me as I limped away to follow the order.

On another occasion, I was told to get a bucket and fill it up from a spigot on the far wall of the stage. I ran over, put the bucket under the tap, turned it on, and received a tremendous torrent of water all over my head. Someone thought it was incredibly funny to block up the bottom of the tap and drill a hole at forty-five degrees in its upper surface, so that turning on the water would drench the person facing it. Again, I looked around and realized the crew around me thought this was the funniest thing they had ever seen. Welcome to apprenticeship 1966 in the United Kingdom.

I gritted my teeth, did my job, and eventually someone even more junior than I was hired. I never bullied him even though I could have. By age fifteen, I already thought bullying was bullshit.

Bullying is done by insecure people to feel better about themselves. What I did not know at the time is that if you stand up to a bully, they almost always will back off. If you cower from them, they go from strength to strength and get worse. There is normally a leader of the pack of wolves, and several kiss-ass acolytes around them. They wind themselves up further every time nobody stands up to them. There were similar groups of bullies at my middle school and high school.

I went to St. Mary's Church of England Primary School until I was eleven. Then I interviewed and took an exam for a place at University College School for middle school and high school. Every morning I would go there on the Tube, in my red-and-black-striped uniform blazer, collared shirt, and tie.

When I got my scholarship to Cambridge University, there was limited bullying, and what little I experienced was based on my not being born upper class, and also being Jewish and encountering antisemites. More on that later.

Chapter Takeaways and Reflection Questions for You

- Have you experienced bullying? What did you do about it? (Clue: Don't keep it secret. Talk to your mentor, teacher, group leader—someone who can help and advise you.)
- You don't generally help yourself deal with a bully by turning your back. Unless you think you may be seriously hurt, standing up to a bully is often your best course of action.
- Everyone feels insecure from time to time. What is the best we can do to rise above this without lashing out at the people around us?
- Have you ever bullied anyone? Was it because of your own insecurity? Did you ever make it right? Did you learn from it?
- How can we avoid becoming as bad as those who bully us?
- Reflect on your experiences on both sides of bullying.
- How can we avoid falling into behaviors that harm others even when we are feeling mistreated, enraged, insecure?
- What purpose does bullying serve?
- Have you ever reached out to someone that you saw being bullied, to help them survive it?

CHAPTER 9

How Do You Find Your Mentor?
Mr. Lund, Who Lifted My Self-Expectations

I was privileged to be taught English by Mr. Lund in year ten. I remember, as though it were yesterday, Mr. Lund instructing me in class to see him after school. With some trepidation, I showed up in his study. He poked me in the chest with his finger and said, "If you work about twice as hard, I really think you can get into Cambridge University." I burst out laughing and said, "Mr. Lund, thank you, but nobody in my family ever went to college."

But I did work twice as hard. He mentored and tutored me. I sat the Cambridge Entrance Examination, a series of very long sessions taken over several days at one's school. The essay required three and a half hours to write about one of ten given subjects. When I opened the packet, I realized to my horror that I did not know enough about any of the subjects to write a Cambridge-place-winning essay for three and a half hours. I scratched my head for twenty minutes, and then decided that I would write about the one about which I knew *the least*. Question number ten simply said: "Erasmus. Discuss."

FINDING HAPPY

My opening was this: "I know absolutely nothing about Erasmus. I don't know who he was, when he lived, or what his contributions to the world may have been." I then developed this thought to answer another question: wondering *why* I was completely ignorant about Erasmus. This led to three and a half hours exploring the reasons behind every curriculum: really, that no one had enough brain space to learn everything about everything. And that therefore, curricula were developed to enable specialization and to slim down the sheer overwhelming quantity of knowledge.

I remembered I'd learned from Mr. Lund that King Henry VIII did know everything about everything. When he met with his ministers of state, he could hold his own in any conversation, in however much detail they brought to the meeting. It was a meeting of peers in knowledge. But the Renaissance, the enormous flowering of knowledge that took place beginning in the sixteenth century, changed all that. Knowledge built on itself in an ever-widening web of facts, investigations, results, findings. The total knowledge of all humans rapidly overwhelmed any one person's ability to study it. Our brains simply could not cope. It was impossible.

Thus, it became necessary to specialize. The challenge with specialization is that, ever since, the world has become afflicted by challenges that are incredibly multidisciplinary. Thorny challenges we seek to conquer often need twenty or fifty different kinds of knowledge.

I wrote about all this for three hours, and when the proctor said, "Pens down," I wrote a last line: "And that is why I know nothing about Erasmus."

I remember I came out of the examination room to find Mr. Lund pacing around; he had a lot riding on the time he had devoted to teaching and mentoring me. I told him I'd written about Erasmus. He was apoplectic. "But you know nothing about Erasmus!" "Yes," I said, "that's what I wrote about: my ignorance." He was so angry that he hit me with his newspaper.

When I went to the interview for Emmanuel College at Cambridge University, there sat the senior tutor, Dr. Harvey, and two other dons. A wildly frightening experience. And remember, I had written an essay about what I did not know. Their opening line was, "Ah, Mr. Samuelson,

How Do You Find Your Mentor? Mr. Lund, Who Lifted My Self-Expectations

Emmanuel College, University of Cambridge

who knows nothing at all about Erasmus?" I said, "Yes sir, but now I know an awful lot about him. I've done very little except reading up on Erasmus, because I knew you would ask me questions." "No," said the senior tutor. "We knew you would do that, so we don't want to ask you anything about Erasmus. We want to ask you about the rise of Renaissance Man, the thrall of specialization, and what that means for the future of our world."

It turned out I had a great deal to say about that. "Ah," I began. "It's a core challenge of leadership, isn't it?" I was in there a long time. They were less frightening the longer we spoke, but at the end, they were inscrutable. But I came out feeling that perhaps it had gone quite well. Or not.

Finding a mentor should start with making a list of where to find one. A spider graph can be a perfect way to lay out your pathways graphically, so you can take a good look at each, then narrow them down to individuals to approach one by one. Your inner circle of places to find mentors might say: family, church/mosque/temple, parents and other family of friends, existing mentor of a friend, school, YMCA, After School Activity Center, social media… (See spider graph example in Chapter 2 for a plan to get a safe mentor.)

FINDING HAPPY

A word of caution on all these sources, and especially when finding one online: be very careful. Most grooming by predators, sexual and otherwise, has several steps before the overt "grab." A common tactic is to look like a kind and helpful mentor for a young adult who needs help. Pimps, for example, do a lot of predation parked outside group foster homes. "Are they being mean to you again? You look hungry. Can I buy you a hamburger?" And so it begins. After "pure" helpfulness and kindness, the pimp may tell the target he values her, loves her, and wants to be her boyfriend. After that, he has some friends he'd like to share her with as a favor, part of the "love" that is really increasingly intense steps toward complete psychological domination. And then come drugs, a dependent habit, and under-age prostitution, often with violence and intimidation thrown into the evil mix. All of which creates statutory rape, a serious crime. Much better to avoid falling down the slippery steps.

Always investigate a potential mentor. Don't ever (ever!) put yourself at risk with anyone who might pretend to be a mentor but have bad motives. Every mentor should be vetted. Get help in doing that. Ask if they are accredited and vetted through a reliable entity that is itself trustworthy. Ask the opinion of other adults who know them well. Research them online. Be cautious. Don't share dangerous personal information. Why do they need it to help you? You are smart. Take care of yourself, but ask an adult you already know and trust to vet the potential mentor. Two heads are better than one. Only meet initially in a public place, have a friend keep an eye on you from a distance. If an adult is responsible for you—like a parent, foster parent, or social worker—ask them to help. If you are under eighteen, or in care, there are laws and rules...and your social worker can check someone out in a government database they can access. Set your location alert on Google or Apple Maps so your friends can see where you are. Be cautious. Trust your instincts: *If it looks like a fish, and smells like fish, it is probably a fish!*

The Mentor Project exists to find mentors, vet them, assign them to young adults who need a mentor, and keep an eye on the process. They have all kinds: scientists, engineers, artists, authors, and so on. Every

How Do You Find Your Mentor? Mr. Lund, Who Lifted My Self-Expectations

one is accomplished and would like to be helpful. You can find out more at http://www.mentorproject.org or from info@mentorproject.org

With Steven Spielberg at announcement of a $6-million Coca-Cola donation to Starbright.

Chapter Takeaways and Reflection Questions for You

- Everyone needs a mentor or two, a coach, a wise confidant. Have you got one? If not, where can you find one? Most people will help, but you have to find the right one to help you, and you have to take a deep breath and ask them!
- Think about personal safety, and get help in vetting any potential mentor before you engage with the mentor.
- Once you have a mentor, build the relationship by being excellent and thoughtful. Say thank you, often. Write little notes. Remember that they are donating their time in busy lives. Give them back kindness, follow-through, and intelligent responses.
- It is often incredibly boring to grade school papers or exams. How can you make your work stand out and shine? How do you grip the reader?

FINDING HAPPY

- Where can you talk about your victories over bad life experiences, how you overcame adversity? (Clue: The essay!)

- What role does storytelling have in life and in success? How do you do it? Can you learn it? What compelling things can you say to grab attention, to make them lean in, to give you an A+ on the homework?

- What if you feel checkmated? How can you maneuver past an area where you feel underequipped and challenged?

- Give an example where you were ingenious. Where they gave you lemons, and you made lemonade. Hooray for you!

- Are you a specialist or a generalist? One is not better than the other; they are just different. You can be a brilliant pianist. You don't have to conduct the orchestra.

- Have you experimented enough to know your best direction, the one where you can live a passionate career full of accomplishments and happiness?

- School and college are not only to learn, but to experiment. They give you several years to try different paths with little risk. Are you a scientist or an artist? Which side of your brain makes you happiest? Do you write, or design, or calculate, or lead? Life is choices. This is your time: you are the author of the rest of your life.

CHAPTER 10

What Is Love For, Actually?
And Where Can You Find It?

Occasionally, there is a song written about something other than love. Once in a while someone writes a song about worshiping God, irritation with their job, or some beautiful place they visited. But out of every 1000 songs, roughly 999 are about love: what it is, how enjoyable, how difficult to find, how to nurture and keep it, or what to do when you love someone who doesn't love you back. And about how thrilling and frustrating the whole process is, for most humans. So clearly, this thing called love is incredibly important to us. It dominates our thoughts, arguably like no other subject, and it doesn't matter what your politics are, whether you're poor or rich, nor your sexual preference. Almost every human being wants to find someone to love them, whom they can love back.

Come up to 35,000 feet, and let's look first at the 150,000-year history of human beings. DNA researchers tell us that every single one of us, every race, every color of skin, every tribe, everywhere on Earth, descends from one single woman in Northeast Africa between 120,000 and 150,000 years ago. We are all brothers, sisters, cousins,

FINDING HAPPY

second cousins, and one-hundredth cousins...but cousins neverthe-less. It would be good for the haters to realize that they are hating their own relatives. Charles Darwin and the scientists since he wrote *On the Origin of Species* have all explained meticulously that every spe-cies on Earth seeks to continue to exist. It seeks to lay down seeds, get them fertilized, and then generally take care of the babies, or at least to deliver enough that some will survive and propagate the species. The species that did not take care of their futures don't exist anymore. So, if the first imperative of every living thing is not to be the last of its tribe, then for human beings that would mean that other things—except possibly breathing, eating, and staying hydrated—pale by comparison with taking every step possible to make babies.

How does Mother Nature manage to do that? For almost the whole 7.7 billion people living and breathing on planet Earth, it is done the old-fashioned way, through people having sex. So, if sex needs to take place, how does Mother Nature make it a compelling enough proposi-tion for humans to want to engage in it? This is where nature, by trial and error over thousands of years, has created the most compelling drug on earth: sexual attraction. The wish to have sex with another person causes powerful men and women to make huge mistakes in their careers. It inspires great acts of bravery and also of stupidity. It can be ennobling or corrosive. But in the end, its goal is to cause humans to couple, just like other mammals on planet Earth.

In order to cause humans to pair off and ultimately make babies, it is necessary for them to feel attraction to each other—as Sammy Fain and Paul Francis Webster celebrate in their song, "Love is a Many Splendored Thing." Love is the feeling of attraction that causes a person to wish to spend time with, to help, to nurture, to build some-thing with, to amuse, to entertain, to converse with, to dance with, to hug, to cuddle...and ultimately, in most cases, to have sex with a single other human being. There is indeed such a thing as platonic love, and brotherhood and sisterhood can be incredibly powerful. But what we're talking about here is the process of love, which through court-ship developed a fairly organized way of spending time together—time that allows a process of selection, which has as much to do with physi-cal attraction as it does mental compatibility and harmony. The idea

What Is Love For, Actually? And Where Can You Find It?

that Mother Nature has put forth, by trial and error, is that as many people as possible should pair off in circumstances that will create babies. And society has modified the urge for sex to allow for the raising of healthy babies.

It is not difficult for a young person in their teens and twenties to fall in love. There is a strong yearning to love and be loved. The challenge is finding the right person who will feel the same way in return. Your generation has a huge asset in an array of online dating apps. I lay claim to having invented a very early form in CUDATE during my university years. More on that mad adventure later. I should have commercialized it, and it would have turned into Facebook, long before Mark Zuckerberg. Never mind.

What the apps cannot really give you is more than a slight glimpse, sometimes an illusion, of what the other person is about. Certainly, the X Factor is not present in a photo and a profile, which are often intended to mislead you. No technology has yet been able to accelerate or provide shortcuts in the process of getting to know you, which has to do with such arcane aspects as the way someone smells, the way they look in three dimensions alongside you, their voice, their intelligence, their sense of humor, and their outlook on life. Your teenage years and twenties are the time for meeting an array of different potential life partners, probably committing to none of them, but fully experiencing the amazing and wonderful array of humanity from which you may choose your ultimate partner in life.

It is unhelpful to say about love, "You'll know it when you feel it." A crush is not love. And your love radar is not built in a day but through trial and error, over time. In fact, the problem is the opposite one. You will often feel "love" when it isn't really love, but infatuation or just sexual desire. Remember the role of sex in the procreation of the species. Without sex, there are no more human beings. Relying on sexual attraction as though it was love returned is not your best guide to a stable, long-term life partner. There is much more to compatibility than sexual compatibility, important though that may be. It is one of two or three dozen attributes that need to mesh. What you're really looking for is that relationship where one and one make three. That third thing is what you share, and is bigger than the sum of its parts.

FINDING HAPPY

Where to find love? Ah, there is one of the fundamental mysteries of life. It might be in a bar; it might be on an app. It might be better through the introduction of a mutual friend. It might be at a shared sporting event. But I would suggest to you that the most overlooked way of meeting a really worthwhile potential mate with whom you will find much in common is to volunteer to a nonprofit charity. That's what I did with Starlight. It's how I met Saryl. And as proud parents and grandparents who have been married thirty-five years, it was clearly a pretty strong pathway. One of the things in my life that I love most is that when people meet through my four charities, they quite often invite us to their weddings. And I get to toast them at the party. I see in their eyes, and I hear in their words, that by volunteering side to side to help the unhoused or foster kids or a family with a seriously ill child, they have found a litmus test of common ground that enabled them to get past infatuation and to bond over things that are really the most important: their shared values.

Volunteering creates a common arena to putting energy, intelligence, and love into the society we inhabit and encouraging others to do the same thing. Far from being a mock job, a volunteering position in a charity can closely align with the issues that compel you to help: it can be one of the most richly rewarding things you will ever do in your life. You can do it in your spare time. And you can even work and be paid by a charity. Either way, it is also an incredibly powerful magnetic opportunity to meet your long-term partner through shared activities and the pursuit of common goals. I wish you every good luck! I don't think John Lennon and Paul McCartney had it exactly right when they insisted that love is all you need, but certainly love is one of the prime drivers of a contented life. If you can share your victories and your sorrows, your path forward, as well as dealing with your challenges—if you can be accepted and find unconditional love, and then share it on down to your children—then you have in my view become a great human and done your part to see that good humans inherit the earth. Long may you thrive!

Chapter Takeaways and Reflection Questions for You

- Where might you find love? (Clue: Use a spider graph. Make sure one of the options is a charity.)
- If you think you might have found love, how do you know that it is not just sexual infatuation? (Clue: What do you talk about? What is a common interest?)
- What helps love grow and last? (Clue: Try a sense of humor and a common purpose.)
- When is it too early to have babies? (Clue: When you do not know, with certainty, how you will take care of them for eighteen-plus years and be an excellent parent, as well as fulfill your own education and career steps towards a happy future.)
- What should you do if someone does not love you back? (Clue: Lick your wounds and move on. So many fish in the sea, and time is a great healer.)
- What should you do if someone says they love you, and you just don't feel it? (Clue: Be honest. Don't mislead them.)
- Should you pretend to be in love to get someone to take care of you and pay for everything? (Clue: Shame on you. Of course not. That might be the single worst reason to pretend love, let alone get married.)
- Who can help you understand how to be a great partner in love? (Clue: A wonderful opportunity to ask the right mentor for help. Perhaps an older person with a successful relationship who will understand your situation, because they once experienced similar things.)

CHAPTER 11

First Love, Eloping, and the Telegram

When I was sixteen, I fell in love with a beautiful young lady named Ann. She was my first great love. I was immersed at school with Mr. Lund in the world of medieval English literature: The Knights of the Round Table, Beowulf, Chaucer, Gawain and the Green Knight. The more that ideas of courtly love flew through my head, the more I wrote Ann heartfelt poetry. I had cheap jewelry made for her bearing quotes from Shakespeare. It was precious and pure and extraordinary. A privilege that made me a budding poet!

Ann went off for her Christmas holidays to Geneva, Switzerland, with her parents; and I in my tiny little car, with my brand-new driver's license, followed my parents by road to the South of France, where we stayed in a hotel in Cannes. I learned to water-ski on a single ski, but mostly I obsessed over Ann.

I realized on a map that I ought to be able to drive from Cannes to Geneva in a day, although the map did not make it clear to me that there was a range of very high mountains in the middle—the Alps. I raised this idea with my parents, who said absolutely not, there was no way that their now seventeen-year-old, who had been driving for less

First Love, Eloping, and the Telegram

Only dangerous going over the jump, but I did drink a great deal of seawater. Cannes, France, 1969.

than six months, was going to navigate through three countries in two directions in a tiny car with its putt-putt motor.

This did not sit well with me. And with the impetuousness and arrogance of youth, I decided that I would elope, at least in the sense that I would go to Switzerland without permission. In the middle of the night. I was sharing a room with my brother Jonathan, who was thirteen. I decided that if I told him, he would probably (and quite rightly!) tell my parents, and so I couldn't impose my secret on him. I hardly slept and managed to wake up silently at three o'clock in the morning. I stuffed the bolster in my bed like in a prison escape film I'd seen, and I fashioned a bump under the pillow with a roll of toilet paper, as though it was my head. I slunk out with my passport, a little bit of money, and the car keys.

It was very cold when I got into the car. Off I set for the border between France and Italy, a little over forty miles. When I got there, I was convinced they would take one look at me, realize that I was a child, and not let me into Italy.... This was long before the Europeans did away with frontiers within the European Community. But the

FINDING HAPPY

half-asleep frontier guard just waved me through. Oh dear! Now I was committed.

There I was, driving north through Italy as the sun rose to my right. The further I drove, the less this all seemed like a good idea. I knew my parents would not actually kill me, but I had ominous feelings of very bad consequences when I would have to face the music. By midday, I had made it to Milan, and I decided that my family would be worried and that I needed to phone them. It was long before the days of cellphones, so I navigated to the central Milan Train Station, which, sure enough, had a telephone office where you could prepay for a five-minute call to France, and where you were then put into a little wooden booth to make the call.

I knew that my parents would be irate, but I'd rationalized that Ann was worth it. My heart was in my boots as I was connected. What I did not know then was that that very morning the telegram had arrived from Cambridge University, saying that I had been awarded an academic scholarship to read English Literature at Emmanuel College. My father did not tell me that fact on the call. He told me with a grim voice that he and my mother were extremely angry with me, and that we would discuss it after I reunited with the family. He also told me that my mother had decided to do the one thing I had not thought of that would be a true punishment—which was that she had canceled the holiday for the rest of the family. They would be driving home the following day. And I should calculate where I could join them.

Whoops. Bad Peter. Very bad Peter. Genius punishment. Shame and ignominy.

Because I knew the route that they would take, I decided, "In for a penny, in for a pound"—and that I would carry on to Geneva, where I had one idyllic overnight with Ann and her family. And then, with love in my heart, I set off to drive over the Alps to rendezvous with the family at a place called Condrieu, in the Loire Valley.

But first I had to get over the Alps, driving 150 miles—first, up an incredibly steep set of what the French call "lacets," like laces...meaning hairpin bend after hairpin bend, left, right, left, right, left, right, up three thousand feet to the top of the mountain...and then descending another three thousand feet of lacets down the other side. Near the top,

48

First Love, Eloping, and the Telegram

without warning, there was a big bang, and the entire exhaust pipe and muffler fell off my little car. "Ah," I thought, "this will be good. I will get better mileage. And if I take it with me into the hotel, maybe it will be something funny to talk about when my parents are angry with me."

So, I stood up the whole six-foot pipe with the muffler sticking out of the sunroof on the car. And I carried on to Condrieu. Call me an optimist. Sometimes optimism is all you have to keep going. I remember the smell of the brakes on the descent.

My mother was particularly good at doing what was called by the rest of the family "The Look," which was basically to annihilate you with her eyes. And that, she executed with great skill. She would not talk to me. The exhaust pipe was not helpful. It was just a silly pipe.

I felt terrible. I was ashamed. I had to apologize to my brothers, whose holiday had been canceled because of my idiocy. My father, I thought in one sense, was tipping his hat to my little bit of youthful bravado. Nevertheless, he made it clear that he, too, was very angry. But he also had to place into my hand the telegram from Cambridge University, indicating that I had been awarded a full Academic Merit Scholarship and that they would see me in October of the following year.

Later, when everyone had calmed down, I remember that my dad cried. It was his lifelong ambition, having been forced out of school at the age of fourteen by the family's poverty, to see his children go to university, and I was the first. Thank you, Mr. Lund. I later founded the First Star charity, directly because he had raised my self-expectations and encouraged me to expand and explore what was possible in my life.

So, for sure, a privileged seventeen-year-old with his own car knew in advance that something he wanted to do was incredibly selfish—but did it anyway, ruining his family's holiday, and got away with it through lucky timing. Mad. Shameful. I cringe. But as Shakespeare wrote in *The Merchant of Venice*, "For love is blind, and lovers cannot see, the pretty follies that they each commit."

Then again, he wasn't seventeen when he wrote it....

FINDING HAPPY

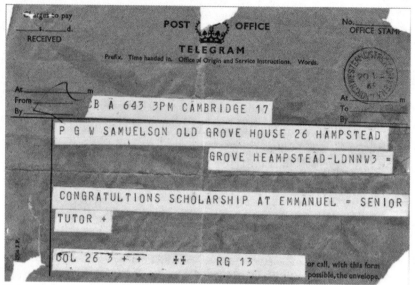

The telegram that made my father cry.

Chapter Takeaways and Reflection Questions for You

- What is love, actually? (Clue: Turns out it is not sex.)
- Have you been in love? How do you know?
- Is love rational or irrational?
- What is the purpose of love?
- Read some great literature about love. Start with *Romeo and Juliet*. That Shakespeare knew a thing or two about love.
- What do you do when apologies don't work? (Clue: Be patient. Time heals. Read the chapter on apologies.)
- What is the best way to find love? (Clue: Common interests and empathy: volunteer!)
- To be selfish is bad. How do you avoid it when you are overwhelmed by the urgency of love?

CHAPTER 12

Get Your Foot in the Door, and Then Don't Blow It. *Le Mans*

In 1969, I finished high school and was awarded my Academic Scholarship in English Literature to Cambridge University. Because Cambridge very sensibly required a gap year, I was faced with a long hiatus to fill between school and university. I spoke OK French, and so with only slight exaggeration, I was able to get a job as an interpreter for the production on *Le Mans*, the Steve McQueen film about motor racing, which was made in 1969–70 in northwestern France. By being in the right place at the right time, courtesy of my father, I met the producer, Bob Relyea, and by great luck, he hired me. You cannot make luck happen, any more than a lightning strike, and often it does not. But you can absolutely try to shine, to stand out, and be ready to grab the opportunity. Bob needed a bilingual assistant, I was standing in front of him, and I made it very clear that I was reliable, energetic, and eager to help. And damn it, if he wanted bilingual, I'd be that too.

You can get an opportunity by luck, but you can only keep it by earning it. You have to make them feel they were lucky to find you! You run, don't walk, to help them, and you are positive, pleasant, and

51

can-do. One of my nicknames among the Americans was the Road Runner... *"Meep! Meep!"* How do you present? Do you look people in the eye? Do you have a firm handshake? Do you mumble? Practice, practice, practice! Impress.

Steve McQueen was a very, very big star. In today's terms, he was as famous as Tom Cruise, Leonardo DiCaprio, and Keanu Reeves together are now, with a bit of Vin Diesel. Steve McQueen was the Taylor Swift of acting.

My entire life before leaving for France was consumed by academic study. I was the teacher's pet, one of the best students in the school, and while everyone else went to the beach on vacations, I sat upstairs in the hotel and read medieval English literature. A full-on nerd! My cultural world was knights in armor, concepts of nobility and honor, and damsels in distress. While everyone else was beginning to experience Flower Power, weed, and the other long-distance effects of Haight-Ashbury, I was reading Chaucer, Kyd, and Shakespeare. The odds against winning a full scholarship to Cambridge in the highly competitive field of English literature were approximately five thousand to one. But as I was actually immersed in the medieval, I really only had to write about where I felt I was living. I could think and speak medieval. Luckily, that shone through in the interview: I was a medieval nerd. And somehow, being bold enough to describe my ignorance on the subject of Erasmus in the essay exam was appealing. At least it was unique.

When I left for Le Mans in France in my tiny little car, I was eighteen and had no idea what awaited. The American filmmakers had not arrived, and I reported to a corrupt production executive who was on the take in ten ways. He imported the prefabricated buildings to make a village inside the race track, because he was receiving payoffs from the Swiss manufacturers. I discovered that there was an empty technical college inside the race track; I realized it was free, and much better

Get Your Foot in the Door, and Then Don't Blow It. Le Mans

My Hillman Imp, and our other cars that went a great deal faster.

than anything we could build. It even had garage bays to lift cars up to service them. Gleefully, I brought my boss to see the treasure I had found. It was raining. White-faced, he put his arm around me and told me, "This will be our little secret." And it was.

I roomed initially in a hotel, but then discovered that by living in a trailer at the track and eating in the commissary, I could keep absolutely all of my living allowance, which was paid in cash and larger than my salary. I had never seen so much money in my life.

My first exposure to Steve McQueen was when I was told by him to hire bulldozers to dig up the ornate gardens of the twelfth-century castle we had rented for him to live in with his wife and children at Viré-en-Champagne, and to turn it into a motocross track. I talked him out of that, but we rented a farmer's field next door to build his bike track. I then flew overnight to Jönköping in Sweden on the private jet to collect two Husqvarna motorbikes for his use. It was bonkers, outrageous, but I knew no better.

McQueen was very, very famous, very rich, and at both high and low points in his life. Fresh off the triumph of *The Great Escape*, he was being directed here by John Sturges for the second time. But there never *was* a script. Writers came and went, and eventually John Sturges resigned and Lee Katzin was brought in to replace him. We never knew what we would be filming the next day because the script never coalesced. We went through *dozens* of drafts, all mutually inconsistent. It was the first and last time I ever saw a call sheet, the order of the day for tomorrow, instructing the crew where to report and what to bring, which under "Scenes to be Shot" said "TBD."

McQueen was energetically promiscuous, and also using substances on a regular basis. All sorts of shenanigans were covered up by the production, with me as a "bilingual" member. To say that he felt entitled was an understatement. There were French laws and rules, and our budget, deadlines, and a schedule. It was very tricky when he did whatever he wanted, and nothing unless he wanted it. Wherever he went, a huge number of gawkers, fans, and groupies followed. I was a key wrangler, with a walkie-talkie and a bullhorn.

One producer of the film, call him Fred, had a terrible problem. He would walk around proclaiming, "I made a million-dollar mistake," and then gnaw at his fingers, with the result that the white cotton editing gloves that he wore new every morning would turn red with bloody splotches by the end of the day.

And then there were the women. From all corners of Europe, rumors spread that a financially profligate Hollywood film, a huge international star, and motor-racing madness had come to a sleepy French town. Women were magnetically attracted from all points of the compass. I went from being a virtually monastic, naïve, teenage medieval scholar to becoming happily bemused as a steady stream of hot-and-cold-running groupies rolled through camp. Hey, it was 1969, and I was eighteen.

At one point or another, three-quarters of the crew was fired. Every time there was a termination, I would be promoted by one notch. When David Piper was hurt in a car accident and badly burned because the fire engine could not reach him, apparently the best person to appoint head of track safety was of course an eighteen-year-old like me, because, by the logic of the film, I spoke French. When my father came to visit, I remember him shouting at the producer, "Peter can't take care of himself, how the hell can he take care of track

Age eighteen, filming in the Pits at Le Mans.

safety? He's a child!" He was right, but I did it anyway, and nobody was hurt on my watch.

The level of embezzlement and pilfering on the film would have been shocking, but of course at the time I had no frame of reference. It certainly did not seem to resemble the courtly manners of some castle in England of the fourteenth century. Everyone in sight seemed to have a miraculously free-of-charge TAG Heuer wristwatch. Cars donated by their manufacturers for on-screen promotion arrived, then mysteriously disappeared.

There was also periodically a slight problem with the financing. The production would run out of cash. On one occasion we were unable to pay the several hundred French extras. These individuals then rioted in the production village. The producer hid in his prefabricated building, sitting on its concrete base. Fifty French extras pushed the entire building off its foundations with him inside it. The police were called. A riot ensued, and in the middle of all of it, Steve McQueen arrived and made matters worse by promising things that no one could deliver. I had to lend the accountant the unspent living allowance I had hidden under my bed. We all chipped in. It was mad, like monopoly money.

The Swiss production manager spoke no French. I remember on one occasion he instructed me to tell the head of the police force for the whole of Sarthe County that "I find his police so efficient, I would hardly think them French." With maturity beyond my years, I told the police chief, "He thinks your police are very efficient."

We could only close down the public roads that made up the Le Mans racetrack one section at a time. One of the things I had to do, as head of track safety, was to ensure none of the Ferrari and Porsche racing cars went back to the starting point of a shot until it was safe. Every car needed to arrive left-to-right first: I counted carefully amid all the noise to see that all of them had arrived—before I released them to drive back to the starting position from right to left! This was a real problem when Steve McQueen would try to drive past me on the grass verge, ignoring my red flag. I eventually had to sit down in the road in front of him to make him stop. I can still hear ringing in my ears: "Peter, get out of the fucking way! My engine is overheating, I have to go." On one occasion, I must have had no earplugs with me. Months later, I found a piece of the Le Mans newspaper deep inside my ear. McQueen

Me and a flag between angry drivers and an accident.

would arrive sometimes an hour late to the set, driving his motocross bike on its rear wheel. He would climb off and ask us, "What are we waiting for?" He was not popular with some of the crew.

My best French back then was mostly medieval, because that was what I cared about and what I read. I had not a lot of vocabulary around cameras and filmmaking. They never spoke in medieval France about flange focal depth or hyperfocal distance. Really, almost none at all. I just winged it, and somehow it worked. The film was a collision of three worlds, all arguably crazy to one degree or another. There were the filmmakers from Hollywood, who were trying to make a film that never had a finished script: it was made up on the spot every morning at six o'clock, while everybody else stood with their hands in their pockets. The second world was that of racing-car drivers. It is rather an existential profession, because life expectancy is not high. They do extraordinary things behind the wheel, and often dangerous things in the rest of their lives. As I was the one who could speak French, I spent quite a lot of my time down at the police station, apologizing to the local police for mechanics driving a thoroughbred racing car—a Ferrari, a Ford GT-40, or a Porsche with no muffler—at 3 a.m. through the center of Le Mans at 150 miles an hour, to show off to the girlfriend they met in a bar. The third world in collision was that of the local Le Mans people, whose entire goal, as far as I could see, was to take as much money as possible from the Americans before they left town.

I found myself in this sleepy little French town, electrified by the arrival of Steve McQueen and his entourage, and I had a fine old time for ten months. On one memorable occasion, I used a loudspeaker system to tell approximately two thousand extras—Americans, Canadians, French, and every tourist in the region—"Open your parasols, put on your caps. Ladies and gentlemen, we are ready to shoot." I should have used the word *"kepi"* for cap in my French translation. Unfortunately, I used the word *"capote,"* which is the French word for a condom. I had to explain to the crew why two thousand French extras were hysterical.

Every fourth weekend I would drive back up to London and thrust the accumulated living allowances into my father's hand. "Here, Dad, please keep this for me."

Me, and the flag that Mr. McQueen mostly ignored, trying to prevent a head-on collision.

I learned that every time I was given an order by Mr. McQueen, I should smartly reply, "Yes, sir," and then run around the nearest corner of a building and find someone who really knew what was needed. I learned not to disturb the Swiss production executive and his money-making schemes, or his enjoyment of a large cache of pornography. I learned that the absence of a script was no excuse for not busying the crew, especially when the financiers from CBS arrived. I learned that motor-racing crews were even crazier than the film people.

In 1969, there were only twelve international telephone lines out of Le Mans. Part of my job was to constantly deliver flowers to the telephonists in the central telephone exchange so that we'd be given lines. I chartered aircraft to fly in the film equipment, Super Constellations out of London. I apologized to the French F.C.C. when they discovered we were illegally using shortwave radios to communicate with the United States.

I spent a considerable amount of time trying to keep track of various young women and did not really succeed in developing a stimulating intellectual relationship with any: I noted that they knew nothing of medieval literature. But I soon realized they didn't seem to care, and right after that, neither did I....

And then it all came to an end. The fall semester at Cambridge University was about to begin. I left Le Mans and dropped the car in

Get Your Foot in the Door, and Then Don't Blow It. Le Mans

Negotiating in my best (not very good) French with the farmer who wanted money to not park in the middle of the road that was also the race track. Extortion!

London, because undergraduates could not have a car at Cambridge, a city of soaring spires but ridiculous traffic jams with near zero parking. I took the train to Cambridge and moved into Emmanuel College. Not twenty-four hours after a raucous farewell in the main tent of the Le Mans production village, I found myself standing in the refectory of Emmanuel, where, as was my duty as a scholar and wearing a long black academic robe, I recited Grace in Latin before the meal:

Oculi omnium in te sperant Domine,
Et tu das escam illorum in tempore opportune...

My academic career resumed, but, touched by the Hollywood and racing lunacy, I grew up suddenly. I came of age in Le Mans and for sure felt older than eighteen. Steve later wrote to me, "I think we may have the greatest film shot about motor racing"—and I believe he was right, at least in the footage of the cars, which was remarkable and entirely filmed in real life, not using special effects. And I first met America in France. Weird but true.

Chapter Takeaways and Reflection Questions for You

- What does being in the right place at the right time mean? How can you do that? (Clue: Keep trying!)
- How can you shine in the first ten minutes when you need to make a strong impression? Would *you* hire *yourself*? Practice!
- How do you present? How's your handshake? How do you dress? Do you mumble?
- Are you a good, responsive listener?
- When you get your first break in a serious job, how should you behave?
- How do you use the first job to build a network, to help you get the next job?
- Do you perform excellently, so that your bosses want to hire you again?
- What do you do when a person above you with power tells you to do something either wrong, unhelpful, immoral, illegal, or unethical? (Clue: Run around the nearest corner and get advice from people you trust.)
- Always think two steps ahead. Beware the Law of Unintended Consequences. What does that mean?

Discussing the next shot with assistant directors, including Jean Pierre Avice (in hat), who became my great friend and often my fellow career producer for fifty years. R.I.P., JPA.

Get Your Foot in the Door, and Then Don't Blow It. Le Mans

November 6, 1970

Mr. Peter Samuelson
Emmanuel College
St. Andrew's Street
Cambridge, CB2 3AP, England

Dear Peter:

Hope all is going well and you have settled back in school and am sure you miss the sound of racing cars every morning and during the day.

LE MANS is coming along just dandy. I think we possibly have the greatest film shot about motor racing.

In reference to your letter, I would be more than delighted to come and have a round-the-table chat about film. It will all depend upon my schedule and previous commitments in the United States, so I will keep you posted and if I am in England and you are around, it would certainly be my pleasure.

Thank you for being so kind to my wife in London, and my best to all of your chums who one of these days will be making the right decisions about the world we live in.

My best,

Steve McQueen

CHAPTER 13

What Is University For? Cambridge

Cambridge was a complete shock after ten months in Le Mans. I went from one alternate reality to another. I realized on the train that I knew no one else among the undergraduates. There was a real opportunity to reinvent myself to be exactly whom I wanted to be. I boarded the train as one person, and arrived an hour later as another.

I did not at first realize that the college, quite reasonably, would expect me to "sing for my dinner," to perform for my scholarship. I had decided in France that I was a filmmaker, and that somehow or other I was going to make that my first career. My scholarship at Cambridge, however, was based on being really good at English literature, especially medieval English literature. That was where the senior tutor and his colleagues expected me to devote my time. How could the making of films and the study of literature coexist? I did not know, but I aimed to find out.

In the week that I arrived at Cambridge, I was ushered with the other freshmen undergraduates on scholarship into the library, where there was an imposing row of leather-bound volumes dating back to the founding of Emmanuel in the year 1584. I was invited to sign my name as a scholar on the next blank page of the last volume, and I did

What Is University For? Cambridge

Emmanuel College, Cambridge University, Freshman Class 1970. Fourth row, third from left.

so with great pride, wishing my father could be present. The college master, Dr. Derek Brewer, who later became my tutor and mentor, showed us where the then eighteen-year-old John Harvard had signed his name in an earlier volume of the same series of leather-bound scholar books—also when he was in his first week as an undergraduate at Emmanuel College, Cambridge, and well before he sailed off to Boston, Massachusetts, to found his eponymous university. It wasn't intimidating, but it was certainly strange and different.

I made friends and set about making the most of being privileged to attend one of the world's truly great universities. I was not at all happy to discover that there was not a single woman at Emmanuel, and that in a freshman class of perhaps 160 students, there seemed to be only a tiny handful who were not white men. Not only that, but the official view of English literature was that the last important work was written in the 1920s. But this was the 1970s, the first decade after John Osborne's *Look Back in Anger*. Change was in the air, and a new wave of writers were breaking through traditions and creating whole

FINDING HAPPY

new genres, especially in English drama. There was dynamic tension between what I wanted to read as a young man and what I was required to study. In the end, that was resolved by doing both in parallel.

But then there was Dr. Brewer, a truly brilliant scholar who took me under his wing, deduced what would interest me that was part of the approved curriculum, and propelled me into its study. A truly amazing human being, and an inspiring teacher.

I took steps to address the lack of women to pal around with at Emmanuel College. I decided that what was a challenge for me in a university of twenty thousand students, under two thousand of whom were female, must be a problem for other men in the same situation, and perhaps for some women as well. I created a questionnaire that I called CUDATE, the Cambridge University Dating Service. I dreamed up twenty questions that an undergraduate could answer to describe their personality and interests...that one could use, I thought, to match them up with someone to take for a coffee. The questionnaire invited the person who filled it out to attach a headshot and a five-pound note, and to mail it back to the post office box I opened on St. Andrew's Street. I printed ten thousand copies of the questionnaire and went around to Cambridge colleges on my bicycle, its panniers stuffed full of questionnaires. Each college had ancient, rectangular wooden boxes in racks called pigeonholes, one for every student. Into each of these I thrust a copy of my CUDATE sheet. And then I held my breath and waited for results.

When I went back a couple of days later to the office where I had rented the box, the person in charge was angry. "This is ridiculous," he said. "You rented the smallest and cheapest box, which only holds a few envelopes. We have sacks of responses. You should have thought it through and rented a much bigger box."

So I did, and I struggled back to Emmanuel with several sacks stuffed full of completed questionnaires. I was staggered by how many I received, even just in that first week. There were something like two thousand responses! Each of them attached a stapled pound note as well as a headshot. I took two thousand pounds to the bank, an enormous amount to me, but also realized I had bitten off a frightening responsibility!

What Is University For? Cambridge

I was faced with the challenge of how to match people up. Few women, many men. And most who responded were heterosexual. I pulled in my friends and shared the wealth. Together we sat on the floor with beers and tried to develop a system for intelligently matching up our CUDATE clients. The first problem was that over 90 percent of those who filled in the forms were men and wanted a date with women. Very few women had completed the questionnaire. So, we needed to keep our women clients very busy! We had promised people

FINDING HAPPY

three dates each, but our ladies got twenty each. We started by trying to match up interests, life outlook, and so forth. We ended up being a bit more rudimentary: "She's a tall scientist, he's a tall scientist. They should go have a coffee." We did the best we could, and it was much better than nothing. We even got fan mail. The women members were kept very, very busy. I don't know how they did academically at the then women-only colleges....

All went well, until I was called in by the senior tutor, Dr. Harvey. He had a stern and exasperated expression on his face and explained that I was "...not permitted to run a business from my room in the South Court of Emmanuel College, sir." I had to find a way to keep CUDATE alive, but not to run it in conflict with my obligation to study a vast swath of English literature every week. What to do?

There was a secretarial bureau on Rose Crescent off of Market Square, run by several amusing and jolly middle-aged ladies. I had been using them sometimes to type up my homework. I approached them with the proposition that they would run CUDATE and would take half of the revenue. They would do all the work and pay any expenses, and I would take the other half of the money for having invented it. And so quite possibly the first undergraduate dating service in the world began. Mark Zuckerberg wasn't even a twinkle in his parents' eyes. CUDATE gave me more than pocket money. Alongside my scholarship, I could actually afford to take my own dates out to a pretty good dinner. And I had money to buy Kodak 16mm film stock. Apparently, Dr. Harvey was mollified. And the notion that I could invent things was born. I realized that if there was a challenge affecting many people, I could dare to be the one to fix it. A heady concept, for sure.

The challenge of my scholarship was that it paid room, board, and tuition but gave me no pocket money. One of the ways that I made the wherewithal to run my increasingly ambitious life, alongside CUDATE and the money left over from Le Mans, was by working as an interpreter. In the ten months I worked on Le Mans, I'd become quite proficient translating live, and in both directions. In interpreting, you market yourself exponentially; everyone your client meets is a potential client. You give out business cards, and they often contact you later, when they are to meet someone other than your original client.

What Is University For? Cambridge

So I was already building a network within the American and French film industries. When someone who only spoke English would need to do business with a counterpart in France or North Africa, I would attempt to get myself hired to be their interpreter. If this was during term time at Cambridge, I would do it by conference call. Somehow it all worked out, and I had good pocket money as a result of that and CUDATE. Dumb luck was probably part of it, but you have to position yourself for the good luck to strike.

What made saying Grace in Latin challenging was the frequent bad behavior of one's friends. Academic gowns had to be worn, then as now, in the dining hall. One stood facing High Table, where the faculty sat (think Hogwarts). My fellow students would crawl up behind me, then progressively pull me downwards by yanking my academic gown towards the floor, the goal being to make me mess up the Latin. They sometimes succeeded.

I made two decisions: I had to get a car permit, and I had to make films. Satisfying both of these goals, I successfully applied to the Proctors, who are the police force of Cambridge University, for a permit to open an official student club. Thus was born the Cambridge University Film Production Unit, known affectionately as CUFPU. One advantage was that the secretary of the club was allowed a permit to bring an automobile to Cambridge, so long as it was parked off the street. So, with the money from CUDATE and interpreting away-days, I rented the garage of a house on the Hills Road, where my Hillman Imp lived. We made short films on 16mm film stock. I would drive down to London on a Friday night, borrow equipment, and drive back to Cambridge. We would spend the weekend turning a script into celluloid. On one occasion, I so overloaded the car that the middle of it touched the ground, and I had to unload until the wheels would turn.

I was the CUFPU cinematographer, sometimes the writer, and most of the time the editor. And I ran it, becoming the producer by default. My friend John Harris directed. Michael Jordan, later a leading British anesthesiologist, recorded the sound. I operated the camera, produced the films, and arranged the screening space to show them to anyone who would pay a few pennies to come and see our masterpieces. We were so short of money that on one occasion we could not properly

FINDING HAPPY

dub the film to remove the clicks and pops on the soundtrack. We rehearsed the crew to cough and sneeze in the audience at the appropriate moments, and these splutterings successfully masked whatever was deficient on the soundtrack. I learned to produce on a tight budget: deliver the goods and bring it home within the money available.

I fell in love with a beautiful, smart, Lebanese-Egyptian-British lady who was a premed student. Carol has since made an illustrious career as a doctor and writer. We shared the rent of a flat overlooking Market Square. I was the Jewish kid, and she was the Lebanese Egyptian, and together we filled our dinner table with very diverse students, and had a spirited time finding the middle in intractable political and geopolitical differences of opinion. And we took an oath always to stand up to prejudice. I've burned bridges since by honoring it. Tricky stuff, but some things need to be absolutes.

I joined the Cambridge Union, a venerable debating society. I learned to debate under the leadership of the young Arianna Stassinopoulos, who later married Michael Huffington and became Arianna Huffington, the founder of *The Huffington Post*, for which I later wrote a regular column for years. I learned to argue both sides of an issue, changing between them whenever the gong sounded. I debated great visitors to the Cambridge Union, including Michael Foot, then deputy leader of the Labour Party, and other luminaries. I got more than a taste of debating around great thoughts with really smart students and visitors. Heaven! My head was exploding, in a good way.

I did get into trouble from time to time with the Proctors. Often, this had to do with climbing in and out of college after the curfew, which was at a very unreasonable 10 p.m. I became adept at quickly climbing over the twelve-foot gate of South Court in the dark in both directions, but I was occasionally caught. The punishment of the Proctors' Office was a fine, which was expressed in nobles. A noble was an archaic form of medieval English money, at the time worth six shillings and eight pence. There were twenty shillings to a pound, and twelve pennies in a shilling. Nobody had actually possessed or used nobles for several hundred years, so you paid up in modern money, but it was calculated as the equivalent of the number of nobles specified in the fine. There you have Cambridge and its history in a nutshell. I loved the whole thing, in all its eccentric and often Monty Python-esque glory! It was

What Is University For? Cambridge

a wonderful three years, and at the end of it, I came back to London determined to make a career in film. In Le Mans and Cambridge, I had caught the bug early, and happily, I have never recovered.

I learned early and often to find and nurture mentors, the encouragers and facilitators for young people. As an example, Carl Foreman was a famous American writer and sometimes a career producer. He wrote *High Noon* and *The Guns of Navarone*. In the evil times of the red scare that swept through the American film industry in the late 1940s, when he was accused of being a communist and was exiled to the UK, he had a cutting room and offices on Jermyn Street in London. He took an interest in CUFPU and asked how he could help. With one eye on his state-of-the-art Steenbeck horizontal editing machine, I impertinently asked whether we might be able to use it for our student films. Realize how big an ask that was: He had his own 35mm film meticulously laid out throughout the cutting room. I was asking if we could pack it up, change over the dual-gauge Steenbeck to 16mm, edit our film, and then change it back. He said yes! So, every Friday night for weeks at a time, Mike Jordan and I would drive down in my Hillman Imp, take Polaroid pictures of Carl's setup, pack it all away, convert the machine, edit continuously except for sleeping on his sofas and eating in cafes on Jermyn Street...until 6 a.m. Monday morning, when we'd pack up our stuff and use the Polaroids to reinstall his. A giant of a man, Carl was my encourager, a lovely human being, and a brilliant filmmaker I'm proud to have known.

As I write this, I am fighting jet lag, just back from a UK trip for First Star, which included a day of meetings in Cambridge. To my great honor and delight, after much discussion, we have now agreed to launch a First Star Programme for Looked After Youth, in partnership with Emmanuel College, at Cambridge University. More about First Star later. Doug Chalmers, the master of Emmanuel College, and I shook hands on the deal in the Master's Garden behind the Christopher Wren Chapel. It is an understatement to say how much joy it gives me, in the sense of full circle, to enable the extraordinary Cambridge experience of high achievement and excellence at Emmanuel College, the very same college where I was awarded a scholarship at age eighteen, fifty-three years ago. Humbling.

FINDING HAPPY

Shaking hands on the partnership bringing First Star to Emmanuel College, Cambridge University, with the master, Lieutenant General Doug Chalmers.

Chapter Takeaways and Reflection Questions for You

- What is University *for*? Alongside learning the academics and perhaps pursuing a career, is it for experimentation? How do you do that?
- What other advantages are there? (Clue: You have somewhere to live for an extra three or four years.)
- What is your plan? Not your outcome. Not even your best outcome. But what are the alternate paths you aim to explore? Try a spider graph.

What Is University For? Cambridge

- What are the baby steps of your experiments? How far can you go before you become too promoted to return to the crossroads and try something else at entry level?

- How old does an entrepreneur have to be? What about a leader?

- Have you experimented with being an entrepreneur or a leader, to understand the boundaries of what is possible and personally happy for you? Go for it! Find out!

- You have nobody to please but yourself. You are the author of your own life. Agree?

- If you are first generation in this country, growing up in a culture that is different from your family's before they immigrated, do they expect you to choose career, marriage partners, locations, and other important things in service to the family culture? Is it different? Is that stressful?

- If yes, have you talked confidentially to older people who share your "family first" culture but are leading lives you admire?

- Are you preoccupied with what others think of you, or letting others discourage you?

- Who are the people who limit you, and how do you get past the naysayers? There is usually a way if you are smart and don't give up.

- How do you find the courage to actually ask people you admire to help you?

- Regardless of age, but especially when we are young, we often think our problems are unique. They almost never are. Somewhere out there is a wise mentor who has walked in your shoes and can help. Go find them. Thoughts?

CHAPTER 14

When Should You Take Risks?
How to Survive Your Risk-Taking Years

What is brave? What is stupid? Young adults, especially young men, often die in avoidable accidents. Why is that? Let's talk about your human brain. Your brain has a front and a back. Which keeps you safe?

Key for any young adult is assessing risk: "Could I, should I, would I...?" At the back of the brain, in the brainstem, there is a part called the amygdala. It is the primeval, instinctive, and instantaneous decision-making mechanism, the rapid chooser between fight and flight in any danger. It is what a caveman or cavewoman used most often when about to be eaten by a saber-toothed tiger, to decide instantly whether to enter into mortal combat with the predator while armed only with a stick, or to turn tail and run in the hope that they could outrun the tiger. If there were two cave people, it went better for one of them, as they did not have to outrun the tiger, but only the other cave person.

The amygdala has no concern about long-term consequences, thinking only in the moment and of the moment, with no regard for the future. But at the other end of the brain, behind the eyebrows, is the

72

prefrontal lobe. In human evolution it developed much later. The prefrontal lobe is the poker game and the chess game of life. It attempts to think three and four moves ahead and to assess consequences. "If I do X, and then they do Y, will I do Z or not, and what will be the consequences of those?" And on and on. It is what makes us human, smarter, and frequently makes life more complicated, because we use it to think ahead.

The prefrontal lobe, if confronted by the tiger, will not only think about fight or flight, but also whether by making a lot of noise, warriors might arrive quickly from our nearby cave with bigger sticks and join forces to scare off the tiger. The prefrontal lobe realizes there might be enough time to get an arrow out of the quiver and get it into the bow to fire at the tiger before it jumps. The prefrontal lobe allows us to think in the long term and to place short-term events, crises, challenges, and opportunities in the context of the whole rest of our life, as it may affect and be affected by future events. It is where we wrestle with and assess the relative value of uncertainties. Perhaps it is the prefrontal lobe that makes us realize we don't have to outrun the tiger, but only the other person...can the tiger only eat one victim at a time? But what if you feel compelled to defend the other person? Oh dear, life is complicated! That's why we grew the prefrontal lobe. A grand master can understand and judge a game of chess ten moves ahead.

The challenge for young adults is that the prefrontal lobe of the brain does not fully develop, especially in a human male, until around the age of twenty-five. Before that, all we have is fight or flight without any of the calculus of consequences. This has many downsides. It is why insurance premiums are higher for young drivers: they take more risks! It is not a coincidence that the soldiers in a war, who are required to jump out of the trench and charge towards the enemy machine guns with nothing but a rifle, are usually less than twenty-five years old. It is not a coincidence that the chants and rallying cries of every army are designed to mask higher reasoning, to have the young soldiers simply obey the general, who follows but almost never leads them into battle. The general is older and has a prefrontal lobe that is fully developed. He knows that the possibility of death is a strong likelihood and acts accordingly. Younger men charge ahead, emboldened by the amygdala, the whistle that the sergeant major blows, the sound of the military drums, and the fact that they are all wearing the same uniform. They have given their decision-making over to the military high command at that moment and in that place...and that is how the army wants it. *Hoorah!*

Young adults can frequently achieve extraordinary things because their lack of fear enables them to try many courses of action, which in later life seem too risky. This is not necessarily a bad thing, so long as they survive. In our First Star Academies, we teach foster youth in years ten through thirteen (UK), and in grades nine through twelve (USA), to use the university opportunity we make possible, not only to learn a skill and widen their knowledge of the world they will inherit, but also to experiment. To take risks. Be safe, but try alternatives. If you fail, try another one.

In one of the classes I've taught, I suggested that it is like being in an envelope in the dark, with only a pencil to feel your way. You don't know where the edges of the envelope of possibility may lie. But if you poke with the sharp end of the pencil, you will be surprised that there is abundant scope for you to expand. The envelope is bigger than you thought. For sure, once in a while you will hit the edge of the envelope and your pencil will poke through. But that doesn't really matter. All it does is tell you that you've reached the edge of the possible: you can pull the pencil back, turn through ninety degrees, and go off in a different direction. But had you just sat cross-legged in the middle of the envelope, you would never have known how vast were the possibilities open to you as a young adult.

The first step is to get an education, develop a network of supportive people, and seek the unconditional love of either members of your birth family or, in the case of First Star, your equally real First Star family: your fellow Scholars, your Youth Coaches, your tutors, your teachers, our staff and volunteers...all who help you thrive and climb

When Should You Take Risks? How to Survive Your Risk-Taking Years

the ladder to your own highest and best success. If you have neither a loving, supportive birth family nor a First Star family, the task is to seek out those who have compassion and empathy and build your own support system. It is harder, but many people have been able to do exactly that. Don't be afraid to ask. Most people would like to help.

One way of looking at adult entrepreneurs who are successful is that they have not fully developed a sense of fear. They have not become subject to a fully built-out, reasoning, front part of the brain to tell them what they should not even attempt. They are not fearful. Thus, they stride forward to new possibilities, be they Steve Jobs, Bill Gates, Thomas Edison, or all the rest. Sometimes their ideas and inventions will work. Sometimes they will fail. But had they not even tried, they could not have found their successes. Many are neurodivergent, and their mental process consistently makes them stubborn, pushy, and resilient in failure. They can sometimes be real assholes to those around them, whom they bulldoze aside in their single-minded quest to succeed. And they can often focus intensely for long periods of time.

It is usually easier with hindsight to recognize bad choices that create great risk. Preserving your own life and the lives of those around you is the most important overarching purpose for any human being. Life is precious! We cannot safely assume that we have more than one of them, so best to focus on maximizing this one.

In my teenage years, while still living with my parents, I realized I was locked out of the house at three o'clock on a Sunday morning, after a Saturday night out. It would have been more intelligent to remember to take my keys. Faced with the impossibility of getting into the house without waking up my parents, I should have slept in the car if I didn't want to risk my father's anger. But at the age of sixteen, my amygdala was blinding me to the nature of physical risk. There was a wall at an angle to the house that went along the edge of the garden, getting higher and higher as it reached the corner of the house. At the top of that wall, there was a drainpipe that went up the corner of the house, all the way past the third floor. It was dark, but I thought perhaps I could carefully balance my way along the top of the wall and then climb the drain pipe to the top-level floor, where my bedroom was located.

FINDING HAPPY

I did indeed make it up the drain pipe without it falling off the wall, and only then realized that all of my bedroom windows except the furthest one were closed. So, with the stupidity of youth, I inched my way sideways on a decorative brick ledge that was an inch wide and that stuck out from the back wall of the house. I balanced by holding on with the fingertips of both hands on the top and bottom of a higher row of bricks. In this way I shuffled slowly along toward the open window, past those that were closed. I eventually reached the far window, climbed in, got undressed, and went to bed.

Later in the morning, I went down into the sunken garden where there were flagstones under the back face of the house and looked up at my third-floor bedroom windows. I realized that if I had fallen, which was more likely than not given my precarious grip of the bricks, I would certainly have been killed by smashing my head on the flagstones thirty feet below. I felt so ill at the risk I had taken that I threw up in the flowerbed. Stupid is as stupid does.

Years later, after Steven Spielberg and I founded the Starbright Foundation, we recruited Kathleen Unger as our executive director. She and I came out of a meeting with a philanthropist on Pico Boulevard in Los Angeles. As we walked through the parking lot, a tall, muscular man strode up to us, snatched Kathleen's handbag, and ran away down the alley. I went after him. I did not use my long-term thinking of consequences; I simply wanted to return the handbag to its rightful owner, who was my colleague. The man ran fast down the alley, but not faster than me. A few hundred yards into the chase, I started using the front of my brain and asking myself what the hell I was going to do if I actually caught him. Did I remember enough of the game of rugby to lock my shoulder and arms around his lower legs and bring him to the ground? And if I did, he was much bigger than me...he could probably hurt me a great deal.

I began to have second thoughts about catching him. We arrived at a Volkswagen minivan. He leaped into the driver's seat and sped away. I stared intently at the license plate, only to realize that he had covered it up with a piece of paper. As I staggered back out of breath to Kathleen, who was industriously calling the police, I felt I was very lucky to have *not* caught the thief!

When Should You Take Risks? How to Survive Your Risk-Taking Years

Le Mans, 1970. I wondered if a car hit me, would I have time to jump on the hood?

It is challenging for any young person to assess risk. May we agree that the most important thing is to prevent your own death through making a mistake in assessing risk?

Chapter Takeaways and Reflection Questions for You

- What's the most dangerous thing you've ever done?
- Are you proud or ashamed of it?
- Did you do most of your dangerous things before the age of twenty-five?
- If you're under the age of twenty-five, how can you think things through to avoid jeopardizing your life or that of someone else? (Clue: Ask someone who is reliable and older.)
- Is it better to sleep on risky decisions before making them in the morning? (Yes!) Why?
- While it may be true that what doesn't kill you makes you stronger, it is also true that if it does kill you, then you have thrown away your life.

FINDING HAPPY

- Do you have a guardian angel? Should you rely on the angel, or try not to do stupid things that are incredibly dangerous?
- Is it ever worth it to risk your own life or the life of someone else?
- Be safe, young people. Your futures are bright. We need you alive and lifting up the world. Please.

Ever Tried. Ever Failed.
No matter. Try again.
Fail again. Fail better.

—**Samuel Beckett**

CHAPTER 15

How Can You Dare to Do?
Marrakech to Monte Carlo

In the early stages of my professional career as a filmmaker, I was a unit production manager, or UPM. Nobody was ready yet to trust me with several million dollars as a career producer, and I was not ready either. I was instead hired by other career producers to do the busy, detailed work of physically organizing a production: a new script with a new crew in the new country at a new time of the year with new challenges and hopefully new opportunities to solve them.

Thus, aged twenty-one in 1972, I was hired by a man called Tony Busching as the production manager on what must have been some of that year's most expensive thirty- and sixty-second American television commercials, to further the business of Chevron, the American oil company. With the wisdom of history, we were on the wrong side of what turns out to be the only path forward to survival for the planet, where we stop burning hydrocarbons and melting the icecaps. But we were hired to help Chevron sell more gasoline, so that is what we did. Very sorry. In 1972, we knew no better.

The script called for the winners of the 1971 Monte Carlo Rally to recreate their route in standard American production automobiles,

FINDING HAPPY

using Chevron gasoline. So, Paisley Productions hired the two rally winners, Ove Andersson and David Stone, to drive the cars at high speed on dirt roads and highways, and they hired me to organize the logistics: starting in Marrakech, Morocco, winding our way up to Tangiers, crossing by ferry to Spain, landing at Algeciras, driving along the winding coastal road to the French border, across into the South of France, past Marseilles, and ending up in Monte Carlo. Just like the actual rally.

David Stone, the navigator, was British. Ove Andersson was a Swede who, as a bored air force pilot waiting to be scrambled on some snowbound Swedish military runway, had learned that he could drive his car very fast on the ice. By using the handbrake and the steering wheel, he could be sliding sideways, so that when he came to a turn he was already facing into it at ninety degrees to the road just traveled. He would then use the accelerator while releasing the handbrake in order to achieve just enough traction to zoom off, thus having navigated the corner much faster than if the wheels kept a linear relationship with the road surface. To sit next to him in any car while he did this was one of the scariest experiences I've ever had. Rarely was his car in a straight line with the road! It was mostly at forty-five or ninety degrees, and occasionally it was facing backwards, in order to arrive at the apex of a hairpin bend, just in time to accelerate out of it down the new stretch of road. Quite an experience, especially right next to a cliff edge, a sheer drop of hundreds of feet!

The first thing I realized as the UPM on this epic commercial project was that we would need American production cars in Morocco, followed by Spain and France. This was accomplished at vast expense, by my colleagues in the United States shipping three brand-new, fully assembled, and functional Pontiac Grand Prix cars (Grand Prix was the name of the model, not the nature of the car). These were lumbering, whale-sized boats of a car, basically a ship with four wheels that delivered something like nine miles per gallon. They were flown by freight aircraft from Detroit to Paris, and then on a different aircraft to Casablanca in Morocco. They were slightly wider than the freight door on the second plane, and we had to pay the airline to remove and replace the doorframe before and after the flight. We took delivery several weeks before the crew arrived, and we put the three of them in a Casablanca warehouse, after making sure that they were not damaged.

The next problem was rather more challenging to solve. I suggested to Paisley Productions that no one would really know what gasoline was in the cars. A car is a car. And so is gasoline, when you really come to understand it: the same thing whether you buy it in Morocco or Detroit. No, said Tony Busching. We would have with us a lawyer from the Legal Compliance Department of Chevron to make sure that we really did use the Chevron gasoline every inch of the 1,516 miles from Marrakech to Monte Carlo. But it emerged that there was an aviation rule that no more than a single five-gallon can of any petroleum product, including gasoline, could be on any freighter or other aircraft flying commercially from France to Morocco. And so it was that for several weeks, every aircraft that landed nonstop from Paris to Casablanca or Marrakech carried just one of our black five-gallon drums of Chevron gasoline. The shipping broker in each city made a fortune in fees by sending and receiving these. And the airlines must have thought we were raving mad. Which in a way was true.

There was an even worse problem: a government gasoline monopoly in Spain meant that it was completely illegal to import any quantity of gasoline at all from anywhere into Spain. You simply could not do it. I hired a fellow career producer I had first met on the Steve McQueen *Le Mans* film three years earlier, Jean Pierre Avice, and he went around government ministries in Madrid trying to get permission to import five hundred gallons of gasoline from Morocco into Spain. He was turned down by the government at every turn.

I spent a lot of time trying to work out what to do. I was twenty-one years old and had no sense of what was truly impossible; surely there had to be a way? If we couldn't get the gasoline into Spain, and if that was the only gasoline we were allowed to use, I was checkmated...but I was too young to accept that!

One of the things that works very well for me in trying to noodle a new solution to an old problem is to be half awake and half asleep. I often come up with my best solutions, my best hypotheses, in those few minutes while I am waking up, because everything is possible then. There are often lateral leaps of the imagination. In solving things,

FINDING HAPPY

imagination is often more important than knowledge. I woke up thinking that there was one category of gasoline that was absolutely allowed into Spain: surely, the contents of the tank of a vehicle on the ferry from Tangiers to Algeciras in Spain had to be allowed? They couldn't possibly require you to drain the foreign gasoline and buy Spanish: you had to be allowed to arrive with whatever was in your vehicle. But doing the math, using a fleet of cars with drivers was much too expensive... and then we'd have to send them back again. And there was no time. Oh dear!

So, I dreamed up the idea that if we bought a cheap truck, we could weld fifty-five-gallon drums underneath it, and plumb them to the engine of the truck. If challenged, I would say that this was a trans-Sahara truck. "There are no gasoline stations in the Sahara Desert," I would say, and therefore this truck had to carry with it enough capacity in its main tanks to get itself long distances until it could refuel.

I phoned Los Angeles, and a rather bemused Tony Busching said, "Peter, I trust you. If you think we need a truck, and that is the solution, go ahead and buy it." He wired me yet more money, and in a second-hand truck dealership in Casablanca, in my best Arabic-accented French, I negotiated to purchase a ten-ton vegetable truck. Mickey McClay, the key grip on the commercial (the professional who rigs the mechanical stuff on a film), and I navigated this behemoth back to the hotel. Thinking about it, I decided there was one other thing that we should do, which was to put a metal roof on the truck, so that we could put the camera, grip, and electrical equipment inside it. This would mean not only that we would need one less truck, but in addition, it would give me more plausibility at Spanish customs that we had a good reason to be taking a secondhand truck on the ferry to Spain, where they have many secondhand trucks available. It would have our equipment inside it!

It was relatively easy to get a garage to steam-clean fifty-five-gallon drums and to strap them with steel bands underneath the two sides of our ten-ton truck. They also were able to put pipes with stop-cocks from the tanks so that they all supplied gasoline to the engine. My idea to put a metal roof on the truck was at the last minute, because we were supposed to arrive two days later in Marrakech to meet the rest of the crew, who were coming directly from the United States via Paris.

The problem was that what I had already bought was called a stake truck, with sides and a back but no top. In its previous life, it had belonged to a farmer and carried produce to market. When I had the idea to put a metal roof onto it, it was already six o'clock in the afternoon. I realized that the idea was going out of the window unless I could find someone to weld on a roof through the night and the next day, and to get it done before we would need to leave for Marrakech. We went from garage to garage, and everyone was either closed or unwilling to help us for any amount of money. And then Mickey, bless him—out of the corner of his eye, in the gathering darkness of Casablanca's industrial district—saw the flash of an oxyacetylene welding operation in the distance. We made a beeline for it and discovered a man and a couple of assistants who were welding together wrought iron gates for a convent. They did not have any work facility at all; they were simply squatting on the sidewalk with metal bars, a machine to bend them, a rough design on paper, oxygen and acetylene cylinders, and a gas arc welder. I made a deal for them to find some sheet metal and cover the truck!

Anywhere in the world, people who have never worked together don't really trust each other. The way this was dealt with in Morocco, especially in the dark at 8 p.m., was that the bank notes to pay the entire amount for the contract were torn in half. The left-hand halves went to the supplier and the right-hand halves were initially withheld by the buyer, which was me. In that way, both sides of the transaction would know that the other one couldn't defraud them, because they would not have money of any value, just some torn-up halves. That was why almost all Moroccan dirham bank notes were torn in half and taped back together.

I still didn't entirely trust a welding operation run on a sidewalk, and I asked Mickey to disable the truck, which he did by removing the rotor arm from the engine. We took it back with us in the rental car to the hotel. The following morning, full of good cheer after breakfast, we came back to see whether they had done substantial enough work on our truck. There was the convent. There was the sidewalk. But there

FINDING HAPPY

was no truck. There was no welder. There was no team. There was nothing but an empty sidewalk. And I thought, now I have to phone my boss Tony and tell him that I bought a truck and it has been stolen!

Then a little boy came up to me, looked up, and said in French, "I know where your truck is." I paid him, and we followed him around the corner, perhaps two blocks, and then around another corner. There was our truck with a shiny roof almost finished on top! A big relief. And there was the man with a big smile on his face. In the middle of the night he had run out of acetylene gas, and so the welder wouldn't work. He got his family out of bed to help him, and twenty of them had pushed the undriveable ten-ton truck a considerable distance in the middle of the night, to get it to an electrical socket so that they could use an electric arc welder and finish the job. But they had done it. I loved that man! I gave him the other half of the money and a bit more.

Mickey and I looked incredulously at each other for what we had accomplished. Then we set off, with me driving the rental car and him driving the truck, on the four-hour, 150-mile trip to Marrakech, on a road not known back then for its smooth surface. We got about half-way there and stopped to refuel. Mickey asked me to interpret what a local man was trying to say to him. I told Mickey, "This gentleman is attempting to sell you a little girl. You have to say no." Mickey said, "But I could take her back to America and give her a better life." And I said, "No, you will be arrested as a sex trafficker. So no, we won't be doing that. Our job is to get the truck to Marrakech. Say goodbye."

We drove for about another thirty minutes, at which point the truck, with me behind it in the rental car, rolled to a stop at the side of the road. Mickey told me the head gasket had blown in the ancient truck engine. The top of the engine was under a cover in the cab, and we drove the rest of the way to Marrakech with Mickey pouring water into the radiator out of jerry cans and bottles, while I beetled ahead in the rental car and negotiated for Bedouin folks to sell me water they pulled out of wells. I would then catch up with the truck and exchange Mickey's empties for the full ones.

I was feeling as though I was Yogi Bear in that famous cartoon where he walks off the edge of a cliff. Until he looks down, there is no gravity and he whistles to keep himself cheerful as he continues horizontally in the air. Will he reach the other cliff before the gravity exceeds his optimism?

As we reached the outskirts of Marrakech, the truck engine seized up and would go no further. I found another truck and paid its driver to tow us the rest of the way to the hotel, using an old tow rope. We almost got there, but not quite. It was now dark. We were stopped by a policeman. "Monsieur," he said "you have no lights on your truck." "Yes, sir," I replied, "the engine doesn't work. The battery is flat for that reason. And so we have no lights. I am terribly sorry." The policeman said, "Because you are guests in my country, I will not arrest you, if you will buy a book of raffle tickets from me." At this point, I was ready to do almost anything. We negotiated a price for the raffle tickets. He gave them to me and I gave him the money. I stuffed the tickets in my pocket. We drove the rest of the way to the Hotel Mamounia.

We arrived there at about eight o'clock at night to find Tony Busching and the American and British crew having dinner. Dirty and disheveled, Mickey and I staggered into the dining room and sat at the table, regaling the rest of the crew with our adventure in solving the problem of the gasoline overnight and during the second day. Tony Busching interrupted me when I got to the bit about the policeman, and he said, "I believe your whole story, but you cannot possibly be telling the truth about a policeman who made you buy raffle tickets." "Well," I said, "it so happens that in my pocket, I have them." I placed them into his hand and carried on telling the crew how we were going to get the petrol into Spain, under the truck. Tony said to me, "I don't read French, but what's this date on the tickets?" I had a look for the first time and I said, "It appears that the policeman, as a polite pretext for *baksheesh*, or bribery, has sold us raffle tickets which expired five years ago."

We had the truck fixed in Marrakech and set off successfully with Ove Andersson and David Stone driving the Pontiac Grand Prix cars,

FINDING HAPPY

the crew in minibuses, and the equipment now in my long-distance-desert, ten-ton vegetable truck with a roof. We arrived at Tangiers after filming on the way. We filled the fifty-five-gallon drums under the truck from the five-gallon Chevron cans we had brought from Casablanca and Marrakech. We put the truck on the ferry and crossed over the eastern edge of the Mediterranean, north to Algeciras. The Spanish customs paid no attention to us at all! Honestly, we could have just had the drums in the back of the truck; they never even looked. But there we were. Past the customs, my colleague Jean Pierre Avice stood incredulous that we had somehow found a way of getting the petrol into Spain, where the government forbade it.

The following day, we set off for Monte Carlo after decanting the fifty-five-gallon drums into jerrycans so that it would be easier to fill the cars on the way. Unfortunately, the jerrycans that Jean Pierre had bought were made of plastic, and they interacted somehow with the gasoline and began leaking. So he had to run ahead in a rental car, find metal jerry cans, and quickly bring them to us. We again had to decant the gasoline, shouting that no one was to smoke in the vicinity of this rather hazardous job. I told the Chevron lawyer that it was his fault! He said, "No, it's my job."

So it was that we arrived in Monte Carlo and completed the commercial. The advertising agency got a bonus from Chevron. Paisley Productions received a bonus from the advertising agency. I got a very nice bonus from Paisley. And I had further solidified my reputation with Tony and the Los Angeles team: in case of an impossible situation, Sammy Samuelson, nicknamed by them The Roadrunner, was the one that you wanted to sort it out.

It was at the end of that job that Tony Bushing said to me, "Why don't you come back to Los Angeles, after you wrap the production and sell the truck? Maybe you'd like to see how we edit, and experience Los Angeles a little bit?" I was young, I was single, and I said yes on the spot. And thus, in 1973, right after Cambridge, I found myself on the way to Los Angeles via New York to take up the most junior position at Paisley Productions on Sunset Boulevard. I made television commercials all over the United States and fell in love with America and Americans. I was twenty-two years old.

How Can You Dare to Do? Marrakech to Monte Carlo

I think for this chapter to work, you need to make it feel less like an adventure yarn and more like a lesson in perseverance and creative problem-solving.

Chapter Takeaways and Reflection Questions for You

- How can you best make your boss really appreciate you?
- How can you go the extra mile to achieve success?
- Is imagination more important than knowledge? Was Einstein right, or not?
- When you get a job, how can you excel?
- What are planning, hard work, daring, and ingenuity, and how do you combine them?
- When the door is closed, can you find an open window?
- What is ingenuity?
- Are you ingenious?

CHAPTER 16

How Can You Seize the Day?
The Return of the Pink Panther

I met an important American director, Blake Edwards. He was planning a period film set in early Canada: British versus French soldiers in the snow, among the Iroquois indigenous tribes. I was game for anything, I listened carefully to what he wanted and said a bold "yes" to that. He hired me on the spot. A month later the film was cancelled. But Blake immediately hired me as the production manager on his next Peter Sellers film, *The Return of the Pink Panther*, which was an even bigger break. It helped that by then I could speak current French as well as the medieval version, and that I had already filmed in Morocco. But the studio and some of the middle-aged British crew were resentful; they thought I was too young at twenty-two. They were right! I worked twice as hard to prove Blake chose the right man. It was a heck of a responsible job, and everyone reporting to me was at least twice my age. I often slept in the office.... I worked eighteen hours a day.

I got it done.

I loved Peter Sellers. Back then, he was as famous as, say, Adam Sandler, Ben Stiller, and Steve Carell would be now...if you combined

How Can You Seize the Day? The Return of the Pink Panther

them. He was also the first real genius that I ever met. Truly, truly gifted. An extraordinary human being whose talent took your breath away.

But he was also a bit challenged in various eccentric ways. He was very superstitious. Crazy scared of weird stuff. One of the things that I had to do each morning before he arrived on the set was to make sure we would not provoke his superstition. I would go around and stare at all the members of the crew and anyone else who was there. If they were wearing the color green I would have to say, "Harry, do you mind going to wardrobe and changing your socks? Because, you know, Peter, who will be here any minute, will not work if anyone is wearing green. Peter doesn't work with green. So if you could please go and change your socks quickly, that would be a blessing."

The script called for a chase on the rooftops of a museum in Casablanca, where the Pink Panther thief, played by Christopher Plummer, was stealing a gigantic diamond. I needed to import six Sterling submachine guns, two Luger pistols, and ammunition into Morocco, from Bapty Armourers in London. So, taking a deep breath, I took my twenty-two-year-old self off to the central police station in Casablanca and met the chief of police. It was illegal to bring machine guns or pretty much any kind of gun into his country, he said, and he would not issue me a permit. I had a letter from the prime minister of Morocco encouraging us to film there, and I showed it to him. This did not work: He asked me, "Just exactly who the hell do you think you are? You think you can intimidate me with this letter?" "No," I said, "not at all. I just want you to know that we are guests in your country." The chief said, "I am in charge of the law in this city, not the prime minister, and I will decide what to do without that influence."

Checkmated. But after some discussion about how important the film was for the local economy, and how we would need to hire a large number of local police officers to keep good order, he called a typist and dictated a permit, whereby I was indeed allowed—on my personal undertaking of safety and good faith—to import two Sterling submachine guns and accessories, which I was not to allow out of my sight until they went safely back onto an aircraft to exit Morocco some weeks later. I had to give him my mother's maiden name, and in the affidavit I was required to swear on her life! If Doris Cicely had known that her name was used to bring machine guns into North Africa, she would not have been amused.

In due course, the crates with the machine guns arrived. I signed all the paperwork and escorted these dangerous weapons to the hotel. I felt like a gunrunner. I did not know where to keep them safe and ended up putting them under my bed in the hotel room. There they stayed until we used them, and I was able to get them back to the airport and on a return flight as quickly as possible. I sure as hell was not going to get locked up indefinitely in some Moroccan prison.

A young person, specifically a young man, does not really have a well-developed sense of prudence, of care, of diligence, nor of caution, until he reaches his mid-twenties. Women are much smarter and shrewder at an earlier age. I was sitting in my office late one night after everyone else had dinner and had gone to bed. I had gone back up to my office to carry on working, to get a jump on my insuperable

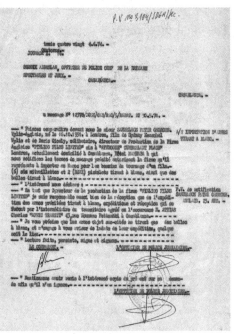

list of tasks for the next day. As I sat at my desk in the silence of the Marrakech night, with only the noise of cicadas and my pen on paper, I heard a cat meowing. It sounded like a tiny kitten. I tried to ignore it and carried on working on the budget, but I eventually had to go and find out what was going on with the cat. I followed my ears into the office bathroom. As part of the wall there was a kind of cupboard that, when one opened the doors, contained a number of conduits and big pipes carrying wiring, water, gas, and sewage vertically up and down the several floors of the hotel.

Looking down into the dark and using a flashlight, I could see two little yellow eyes looking back up at me from the cellar, three floors below me. There was the kitten trapped down there. I looked down and realized that it was a long way, and that it was also incredibly dirty, not having been cleaned since the hotel was built as a royal palace, hundreds of years earlier. I went back to my desk and tried to concentrate on the budget. The cat continued meowing, and eventually I couldn't stand it any longer. I stripped down and, naked, held my flashlight in my teeth and climbed down the pipes several floors into the basement. As I reached the bottom, the kitten ran away through a lateral duct, and I never saw or heard it again. Cursing and thankful that there would be a shower once I got back up into the bathroom, I started to try to climb back up, gripping the pipes.

Unfortunately, I had not really thought through the difficulty of climbing back up, which was considerably worse than going down. I would go three feet up and then slip two feet down. Sometimes four feet down. It did not go well. About half way up, sweating like a pig, I realized I no longer had the upper body strength to get myself back up to the beckoning light of the office bathroom. I wedged myself in among the pipes and had a think. I also noticed that there were rats that were considerably more adept at climbing up and down the pipes than me, and that there were many very big ones. They were not scared of me, but I was certainly scared of them. After I had a rest, I carried on, trying only to move upwards three inches at a time and not to slip back at all.

In this way, around two hours later, I fell through the doors, out of the pipe duct, and onto the floor of my bathroom. Covered in muck from head to foot, I crawled into the shower, then finally got dressed. I staggered back to my desk, collapsing into the chair. By now it was getting light. There was a knock on the door, and I said, "Come in!" One of our electricians entered with an envelope full of receipts, asking if I could please reimburse his petty cash? I never told him or anyone else

FINDING HAPPY

how stupid I was in climbing down a pipe duct in a Moroccan hotel in the middle of the night. I don't recommend it.

When I worked on the *Return of the Pink Panther*, I realized that literacy was a key to the door of life, and that people were handcuffed without it. A large proportion of the Moroccan population was not able to read or write, and that included the twenty-five or thirty drivers of all our trucks and cars. But in the town square of Jemma el-Fnaa in Marrakech, there were ten scribes sitting cross-legged on rugs. If someone paid them a few dirhams, they would take dictation and produce a letter typed on an ancient manual typewriter.

One morning, halfway through the shoot, I received a typed letter from the drivers. It read:

"Dear Mr. Samuelson, May Allah in his infinite power protect you, your children and grandchildren. And may you live under the divine benevolence of a happy life, and may your family be many. Mr. Ben Daoud the Transportation Captain has not been paying us our wages. We implore you to please make him give us our money that we have already earned, as we need it to feed our families."

I was appalled. I had no idea that this was going on. I strode off to find my transportation captain, and he immediately agreed that he had been accumulating the pay of the drivers and now had a lot of cash in a safe. But he said, "In our country, we do not pay the drivers until the end of the shoot." I replied with some anger, "Well, I don't care. On one of my films, when people earn money, we pay them promptly. These people have families to feed." "No, sir," said Mr. Ben Daoud, "you have this wrong and you will see there will be bad consequences." I said, "Well that will be my responsibility, won't it? Tomorrow at wrap, I want you here with all the money, and the drivers will form a line, and you will give each of them all of their accumulated wages. And that's the end of the discussion."

Which is exactly what took place.

The following morning, not a single driver could be found anywhere. The vehicles were empty, still parked in the transportation compound. The drivers had disappeared. The crew from the United Kingdom had to drive the trucks and the cars to the location. It turned out that with this amount of cash, our drivers had decided that they should party long into the night, and they did not care that they had a call time they should observe. I learned that one simply cannot carry cultural differences from one country to another. And that was one of those occasions.

Peter Sellers was a massive practical joker. I didn't realize it when he directed this at me. We were still in Marrakech and just finishing up filming there. It had gone very well—we were on schedule and on budget. We were flying to Switzerland for the next segment of filming. I had chartered a Boeing 707 to take most of the equipment and the whole crew up to Gstaad via Geneva. Peter came into my office in the Hotel Mamounia bright and early one morning and said, "You're going up at the end of the week, but I'm going on the private plane today. And I have so much baggage! Would it be okay if I asked you to take a bag for me when you go on the charter?" And I replied, "Of course it would." So he fetched a rather small, briefcase-sized bag. I said to him, "No problem at all. Just put it on the credenza, you'll see it again in Gstaad."

I said to the crew, "You know, we're flying nonstop on a charter. We're a film company, and we're going nonstop from Morocco, home of hashish and marijuana and God knows what other drugs, and we're going to Switzerland, which is not known for its accommodating police and customs authorities: they have zero tolerance in matters of illegal drugs. So you'll not take anything with you that you wouldn't want the Swiss police or customs to find in your bag."

Peter Sellers went off on his Learjet, and I sat there the rest of the day looking at the credenza. I'm looking at his bag, and eventually I'm thinking that I know what he's done. It's going to be full of blocks of hashish. And I'm going to go to prison in Switzerland for several years because of Peter Sellers. And he'll write me a note of apology and send me food, but I'll be the one in prison because I'll be responsible for taking the bag on the charter. And I thought that actually I was not prepared to do that, even for my star. I looked and looked again at it, and in the end I tried to open it. It had a leather strap that went through the handle from one side of the case to the other, and of course it was locked. So I went back to my desk and I stared at it again for several hours.

FINDING HAPPY

In the end, I decided, "The hell with it. I'm not going to prison for Peter Sellers. Sorry." I took my desk scissors, and I cut through the leather hasp and opened his case...which was full of his dirty underwear and socks. Nothing else. That was all that was in there.

I thought, "What am I going to say to Peter Sellers? He's going to know that I didn't trust him!" I took the mutilated case to Switzerland. When I next saw him, I gave him the case, and he saw that the hasp had been cut. He said, "Ah, Sammy, you didn't trust me!" I blamed the Swiss customs for cutting the strap. He thought it was very, very funny. And I realized he actually had done it all on purpose, because he wanted to see what would happen. He was testing me. And of course I had played into his joke by cutting the thing. I don't think he believed for a moment that it was the Swiss customs agents. He thought it was me!

We made it to Switzerland. I had to go to Blake Edwards very early one day, while we were filming at the Palace Hotel in Gstaad. I had received a phone call even earlier from an assistant in London, who told me he couldn't get the actor who was to play the Clothing Thief onto the plane because there was fog at Luton Airport and all flights were cancelled. I couldn't reschedule; we were almost finished in Gstaad. I had to go to Blake and say, "I'm terribly sorry, but you've got to cast someone here because I can't bring in the actor to do the Clothing Thief...and I'm so, so sorry."

He was actually quite angry, or possibly he was pretending to be so. And he said, "Okay, your punishment is that you will be playing the Clothing Thief." And I said, "No, no, no, no, no, no, I can't act. Blake, he's got lines and everything." And he said, "You'll have to do it in an Italian accent. You're it, and you get one rehearsal."

In the scene, Peter Sellers as Clouseau, the bumbling French detective, comes through the hotel's revolving door. He gets his case stuck in the opposite quadrant. Eventually he gets that sorted out and falls into the foyer of the hotel. My character comes up to him and says, "*Mi scusi, Senõr!* May I take your coat?" and Clouseau replies in his thick French accent, "*Ah, oui.*" He gives me his coat, and I say, "And your hat? And your gloves?" He hands them over, and then bemused, watches me through the big picture window, while I quickly run out and jump into an open-top sports car...and then drive away with his clothes, waving

94

back at him. Peter goes over to the reception desk and asks the reception clerk, played by the late, great Victor Spinetti, "Who is that man?" Victor replies, "He is Senõr Fabrizzi." Sellers asks, "Who is Senõr Fabrizzi?" The receptionist replies, "He is a secondhand clothing thief from Milano." That was the scene. In editing it, Blake thought it didn't need the explanation, so Victor ended up on the cutting room floor. But my bit is there: the only time in my career anyone got me in front of the camera while it was turned on. Definitely the last time too, but opposite the most famous comedian in the world!

We completed the location portion of the film at Victorine Studios in Nice, France. I had a great deal of fun filming in and around Nice, an area I knew well. One of my challenges was to find a swimming pool next to a stately home, and to persuade the owners that it would be really fine if we drove a truck backwards into their pool for a stunt. I knocked on the doors of twenty castles, and nobody would give me the time of day. Then I found a castle that had an irrigation tank, which with a little bit of construction could look like a pool. Better yet, it was at the bottom of a hill, so that the truck would gain momentum before the stunt man playing Peter Sellers as Clouseau drove it into the water. I was quite proud of myself to have delivered the goods for Blake.

It was at that castle that one day Blake bit off more than he could chew. He and Frank Waldman, our writer, had written a tremendous scene where Clouseau, disguised as an inspector from the Nice Telephone Company, drives his ridiculously tiny tricycle truck up to the imposing front door of the castle. He gets out of the truck with his tool belt on and presses the doorbell button. When he removes his finger, the bell continues ringing, and it becomes deeply worrying to him. He has broken it! But then he has the bright idea to reach into his tool belt, take a screwdriver, and lever out the stuck button. Unfortunately, because he is Clouseau, the entire bell-push mechanism falls out of the wall and dangles from its red and black wires. Sellers pulls on the wire, and about ten yards come out of the wall. More and more flustered, he takes a pair of pliers from the toolbelt and cuts the wires. The bell finally stops.

Bent over, he sees that his face is next to a very shiny pair of black polished shoes. As he stands, he realizes that above the shoes is a very tall figure wearing a butler's uniform. This was David Lodge, the wonderful British character actor who always played the butler for Blake in these films. The butler gives Clouseau a withering look. Clouseau holds up the bell push and the mess of red and black wires and says, with Peter Sellers's strangled French accent, "You had a defective bell push. I have a-mended it. There will be no charge." That was the complicated scene that Blake decided we would film all in one shot. Unfortunately, in each successive attempt, or take, whenever after about sixty seconds Peter reached the point where he was face to face looking up at the butler, before he could deliver his line, one or other of them would burst out in hysterical laughter; they got the giggles.

This happened on take after take, until we were really getting behind on the clock. Blake was getting frustrated. He then did a very clever thing, which was to lose his temper and scream at his two actors, scaring the hell out of them, thus breaking their hysteria of laughing and the wind-up of the sixty seconds. He may have been pretending to be upset. We started the shot again. Peter and David were too scared to laugh. But as Peter opened his mouth to deliver the line, Blake Edwards burst out laughing and fell off his seat on the Elemack Spyder camera dolly, jarring the camera and ruining the shot. We never did get that scene all in one! In the finished film, it is made from edited pieces. There was no other choice. It was too funny.

Chapter Takeaways and Reflection Questions for You

- Think seriously about how you take risks. What is the process you generally use, or do the risks just use you? Is your risk-taking just random? Getting this right is one of the most important parts of growing up. If you take no risks, you cannot succeed. If you take the wrong kinds, you can badly hurt yourself or others. How can you tell the difference? (Clues: Ask someone wise. If in doubt, sleep on it.)

- Why do young adults, especially young men, take big risks? What part of their brain is too underdeveloped to think things through in a long-term fashion?

- Whether you are a young man or a young woman, when have you made poor choices? Did you learn from them or repeat them?

How Can You Seize the Day? The Return of the Pink Panther

- How should you behave when confronted with a course of action that might kill you or cause you or others great harm?
- Do humans make their best decisions drunk or in some other altered state?
- Do they know that when in that altered state? (No!)
- What do you do when you are promoted to a position where you are hard-pressed to fulfill all its functions? With hindsight, I should either have said no to Blake Edwards or sought out a mentor on the spot to help me. I was too proud.
- Why is it easier to work with a small company than a big one?
- Why do bullies seek out weakness in a workplace and occasionally make one's life miserable?
- What can be done about that?
- Are Americans more fun than British people? (Clue: Depends on the person!)
- Winston Churchill said that the United States and Britain were "two great nations separated by a common language." What did he mean?
- Why is it important to travel? Why does it grow our mind to experience new cultures, new religions, new societies, new ethnicities?
- What can we always learn from those around us?
- Where does school learning stop and experience of the world begin? Can you do both at once? How? (Clue: Study abroad!)
- Why is it incredibly helpful later to have worked hard developing a second language in school?

CHAPTER 17

Travel as Education. Filming in the Philippines

One of the most exciting, most privileged advantages of making films is that you don't just get to travel to new countries, but you get to work there in depth, far from being a mere tourist for a couple of weeks. You go to a country where you have no prior experience, and you live and work there with local people for between three and nine months, while you plan, pre-produce, produce, and wrap your film. You get the opportunity to work with completely different inhabitants of planet Earth, ones who are living lives entirely unrelated to your own.

So it was that I spent nine months living in the Philippines. I was hired by a very wealthy family to organize a film there called *High Velocity*, starring Ben Gazzara, Paul Winfield, Keenan Wynn, and Britt Ekland. The late family patriarch, Chick Parsons, had been a great hero in the Filipino resistance to the occupying Japanese during the Second World War, and the family owned thousands of acres of sugar cane plantations. The two adult sons, Patrick and Michael, with whom I dealt and to whom I reported, could not have been more different. Patrick was drilled down and business-like. Michael wanted to have fun and rather liked being in, on, and around a motion picture. I found the Filipino people extraordinarily warm, welcoming, and enthusiastic,

98

Travel as Education. Filming in the Philippines

but there were several things that were completely different from anything I'd ever experienced.

On one occasion while we were filming in Manila, we could not drive the generator truck, which we had brought by ship from Australia, anywhere near the location. The Filipino gaffer climbed up a power pole and, with his bare hands, clipped on our main feed cable to the high-voltage line at the top of the pole. And that was how we lit our set. God knows how many volts were up there. I was only partially reassured that he told me, "Do not worry, Mr. Sammy. I do this all the time."

Our film was financed in US dollars. The official exchange rate of the Filipino peso to the dollar during our film was 7.5 to one. I was approached by a man who said that he could give us ten pesos per dollar. I had to meet him while stopped between floors in the elevator of the Hyatt Regency Hotel in downtown Manila, where two suitcases changed hands. I never dared do that again.

The Philippines at the time was operating under martial law. Ferdinand Marcos was, for all intents and purposes, a dictator, and the way that the Philippine constabulary operated was incredibly ruthless and harsh. I remember driving past their headquarters and seeing perhaps one hundred prisoners cutting the front lawn with regular-sized scissors, as punishment. I decided that that would not be something I would want to experience. On the other hand, there was an absolute curfew at 10 p.m. in Manila. Awful though that was for the local people, we—our crew, stunt people, and extras—all had curfew passes. We were able to safely film a spectacular night-time car chase through Chinatown, with no worries of colliding with a civilian. Stunt bliss!

The reason for the martial law was a communist insurgency in the south of the Philippines, in an area of islands called Mindanao. Because we had the encouragement of the Filipino government to make our film, we were able to use military Huey helicopters to get about when

FINDING HAPPY

we filmed in Calatagan, some distance from Manila. If I had a business meeting back in the capital, one of our military helicopters would fly me in to land in a park in the center of Manila. The helicopter would land after hovering overhead, to scatter people in order not to hit them. I would get out, and the car that I had arranged by radio would take me off to the meeting. When we did not need helicopters for the next several days, we would dismiss them. Our military pilots would plead with us to come up with a reason why they could not go back to the fighting in Mindanao. Sometimes when we got a Huey, the inside would have fresh blood on the floor from transporting wounded soldiers down south. The whole experience was sometimes too vivid.

There were also some hilarious experiences. On one occasion while we were filming in the jungle in Calatagan, miles from anywhere, the script called for one of our actors, Ben Gazzara, to eat a chocolate bar. The prop man, shame-faced, was unable to produce the prop. When I asked him where on earth it was, he said, "I ate it." I asked him, "Why did you do that? It was a prop." He replied simply, "Because I was hungry." The enormous economic disparity was everywhere to be seen, between working people who were absolutely dirt poor and the very privileged 1 percent who were, by any international standards, enormously wealthy. The area of sugar cane owned by the Parsons was so vast that they had their own air force and landing strips to fly between. One of their planes was designed to go very slowly, and as you went overhead at only a few miles per hour, you could talk to people on the ground through loudspeakers.

My fellow career producer on the film, Takashi Ohashi, was an amazing man of enormous integrity, with whom I became very friendly as we came to rely on each other more and more. I still miss him very much. When we wrapped the film, we exchanged presents. I gave him a desk set and he gave me a shirt in a box. But when I looked at the shirt, it was a bit frayed around the collar and at the cuffs. At first, I couldn't understand why he had given me a secondhand shirt. Then it was explained to me that this was the highest token of friendship that one friend could give another in Japan: that you would literally give your friend the shirt off your back. I was touched.

Travel as Education. Filming in the Philippines

Ohashi-san spoke wonderful English, but with a pretty strong accent. On one occasion, he screeched to a halt in a company car on location, where the whole crew was gathered. He jumped out and ran up to our production designer, a rather large American called Rob Mitchell. "Rob, Rob, please, immediately I must have your corset!" Rob was perplexed, as were the rest of us by this strange request. Ohashi-san kept repeating it clearly: he urgently needed Rob's corset. Eventually, Rob said to Ohashi, "I do not appreciate you drawing attention in front of the crew to my size. Go get your own damn corset." To which Ohashi-san replied, "Rob, Rob, thousands pardons, not corset. *Call sheet*, please. Urgently."

At one point, as I dashed out of the office to go to set one night, I asked Ohashi-san if he could please create numbers for the cars, because we had twenty identical white sedans, and the American, Australian, and British crew were having difficulty in telling them apart when they needed to requisition transport to get from A to B. I thought Ohashi-san would simply use a felt tip to put rough numbers on pieces of cardboard. But when I came back late that night to the office, Ohashi had fallen asleep on the sofa, exhausted; all around him, drying, were the most beautiful placards, each individually numbered, using pen and ink with the high standard you would expect to see in top-notch Japanese calligraphy. And that was Ohashi-san.

Not everything was wonderful amid the cultural differences. I experienced the different sense of the value of life in two ways. I asked how the insurance premium on the life of one of our Filipino stuntmen could be so inexpensive, a few dollars a week. It was explained to me that if one of them was killed, the family would receive just $1,000. The payout was tiny by our standards. On another occasion, when I arrived back on the set at lunchtime, the Filipino crew were in a circle laughing at something going on in the middle. Someone had tied a tin can to the tail of a puppy, which was driving itself crazy trying to get rid of it.

FINDING HAPPY

Everyone thought this was hilarious, and when I stepped in and set it free, they thought I was nuts.

I am fascinated by my own cultural oversights, instances where, despite my best efforts to be inclusive and to encourage everyone—seeing but going beyond religious, cultural, or racial differences—I nevertheless sometimes trip myself up. When we made *Foster Boy*, we needed to cast an African American lead playing an eighteen- or nineteen-year-old young man. The character had to be able to rap as well as act.

We could not find a known actor who was affordable and available. Our casting department, led by Robert Ulrich, held open casting sessions on weekends, in areas where we thought young men of color would walk in off the street and audition by reading scenes. In Inglewood, South Central, and Compton, anyone who came through the door was considered. On callbacks, our casting team then videotaped perhaps one hundred people. This was reduced down until we had ten and then five and then three and then two. And then we hired Shane Paul McGee, an amazing young Black actor. He was simply the very best of the hundreds we considered.

Knowing that I was going to have a lunch to talk about the film with him, I decided to look online, to see whether perhaps he had done amateur theatricals in high school that might be on YouTube. Sure enough, I found the Christmas musical where he had played the lead in twelfth grade. I had assumed, with massive unconscious bias and cultural insensitivity, that he would have attended a school in one of the three poor communities where we did the open casting. Completely wrong. Unthinking white gaze: he had attended Beverly Hills High and had played the lead in their Christmas musical. He was Tevye in *Fiddler on the Roof!* At our lunch, I learned that he had grown up in a middle-class family and attended USC, where he had trained as an actor. I was really angry with myself for the assumption I had made and determined that I would never make that mistake again.

And yet every so often, I trip myself up and I realize that white privilege is real, and awful, even though not everyone afflicted by it is mean-minded. You can simply be oblivious, and assuming things can be its own kind of widespread bad. *Mea culpa. Mea maxima culpa.* I understand that years ago, a white guest at a formal party in New York asked a man in a tuxedo, whom he assumed was a waiter, for a drink. The man he asked was then senator Barack Obama. Assume nothing! If you'd like to understand further how the white gaze reinforces white supremacy, I strongly recommend you read *Resurrection Hope* by Reverend Kelly Brown Douglas.

Chapter Takeaways and Reflection Questions for You

- Have you ever received someone else's unconscious bias? How did you handle it?
- Have you ever inflicted it? How did you handle it?
- Where have you traveled furthest? How were people different? How the same?
- What are your plans to experience more of the world?
- Do you tend to focus more on the differences between your tribe and others, or on what is the same?
- Can we celebrate and appreciate differences while ensuring social justice and equality? How? Why do some people hate others who are different?
- What is the most embarrassing thing that ever happened to you? How did you handle it?

CHAPTER 18

Value Your Own American Dream. Coming to Hollywood

At the end of the Chevron commercial in Monte Carlo, Tony Busching of Paisley Productions had invited me to come work for Paisley on Sunset Boulevard in Hollywood. I was single, I had no obligations, and I decided to take him up on the offer. It was a difficult time in the British economy, and what few jobs seemed to be available were not terribly interested in my academic qualifications in English literature. If I had had a degree in engineering or architecture, things might have been easier. I also had a father who cast a very long shadow of virtue and high achievement. As a young, impatient man, I was eager to plow my own furrow. The British film industry at the level of crews and operations can be incredibly mean. It seemed to me that I was either criticized for some perceived illusory advantage that I had by being Sydney's son, or else I was scorned as his son if I tripped myself. Either way, the idea of a fresh start in America seemed like a good idea.

I moved into a tiny apartment on Franklin Avenue, and I worked like hell at Paisley, which had a single stage and a staff of about thirty making television commercials and the occasional short film. Mickey

104

Value Your Own American Dream. Coming to Hollywood

McClay, with whom I had worked well in Morocco, was the resident prop man, key grip, and electrician. His workshop at the back of the stage was to me a place of wonderment, with every gadget, knickknack, and souvenir I could possibly imagine, truly an Aladdin's cave. One day I asked him what the object was in the big glass jar. He replied that it was the head of a member of the Viet Cong that he had cut off during his time in Vietnam. I did not go into Mickey's workshop again. I just stood in the doorway, looked away, and talked loudly if I needed something.

I met a cute lady at Reubens, a bar in the Valley, after work. I spent a while telling her about filmmaking, and she ate up every word, until she blurted out, "I have no idea what you are talking about, but I love your accent." It was a hoot.

I experienced firsthand the power of the American Dream. It's a thing more famous in the past, but it certainly still exists. Most Americans seem to have forgotten its value. It is summed up by the famous sonnet by Emma Lazarus on the base of the Statue of Liberty in New York Harbor. "Give us your...huddled masses yearning to breathe free...." It is a sign of the times that more than one politician has attempted to change the phrasing so that it no longer talks about huddled masses but only the highly qualified who might be privileged to gain an entry visa to the United States.

The tall, self-righteous white men have conveniently forgotten that they themselves are descended from immigrants. All of them. We constantly hear their anti-immigration argument loud and clear in all its strident illogic. They pander to under-educated men who seriously believe immigrants steal American jobs and leech off society. They think immigrants don't pay taxes and that if we just rounded them all up and sent them home, or if we made things so tough and scary that they voluntarily left, our economy would benefit. They need to look out of the window.

A fundamental economic pillar on which this country was built was slavery. And immigrants not only made this nation, but they continue to make it function. Immigrants who are undocumented pay sales tax, property tax, excise tax, and if they work under someone else's Social Security number, as is often the case, they pay into the system without any benefit in return. And even more than the taxes they pay, they and

FINDING HAPPY

their children greatly uplift consumer demand for goods and services: these are people who live here, spending money to do so. For exactly the same reason economists pray for a healthy retail Christmas, we should want as many people as possible to contribute to the economy. These are among them. Furthermore, first-generation undocumented aliens often take the millions of menial jobs that Americans reject: ask the farmers how easy it was to get their crops harvested after Title 42 crackdowns scared away their traditional workers during COVID.

The Census Bureau tells us that the US population has inched higher for the first time in several years. But this is not because there are more babies born than people dying. No, the natural growth rate had fallen to a level not seen since the 1930s. Our population only grew because of immigration. Without immigrants arriving, it would actually have shrunk. And a shrinking work force and consumer base would have diminished GNP, impoverished the pension system, and led to further economic decline. Ask the Chinese, with the awful legacy of their one-child policy. Ask the Japanese: no immigration, not enough young people to pay in taxes for the pensions of the elderly Japanese.

So, to those immigrants who arrived this year, I say, "Thank you for coming! We welcome and cherish your contributions to our economy. Please ignore those who want to send you away. There are really not that many of them, they are just loud. Don't watch bigoted TV and websites. They make money by selling advertising, and they attract eyeballs by stirring up outrage. They will upset you, as they do me. Happy Hannukah, Kwanza, Christmas...and Diwali. Come one. Come all. Together we will build a better America."

I am privileged to live here, and I am grateful. I work every day to justify the invitation and to pay it back with a premium.

Chapter Takeaways and Reflection Questions for You

- Where is your family from? Do you cherish your heritage and revel in living in America? You should.

- Do you treat all people equally, despite their family origin, sexual orientation and identity, the way they look, and their faith? That's what smart, thinking people do.

- When you witness discrimination, even a prejudiced joke, do you speak up? Do you push back? Silence equals encouragement. Don't be complicit.

- Are you doing things to make our country better? It's a team sport; do you do your share and then some more? Lead from the front. Civilization is precious and fragile. Do your part, every day, to nurture it.

- Do you apply your discriminating thinking when reading nonsense online? Do you know lies when you see them? How? (Clue: Multiple sources.)

CHAPTER 19

Is Citizenship a Responsibility as Well as a Right?

The American way is exampled in both plain sight and in subtle attitude. It's in moments of routine exchange and in broad expectations. It's in places of historic weight and import and in the small spaces in which we all stand. The American way could be exampled when you respect the law and the rights of all. Because if you don't, who will? When your food is brought to you, will you thank the server? Because if you don't, who will? Would you pick up the litter that has missed the recycling bin? Because if you don't, who will? When you vote your conscience and make sure your neighbor has the opportunity to do the same with theirs, because if you don't, who will? When you make good on your victories and learn from your losses because both are the results of proud and noble efforts, if you don't, who will?

—**Tom Hanks**, actor and author,
Harvard University

Is Citizenship a Responsibility as Well as a Right?

I realized that when I had lived in the US on a green card long enough, America would let me become a citizen. I already felt American. I paid my taxes in America. My philanthropies were born here, and I made most but not all of my films while based in Los Angeles. So, I filled in the forms. There were some memorable questions. Back then, they still asked if someone was homosexual. Another question asked, "Are you now, or have you ever planned to assassinate the President of the United States, or any other elected official?" I believe it was Oscar Wilde who replied, "Sole purpose of visit." Which I imagine did not sit well with the interviewing officer.

I was instructed to report one morning to the Los Angeles Convention Center to be sworn in. The Immigration and Naturalization Service had managed to accumulate an enormous local backlog of people who were ready and qualified to become citizens, but had not yet been given an appointment. To deal with this, they rented the Los Angeles Convention Center for ten days, to swear us in in groups of two thousand at a time. I had honestly thought that this would just be a formality. I thought I would raise my hand, take the oath, and become an American on paper, as I had become American in life a long time previously. But it was much more of a big deal than I had expected. Hugely emotional.

First of all, there were nearly two hundred nationalities present in that gigantic room. Each of us was given a little Stars and Stripes on a stick to wave. We watched rousing videos. There were speeches by famous people, and we sang the national anthem. When it was time to be sworn in, I looked around and realized that to come from Britain to the United States is not to have one's life saved, but in that room, two thousand people cried. My wife and I cried too. There were those who swam through shark-infested waters to escape from communist totalitarianism in Asia. Those who had navigated the treacherous waters to Florida in automobile inner tubes to escape from a different kind of totalitarian government in Cuba. There were political escapees of all kinds and people running from countries where simply your religion would cause you to be killed or imprisoned. There were LGBTQI people who just wanted to be left alone to live their lives, but who realized that in Iran, Uganda, and other countries, they could be hanged, just because of who they were born to be. There were people who had walked a thousand miles, then immigrated in order to feed their children and escape gang violence. I was humbled and grateful.

I felt and continue to feel privileged to have been admitted to this greatest of clubs, the United States of America, where even with all our problems, almost anything is possible if you want it enough, and work hard enough. A man of color was president of the United States for eight years. Gay, lesbian, and transgender people have reached the apex of powerful positions in one generation, and their ability has made that possible. The US rate of admission to university is much higher than in the UK, 61.8 percent versus 37.5 percent. Post-secondary education has helped families pivot in one generation from manual labor as the source of the family income, to doctorates, master's degrees, and highly paid professional careers in the next and subsequent generations.

Freedom is not free, and neither is the American Dream. We have to work for it every day. We need to earn the continuing honor of American citizenship by trying to improve the world around us and the fabric of this, our very own shared civilization.

Don't complain about the government.
Register to vote, and vote.
It's your government.

Is Citizenship a Responsibility as Well as a Right?

Chapter Takeaways and Reflection Questions for You

- Where were you born?
- Where were your parents born? Grandparents?
- Do you feel completely American, or partly American?
- Can you be proud to be American, and also feel affection for the countries where your parents and grandparents were born?
- What is your culture? Your religion? Are they wider and deeper than any one country?
- Who are you, exactly? It does not affect your ability to dream big dreams, but it is always good to know where you are from.
- As you address the story of the rest of your life, you are its author.
- Why is America so polarized? Is it demagogues, brutal leaders who comfort people by telling them that their fears are the fault of others: people who look different, pray differently, dress differently, or live differently?
- Do they sell them on the belief that other ethnic groups are responsible for whatever economic and other struggles they may be having?
- Is it the growth of social media and the ability of maybe six wrong-headed, fascist idiots in one town to put themselves in touch with a different half dozen each in other towns and suddenly become a national movement?
- Is it the huge and disproportionate megaphone of social media that allows them to out-shout everybody else online?
- What can we do about it?
- Do you feel encouraged and obligated to put back into your civilization, rather than just expecting it to take care of you?
- Is it a two-way street, and are you on that street, being helpful? I hope so.
- Which direction is the most traffic going?

CHAPTER 20

Stand Up for Your Rights.
Children Are Not Property

The United States is far, far from perfect. If you care about your society, consider how you can help fix what is broken. I've tried for decades to earn the right to be an American citizen. In recent years, the blind spots in segments of America, including among those with the biggest megaphones, have been...well...deafening. Being flat-ass wrong is bad enough. Being proud and loud about ignorance is worse. But leading people astray for personal profit is the most reprehensible and unforgiveable. There is a lot of it going on. Can you help fix it?

The British satirist Jonathan Swift shocked everyone in 1729 with a modest proposal: in the midst of a famine, Ireland could escape the burden of poor children by...well, eating them. The author of *Gulliver's Travels* pointed out that society was unwilling to actually feed these hungry, dependent children, so what would be so shocking about eating them? The moral decision to let the children die had already been made by default by the government, and thus by the people who repeatedly elected it...so what was so wrong, he suggested, with his solution? If nothing else, it would be less wasteful. It was, of course,

Stand Up for Your Rights. Children Are Not Property

satire, designed to shock the government into feeding the Irish children actual food.

It did not go well for him: thin-skinned people don't understand satire, now less than ever. Swift's *Modest Proposal* was much too shocking and ridiculous for his or our times. So, learning from that, I won't suggest, even as satire, something infinitely more humane and generous for our nation's several million abused and neglected children: that we treat them legally like animals. Nah, people would take it seriously. Satire is tricky.

But consider: We clearly protect and nurture our pets much better than we watch over other people's children. Extensive laws protect animals from abuse and neglect, and in many situations these legal protections are much better than those we apply to children in harm's way. In these United States, a man who beats his dog is uniformly prosecuted, while a man's right to beat his child is legally protected. Let us recall that the very first organization to stand up for children was an animal rights charity. Go figure.

Let's be honest: There is no decisive will in government or among the majority of voters to put kids first. We don't agree with giving children primacy as the future of our society. It would actually improve things for the kids if we applied the existing framework of laws that protect animals. Just define children before age eighteen as animals and bingo, we'll go a long way to providing the protections kids have in most other countries. OK, so we've decided the United States should be the only nation (besides Somalia) of 193 not to ratify the UN Convention on the Rights of the Child. OK, so we have two thousand juveniles locked up for life without possibility of parole, while the entire rest of the world combined has a grand total of two hundred. But at least by giving children the rights we give animals in this country, we might reduce the 1,500 or so who die each year of abuse or neglect, and the several million who suffer, mostly with no right to a lawyer, no right to sue for redress when the government harms them (thank you, Supreme Court in *DeShaney v. Winnebago County*), no right to be heard when their fate is being determined, no right to be safe. And who knows, we might even find a few of those many kids who are wards of a state, and the responsible state has somehow lost them (Hello, Florida!).

FINDING HAPPY

We give an elevated national standing to so many worthy issues. Homeland Security. Rebuilding countries we invade. Hilariously, the constitution we wrote for Iraq, after we dropped a quarter-trillion dollars of high explosives on it, gives their kids important rights our own does not. We find legislative space for tax cuts for very rich people, not to mention pork-barrel projects for politicians of every stripe. These issues, for good or bad, have a golden ticket among our national priorities. Without debating any of them here, why has the position of children—as our gating factor, the glass ceiling of future prosperity, stability, and arguably our only future—not been given at least a couple of golden tickets? OK, so two might be too many. But what about the same little brass ticket we give to pets? I know—crazy, right?

How did we develop this blind spot? Is it that children don't vote? That they don't lobby? That we still viscerally feel kids are the property of their parents? Is it that we still think like medieval farmers, whose laws allowed them to think of their children and wives as chattel, as property to labor in the fields? Why do we still have the Victorian sense that children are imperfectly developed grown-ups, not fully human until they come of age? And are we always to be the nation that believes in fixing things after they break, rather than avoiding breakage through prevention? Can't we find political will to rise above policies that are reactive and rarely preemptive? Do we really believe grown-ups have bigger rights to inflict abuse and neglect than children have to be protected from them? Isn't it totally shortsighted when kids mostly outlive their parents, and when abuse and neglect often rolls from generation to generation? Why does a third of the country think children's rights end at birth? Explain that to me.

We know 68 percent of all adult male prisoners were abused or neglected as children. We know half of morbidly obese women were sexually abused as kids. We know a lack of prenatal care greatly increases the cost of remedial medical services after birth. Why does pro-life stop when the babies are born? We know education breaks cycles of poverty and low adult achievement. We know these things, yet we consistently relegate the fate of children to the bottom of the totem pole. We spend billions of dollars to defend our nation, but a handful of pennies to ensure it will be a safe home to valuable citizens

Stand Up for Your Rights. Children Are Not Property

for generations to come. Where is the comprehensive pro-child plank? It's not rocket science. Every aspect of best practice is found somewhere in the US; it's just the other 80 percent of the 2,250 jurisdictions within the country that ignore it!

Let's be honest with one another: there is no political will to put kids first. I think we have to fix that, whether they vote or not. Can you help? Get politically active!

Chapter Takeaways and Reflection Questions for You

- Is it realistic for young adults to assert their own rights? (Clue: Yes! Google Greta Thunberg, Malala Yousafzai, David Hogg, and many, many others!)
- Where does activism start? (Clue: Research. Find your own truth.)
- Where does it go then? (Clue: Find others to act together!)
- Who protested really effectively? (Clue: Start with research on Gandhi, who threw the British out of India without firing a bullet; Nelson Mandela, who led the largely bloodless overthrow of apartheid in South Africa, even though he was imprisoned for decades while doing it. And Greta T., Malala Y. and David H.)
- How can you help? How can you go beyond hating how things are?
- A chain is only as strong as its weakest link. Think that through in society.
- If children are the future, why are they often treated so badly? (Clues: They don't vote, march, lobby…they have no money and make no noise.)
- Can you stand up for their rights? Why wouldn't you? Just. Do. It!

Never doubt that a small group of thoughtful, committed citizens can change the world; indeed, it's the only thing that ever has.

—**Margaret Mead**

CHAPTER 21

Which American Lives Are Most Different from Yours? Thank You, Navajo Nation

I wanted to make a Western. A cowboy film. It seemed like my further baptism into the American Dream.

I was firmly settled in Los Angeles, about to turn twenty-six, and making a name for myself as a really good organizer for complicated films. I met a man called David Leeds who had a script called *Santa Fe 1836*. We planned to make it in New Mexico, Arizona, and Texas. As associate producer (a promotion!) and production manager, I set off to scout locations and get things set up in the Navajo Nation.

Working across the New Mexico–Arizona border, I could not believe how vast the empty, undeveloped areas were between New York and Los Angeles. It was often just me, tumbleweed, and cacti for a hundred miles. I thought the opportunity to live and work there, and meet so many extraordinarily interesting people, was profound. I saw the United States of America as a huge and diverse nation, the one in which I was proud to be working. I jumped enthusiastically into the American Dream with both feet, and with a strong sense of responsibility to help make it even better.

Which American Lives Are Most Different from Yours? Thank You, Navajo Nation

Casting had begun. A very young Christopher Walken was going to take the lead of the loner cowboy, the first leading role he ever had. Opposite him was the rather beautiful Canadian actress Margot Kidder. The story of *Santa Fe 1836*, later retitled *Shoot the Sun Down*, had a group of outlaws who found Montezuma's golden wheel, a cart-wheel-sized, solid-gold artifact of the indigenous people. They kidnapped a group of about fifty Navajo people as slaves and had them push and pull this hugely valuable gold disc across the desert, thinking that it would make their fortune. We had horses, pistols, and lassos. This was very far from Cambridge! I loved all of it.

My first challenge in wrangling the film together was that in 1976 the Navajo Nation, a vast area of desert scrubland and small settlements, had absolutely no motels or hotels anywhere near Chaco Canyon, where we needed to film. Where was I going to house the crew? I found a Navajo boarding school and made arrangements with the tribal elders to rent it for eight weeks to base the crew there. It was not very comfortable, and its biggest problem was that at night, it was extremely cold and there was no heating. I found a contractor from Albuquerque and arranged for him to install propane gas heating, fed by a big tank next to the building where we would have the rooms for cast and crew accommodation.

All went well until a couple of weeks before the cast and crew were to arrive. The contractor completed the installation. He lit the pilot light to see if it all worked. There was an enormous explosion that blew off most of the roof of the boarding school. Luckily, nobody was hurt, but this created two unforeseen circumstances that I had to solve. Building a new roof on these poor people's school was one, and the other was: now, where on earth was I going to house the cast and crew? My production team and I went off to Albuquerque and rented every Winnebago and other recreational vehicle and camper we could find. We drove these in shifts back to Chaco Canyon. Near the school we had accidentally destroyed, we made an encampment of trailers into which the crew, with quite a lot of complaints, soon moved. And yes, we paid to repair the school. The contractor disappeared.

The next challenge was that the script required a fifteen-foot-tall saguaro cactus, to which our characters tied a victim and used him for target practice. The writer had not done research to discover that there are no saguaro cacti growing in New Mexico. It also turned out to be illegal to bring one of these cacti by road from Arizona, unless it was fumigated against pests. So Mark Burley, my location manager in 1976—who I'm happy to see has since gone on to positions of great leadership across the industry—set off in a jeep and trailer to buy a fifteen-foot cactus in Arizona. He then

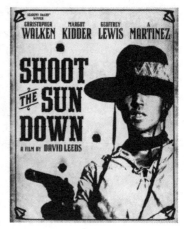

got it fumigated, to obtain the certificate that would satisfy the New Mexico Department of Agriculture. With that, he was allowed to drive it into New Mexico. In the end, we had our cactus, and luckily the fumigation did not kill it.

The script called for the character played by Christopher Walken to be captured by the bandits and spread-eagled between four pegs in the desert, where vultures would peck at him as he screamed in pain. The writer had clearly not researched the behavior patterns of western vultures: They never go near animals that are alive. Vultures only eat carrion once it is completely dead and inanimate. They circle overhead until the animal dies. Our scene had Chris attached to the four pegs in the desert, screaming his lungs out while the vultures moved in to peck at him. An imaginative concept, but completely unrealistic and unachievable. But we did not know that in time.

Which American Lives Are Most Different from Yours? Thank You, Navajo Nation

I made arrangements with the zoo in Albuquerque for us to rent four vultures in cages, together with a vulture wrangler, and they were trucked to our location in Chaco Canyon. In the first take, there lay Chris facing the sky, and the vulture wrangler released Vulture A towards his prone body. The vulture took one look at the screaming Mr. Walken, immediately took fright, and flew away, high into the sky, never to be seen again. The second vulture did the same thing. We were now down to two birds, and I was realizing I would have to pay to replace them at the Albuquerque zoo. What to do?

We realized we only had two more chances, so we re-thought the choreography so that, in the few seconds before Vultures #3 and #4 flew away, we somehow got the scene in the can. Chris helped by screaming valiantly, so we hoped perhaps the vultures' brief cameos would suffice. With an apology, I had to pay the Albuquerque zoo for its lost birds. A significant component of producing is apologizing to third parties who think film people are all mad. At a certain point on most films, you realize that they are more right than wrong. No vultures were hurt in the making of this or any other film I have produced. I hope all four led happy lives thereafter in the wild.

Unfortunately, it was in Chaco Canyon that we had a serious accident on set, injuring a member of the crew. I was that victim.

The script called for the large golden wheel of Montezuma, which was very heavy and shaped like a cart wheel, to be dragged behind a wagon. The wagon itself was pulled behind four horses with the Native Americans pushing it from behind. This was fine for one take. But we were under the hawk-eyed supervision of the National Park Service, who controlled Chaco Canyon and quite rightly its ancient indigenous artifacts. They would not allow us to leave the narrow trail for any reason. The challenge was how to get the horses, the wagon, and the wheel back to the starting position to shoot take two—let alone three,

FINDING HAPPY

four, five, and six—all without leaving the narrow trail. The only way to resolve this was to move the whole ungainly thing backwards on its tracks: to reverse the cart, the wheel, and the horses, without turning them around. The problem with this was that the wagon and the wheel would constantly jackknife; they kept falling over sideways.

I was one of the crew with my shoulder to the golden prop wheel as we tried to keep it moving backwards and not falling over. But the wheel did fall over. I was crushed underneath it and trapped under its full weight. I could feel the ribs on my left side crack and immediately could not breathe properly. As the production manager, I had a carefully organized procedure for what to do in case of an emergency. We were literally in the middle of nowhere, but there was an airstrip for emergencies, and I had arranged for an air ambulance to be available when we called it in by radio if someone was hurt. But the organizer of the solution was me, and there I was, lying on the ground in Chaco Canyon, now gasping for breath, with the instructions in my pocket under me.

Somehow, I managed to get at the air ambulance instructions and gave them to the first assistant director, who then called in the plane on the radio. I was airlifted to Farmington, New Mexico, and rushed by ambulance to the indigenous Native American hospital, where a pneumothorax procedure was done on my left side to relieve the pressure around my collapsed lung. I came to in a ward with various really interesting people, all Native American, and eventually I got enough breath back that I was able to have a series of conversations. I was there about a week, and then, strapped up, I returned to the location in some pain but able to work. A good thing, because we did not exactly have bench depth in the production department to get us back on schedule and budget. I limped around slowly and did my best. It was a relief to leave for the city of El Paso to continue our shoot.

Some weeks later, I was looking at the full-body brace that I had been issued in the indigenous hospital, which I was instructed to wear around my abdomen for six weeks. What I had thought was a smudge on the bottom of it turned out to be the word "top." I had been wearing it upside down for three weeks, but it did not seem to matter! For the many years since the accident, I've actually had about 50 percent lung

Which American Lives Are Most Different from Yours? Thank You, Navajo Nation

capacity on my left side. I don't think we had a really robust insurance package, and certainly I never made a claim against the production. I was the guy in charge of safety, after all! I had nobody to blame but myself. Ever since, my top priority on any set is safety. Easier said than done.

El Paso is the border town across from Juarez, Mexico. I had difficulty keeping my Los Angeles crew in line. On one memorable occasion, members of the American crew drove across the border in a company car on their day off and bought marijuana, which they successfully drove undetected back into the United States later the same day. The following weekend, they drove the same car back into Juarez, with the weed still in the glove compartment. They were arrested by the Mexican border police for importing marijuana into Mexico. Their protestations that it was Mexican marijuana that they were just bringing back did no good, and to get them back into the United States, I had to go to the jail in Juarez and bail them out.

There were also some adventures that required bail for a member of the electrical crew and his experience in a brothel involving a lady with a donkey, but it is best to say nothing about that here. A Los Angeles–based actress, who had a speaking role in our film as one of the kidnapped tribespeople, was arrested in El Paso for shoplifting, and I had to bail her out from the El Paso jail. Honestly, it was a relief to eventually leave El Paso and travel to our final location in Alamogordo, New Mexico.

Alamogordo is an extraordinary place, surrounded by completely white sands and home to a top-secret US Air Force missile-testing base. It literally has hundreds of square miles of pristine white sand, in dunes as far as the eye can see. Our script called for the relentless bandits to force the Native Americans they had kidnapped to drag the golden wheel ever forward. The natives in the script were dying of hunger and thirst. I had checked very carefully that we would have a blazing sun at that time of the year in Alamogordo, and the long-range weather forecast confirmed that it would be hot and dry. It had never rained on that day in history.

But on the morning of the day that we were to film the dying-of-thirst scene, I walked out of the door of my motel room in Alamogordo

and realized that a good three inches of snow had fallen during the night. The entire place now featured white snow on white sand. The only thing we could do was to rewrite the script so that the kidnapped victims would be dying of hunger, but no longer of thirst. Such is filmmaking.

We delivered a rather decent Western on a budget of $700,000, and I thought this constituted my baptism into producing as a future American in America. I also further fell in love with the diversity and rich textures of an extraordinary country, which by then had issued me a green card. I was well on my way to becoming a proud citizen.

Chapter Takeaways and Reflection Questions for You

- Where have you travelled to experience the diversity of a huge country? If not so much, what is your plan? I strongly urge you to make the most of your freedom, before your responsibilities make it more challenging to go see amazing things.
- What was done to the indigenous peoples of America by the European settlers was shameful. Have you read enough about it to understand the real history, in all its cruelty and violence? More human beings owned as chattel.

Which American Lives Are Most Different from Yours? Thank You, Navajo Nation

- Who knew more about ecology and the land, do you think: the settlers or the indigenous people?
- By this time, I had embarked fully on my career as a filmmaker in the production department, without realizing that the decision I'd made felt irreversible. How far can you progress while still being able to back up later, perhaps to take a different path? Cherish your entry-level ability to experiment; it may not last forever.
- Regardless, keep at it, try something different, take some risks, create your own destiny. This is your life.

CHAPTER 22

Should You Pursue a Long Shot?
Crazy Luck: *A Man, a Woman, and a Bank*

Through a lawyer named Paul Migdal in Los Angeles, I met actor Donald Sutherland. We palled around a bit and he proposed that I should join his company. He hired me. I was so sad to read the recent news of his death.

Back then, Donald was having a fine old time. He was Canadian, and the Canadian government had introduced what was then the world's best tax shelter to encourage investment that furthered the training, careers, and financial wherewithal of Canadian cast, crew, and companies. Donald was internationally one of only three notable and recognizable Canadian film stars at that time, the other two being Margot Kidder and Donald Pleasance. Donald's great friend was Paul Mazursky, a fine director and actor. They had always wanted to work together as actors.

We developed a script called *A Man, a Woman, and a Bank* and were able to persuade Avco Embassy, a decent-sized Los Angeles distribution company, to put up half of the film's $3.6-million budget. In our script, Donald's and Paul's characters were thieves who worked out how to tap into the data lines that went into a bank in order to open the doors, and then the vault. I flew up to Toronto and met a lawyer, Rosemarie Christiansen, who was putting hundreds of Canadian taxpayers with significant tax liabilities into film investments, which resulted in a certificate that allowed them to avoid or greatly reduce the taxes due on their other income. Rosemary said yes to taking on our film.

Realizing that we had now fully financed the film, I set off for Vancouver, together with a local location manager and the rest of the scouting team, to work out which locations would be appropriate. Only one film had ever been made in Vancouver by 1979, Robert Altman's *McCabe & Mrs. Miller*. Undaunted, we explored the city. I fell in love with its great beauty and the can-do attitude of the Canadians. It was a great pleasure pulling things together there. And there were terrific Chinese restaurants. Although there was not an abundance of experienced local crew, we were allowed by the Canadian union to bring people in from Los Angeles, USA, though (hilariously) they would not let us bring the same crew categories from Toronto, Canada.

And then a truly horrible thing happened that I had not anticipated: the Canadian government changed the tax code overnight! There was suddenly no longer a deduction available for all those doctors and dentists who had agreed to invest in *A Man, a Woman, and a Bank*. It was just two weeks before principal photography, and I already had fifty or so crew on site, building the sets, sewing costumes, and delivering equipment. Rosemarie Christiansen phoned me and said, "I'm very sorry, Peter, but I can't send you any money at all. And we have to void the contract." I said I was pretty sure laws cannot apply backwards in time. "Ex post facto?" Wasn't it unconstitutional? Rosemary said, "Yes, in the USA...but not, my friend, in Canada." She apologized, and that was the end of it.

I was flummoxed, and immediately flew back to Los Angeles without telling the crew that I was suddenly missing half of the budget

FINDING HAPPY

for the film. In Los Angeles, I went and met with Avco Embassy, who made two things perfectly clear: first, that they were not going to give us the rest of the money; second, that they did indeed own all rights internationally and in all media in return for the half that they were contributing. And if the film collapsed, clearly this was my problem, not theirs.

It made for an impossible situation, because I had nothing to sell except equity. I couldn't pre-sell foreign distribution rights nor any subsidiary media rights, because they all belonged to Avco Embassy. What to do?

I went to the very limited number of people I knew with significant amounts of money. Paul Migdal, Donald Sutherland, and I tried for over a week or so and failed miserably to find the $1.75 million we needed to finish financing the film. I booked my ticket to fly back up to Vancouver, close the film down, and fire everybody. I was devastated. It felt like the end of my career as a full career producer, a career that hadn't even yet started.

Then, that Monday, I opened the *Los Angeles Times* and read a front-page article—a profile piece about a young man, the heir to a great family fortune, who that very day, on his twenty-fifth birthday, had received control of his inheritance. This was Frederick W. Field, known as Ted. It even had his picture, a line drawing on page one. The article continued on a later page of the newspaper and said that he was a student of philosophy at Pomona College, a place I'd never heard of. It also mentioned that he was interested in motor racing and that he loved films.

Disaster makes one bold. It was all I had.

Arriving in our office on La Cienega Boulevard, I said to our executive assistant, Susie Dunster, that we were going to write a letter to this Mr. Field on the off chance that he might want to save our bacon. Susie, a wonderfully ironic English woman who had been working with Donald for years, had a habit of raising one eyebrow when she thought the person she was with was saying crazy things. Such as I was, then: this was one of those occasions. I dictated a letter to Ted, a man I had never met and who had certainly never heard of me. Susie typed it up and asked where exactly I would like her to send it. I said,

"Ah, yes, you make a good point. We obviously don't know his address. We'll have to send it care of the Department of Philosophy of Pomona College." Which is exactly what we did. Susie asked me if I wanted to put a stamp on it and put it in the mail, or to call a messenger. With no idea exactly where Pomona might be located, I said, "In for a penny, in for a pound. Send it by messenger." So, we hired a man on a motorbike for one hundred dollars, who indeed delivered the envelope to Pomona College...or so we hoped.

The following morning, as I prepared to take the flight to Vancouver to fire everyone and close down what was now a useless money pit, the phone rang and the voice said, "Hello, it's Ted Field. I got your letter. Shall we have lunch?" I said, "I would love that. Where are you located?" He said, "I'm in Orange County, but don't worry. Where are you?" I named a restaurant in Westwood called the Bratskellar, where I knew we could get a quiet table.

Ted and I got on like the blazes! Toward the end of the lunch, as we nursed coffees, he asked if there was any film where he might be able to invest and become an executive producer. "Yes," I said, "there is in fact such a film." I was transparent with him. I told him that the film Donald and I were about to make in Vancouver was going to collapse because the Canadian government had cancelled the tax shelter that was good for half of the budget. Ted asked if he could read the script. Could I perhaps send it down to him in Newport Beach? I said I could do better than that. I reached into my briefcase and gave him a hard copy of the script right there, over the lunch table. My instinct was that the lunch had gone well, and I postponed the flight up to Vancouver a further day.

Sure enough, the next morning, a man called me and said, "I'm Tom Baldikoski. I'm Ted Field's lawyer. He's instructed me to wire $1.75 million to you right away. Can you give me the banking instructions?"

I took a deep breath and said, "Tom, thank you so much and please thank Ted. But do you realize we have no contract?" Tom said that Ted and he did realize that, but Ted had told Tom the need was urgent, and to wire it immediately, just on my word, and then sort out the contract later. Amazing. And so it was. Four hours later, the money arrived by wire. A blessed moment. I flew back up to Vancouver, pushed forward

FINDING HAPPY

with the prep and shoot, and never told anyone how close they had been to getting fired. *Phew!* Certainly a squeaker.

After *A Man, a Woman, and a Bank*, Ted proposed funding a company and partnering to make more films. I wrote a business plan where we would develop scripts and then get other people to finance them. At the time, I was a week-to-week, at-will employee with Donald. When I told him that I needed to resign because an extraordinary opportunity to be a principal and to co-run a company had been offered to me, he was incredibly upset. His butler—Susie's husband, Maurice Dunster—arrived apologetically with a suitcase that contained all of the presents I had ever given Donald for birthdays and Christmas. I still have them. Alas, that relationship went out of the window. He felt betrayed. I didn't understand it then, nor ever since. A great shame.

Initially, the company Ted and I set up was called Kinesis Productions, which then transmogrified into Interscope Communications, a subsidiary of the overall Interscope, which Ted created to manage his wealth. Ted was the heir to the Marshall Field fortune, one of the truly great American family dynasties. Ted and his half-brother, Marshall Field V, owned an array of newspapers, paper mills, and substantial acres of real estate. Ted asked me to join him and Tom in a three-person Office of the President. He wanted to divorce his brother in business, implement a Section 337 liquidation, sell everything they owned, and reinvest the resulting large amount of capital.

I said, "Ted, I'm flattered, but I only really know how to make films." He replied, "Well, go and get educated." So I went to what was then the UCLA Graduate School of Business at night and on weekends, and I flew around helping Ted manage his money. It was a heady year: I founded the first of my charities, and I also fell in love with the woman I later married. More on that later.

People would come in to pitch investment ideas. There were so many that we had to limit them to ten minutes each. The three of us would sit in the Interscope board room and listen to ideas, which often sounded completely crazy.

I remember there was a naval captain who arrived in full uniform, wearing medals, and sat opposite us, then with a straight face said, "Off the coast of Florida, in a location I have been able to pinpoint, lies the

128

Celeste. She sank in a storm carrying Civil War payroll for the Confederate troops. I know exactly where she foundered, and I can bring her up." We asked if the ship was just lying on the bottom. "No," said the captain. "She is under thirty feet of silt." We asked how he was going to get at the ship. He leaned forward. "Huge vacuum cleaners," he said. Ted and I lost it completely; we got the giggles. The captain stormed out. In came our receptionist. "That man in the uniform was very angry, and he took the 'N' off our door." We went out, and sure enough, on the leather-covered surface of our outer door, he'd ripped off the "N" of "Interscope." A matching replacement "N" could not be found, so the door had to be re-faced and an entirely new "Interscope" had to be affixed.

The joke was on us. Some five years later, we read in a newspaper that the captain had indeed dredged up the lost ship and found several hundred million dollars of gold coins, the value of which he had split with the state of Florida, making himself very rich. But as they say in business school, you are never hurt by the investments you don't make. Or so we consoled ourselves.

Another man explained to us that he had invented a perpetual-motion machine. He said that through his ingenious mechanical and chemical abilities, he had been powering a light bulb for over a year with no power going into his device. He invited us to Memphis, where he said the machine could be seen on his farm. My colleague Jay Hill and I had to go to New York anyway, so we decided that we would stop off and see this machine, which greatly offended against the laws of physics. Maybe Einstein was wrong?

We flew to Memphis, and sure enough, in a barn with a poured-concrete floor, there stood a heavy, complicated machine, where a flywheel powered a dynamo, which generated electricity and lit a bright light bulb. There was no power entering the machine and no battery that we could see. We said "thank you very much" and continued on to New York. Returning to Los Angeles, we decided that it would be less than clever to invest Ted's money in flagrant opposition to the laws of physics, and so we declined. Around a year later, Jay saw in a newspaper article that the man had raised money and then been arrested for fraud.

FINDING HAPPY

When the police lifted up the machine in his barn, it was plugged into an electrical socket set into the concrete floor underneath.

Chapter Takeaways and Reflection Questions for You

- What role does luck have in success?
- How do you maximize your chance of having your share of luck?
- When is it foolish to pursue a long shot, and when is it worth having a go? (Clues: What could be the best outcome? What could be the worst? Ask people you trust. Sleep on it. Try a spider graph. List and score the upsides and downsides.)
- Do you owe it to anyone when you have no agreement to continue working for them if a better opportunity arises?
- Can you act in your own self-interest, or do you have an obligation to stay where you are and let the other opportunity pass you by?
- Young people are often confused and get stuck because they feel obligated when they are not. Unnecessary guilt comes up in the workplace a lot, often a habit formed in one's relationship with parents who were shaming or guilt-provoking or instilled rigid rules. What are your thoughts on this?
- Is scientific truth absolute? We live in a time of wild untruths, fueled by culture wars, racism, and the internet. Everyone with a keyboard can lie to thousands of the credulous. How do you apply critical thinking when you hear wrong thinking, often shouted loudly online or off?
- Why is research incredibly important? Start dubious, research, read multiple sources, apply your own critical thinking: seek the truth! In the end it is not a matter of opinion. Find it.

CHAPTER 23

Is Failure a Matter of Opinion? What Is Success? Revenge of This Nerd

By 1983, Interscope had a staff, a much too beautiful and expensive floor of offices above Westwood, and a whole development slate. One of the lead projects was brought to us by Peter Bart, who had started his career an assistant at Paramount, and who later went on to become the editor of *Variety*. It was originally called *Brainz*, a youth comedy set at a university, designed to follow the same highly successful scatological course as *Animal House* the year before. We developed what we thought was a strong script by Miguel Tejada Flores and Tim Metcalf. Joe Roth, who was running Twentieth Century Fox, agreed to take the risk and fully finance the film.

The first problem was that we approached perhaps twenty universities for a filming permit; but given the ribald content, once they read the script, they all refused to let us shoot. Eventually we managed to persuade the University of Arizona in Tucson to give us a permit to film, on the strict condition that there would be no identifying of the university anywhere onscreen or off. We were scrupulous in this regard, and it was with horror at the premiere of the film that I realized

FINDING HAPPY

that in the first scene, Jamie Cromwell—playing the father of one of the Nerds and driving the family's wood-paneled station wagon along the interstate at thirty-seven miles per hour—drove straight past a billboard that clearly advertised an FM station in Tucson.

Making films is frequently a roller coaster. You have something, and then you don't. You have nothing, and then you do. The erratic nature of your expectations is one of the challenges. We were quite pleased by the film, by now called *Revenge of the Nerds*, as we edited it. It made us laugh (a bad sign, it turns out). We flew on the Fox jet to a National Research Group test screening in a multiplex in Phoenix, Arizona. In the screening, I noticed that nobody laughed, even in the bits we thought were hilarious. After the screening ended, the NRG guys quickly tabulated the result of the audience questionnaires and handed us the results sheet, where the significant score is the percentage in the top two boxes: the Excellent and Very Good votes. I went to the then-head of distribution at Fox, Tom Rothman, and asked him what he made of the score. "I have no frame of reference, Tom; how is this?" I asked. "I don't want to be cruel," replied Tom. "But this is the worst score I have ever seen in the top two boxes in all the years I've been with Fox in distribution." The color draining from my face, I asked him, "How many years have you been with the studio?" "Thirteen years," said Tom Rothman. In high dudgeon and silence, our group flew back to Los Angeles.

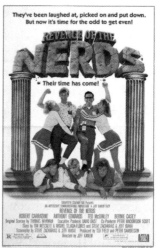

The studio, with good reason, decided that our film was a bust. They halved the number of screens and the advertising they had booked. I was pretty sure again it was the end of my career, and possibly the end of the company. The film opened with two times on a Friday evening. On the Saturday morning, someone from distribution at Fox phoned me and said there was cautious optimism because the film had done much better at the second Friday screening than at the first. On the Sunday, the same man phoned and said that Saturday had been spectacularly successful, apparently because of excellent word of mouth from the people who had seen the film on Friday, as they hadn't seen much advertising!

On the Monday, the studio doubled the number of screens and ramped up advertising. *Revenge of the Nerds* went on to be the most successful comedy of the summer of 1984. What I learned from the experience is that comedy is the trickiest genre to judge. It has to do with whether someone with a loud laugh finds the film amusing and effectively gives permission to the rest of the audience to laugh. Once that happens, you can have a success. But if nobody laughs in the first few minutes, your film is dead. My wife has such a crazy laugh, and from time to time when watching comedies, that has been really valuable. The noise she makes gives the audience encouragement to laugh themselves. *Go team!*

Making a complete ass of myself with the 1984 Olympic Torch, as PR for the film.

FINDING HAPPY

Chapter Takeaways and Reflection Questions for You

- When the success of your product is at best erratic and unpredictable, does that make it a bad business? (Clue: No, you need to do enough of it, make enough films, to receive your statistical chance of success. Diversify.)
- Is research always right? If not, why is that? (Clue: The sample is wrong.)
- Can you measure human psychology, or only numbers?
- What is humor? Why are things funny? (Clue: Read the book by Sigmund Freud, *Jokes and their Relation to the Unconscious*.)
- Why in our times does some of the most incisive political commentary come from comedians?
- *Revenge of the Nerds* does not hold up well against current, more-evolved societal norms. I'm ashamed of some parts of it. Is comedy any defense against poor judgment? I'd say no. We should do better. What do you think?
- In Silicon Valley, potential investors ask about earlier failures as much as about successes. What is the role that failing can play in making us better in future? How do we learn to succeed?
- Can there be success without failure?
- What can we learn from failure?
- How do you never give up, even if you do take a better path?

CHAPTER 24

What Is an Entrepreneur?
What Is Leadership? Starlight

I don't really know how the Starlight Children's Foundation grew so big. For sure, by now it has become the work and the volunteer effort of thousands. It is they who have made it grow to become so huge, valuable, and powerful. Coming up on our fortieth anniversary, the Starlight family of organizations, including the sister entities in Canada, Australia, and the UK, have raised well over one *billion* dollars! Starlight is the work of many, many volunteers and professionals across those countries.

Starlight began with one fragile little germ of an idea. In 1979, my nineteen-year-old cousin Emma was still living in England. I was twenty-eight, and I had already moved to the United States. She was making the beginnings of a career as an actress. Our family had experienced enormous grief and loss with the death of Jamie, Emma's brother and my cousin, as a little boy. In July of 1979, Emma appeared in a film called *Arabian Adventure*, in a cast including Christopher Lee, and the film was screened to the patients of Great Ormond Street Children's Hospital, where Jamie had been a patient. The following day, she first

135

FINDING HAPPY

met a very ill little boy there, Sean. She continued visiting him, became friends with him and his family, and on a subsequent visit—now knowing his surgery had been unsuccessful—she asked him, "What would make you really happy, Sean?" Sean, about age ten, replied quick as a flash, "Oh, that's easy. I want to go to Disneyland." I remember Emma phoning me and saying, "We have to do this." And I said, "You are right. We'll bring him to Los Angeles...I'll help."

This was not an inconsiderable thing to bite off, because Sean was terminally ill. But Sean and his mum, Brenda, did fly The Pond and come to Los Angeles. We didn't think we should put them in a hotel, and Emma's apartment was too small, so they moved into my apartment, as did Emma. We spent two weeks arranging everything that you probably shouldn't do lightly with a terminally ill child. Sean had an extraordinarily wonderful time; he enjoyed the heck out of it, and so did his mum. We realized this was actually as much a gift to her because she would have something happy to remember when her son passed, which indeed sadly happened after they went back to London.

We felt we had done something really important that, honestly, was not that difficult. It would have perhaps ended there, but I called a meeting one evening in the boardroom at Interscope Productions, where I was by now an executive vice president. Career film producers call meetings. It's our best thing. We stood at the end of the conference table, passed around the Polaroid pictures, and asked, "There must be other sick kids in the world. Why don't we find them, probably through hospitals? And a few times a year—you know, five times a year, maybe something ambitious like that—we'll ask them what would make them happy, and then we'll do it." Everyone nodded earnestly.

This was back in my single days. There was a lady there with whom I had had one date. Saryl was very smart and very pretty. I had neglected to call her...but then I remembered she had said that she was an accountant. I needed an accountant for the meeting. So, I phoned her and said, "I'm so sorry that I didn't call. I've been away. I've called this charity meeting, and I wonder, would you like to come?" Functionally, that was our second date.

And when the lawyer I'd roped in asked, "What do you want to call the charity?" Saryl said, "You know that children's rhyme: 'Starlight,

What Is an Entrepreneur? What Is Leadership? Starlight

starbright, first star I see tonight. I wish I may, I wish I might, have this wish I wish tonight.'" She asked, "Why don't we call it the Starlight Children's Foundation?" I said, "Thank you, Saryl. That sounds fantastic. It's sort of happy." There was another lady who said, "One of the things I do in my spare time is design logos. And I can already see the logo in my head. It's a silhouette of a child reaching for a star because it's Starlight." We all loved that. I said, "Look, we already have the design for a letterhead, and we don't even exist yet."

Here is the 1982 logo and (right) the current one:

That was our beginning in 1982. My then partner Ted Field put up the first funding. I ran it hands-on, Emma's career took off, and we both talked it up in every direction. The tremendous power of a big idea: delivering happiness to seriously ill kids and their families. At a pretty rapid clip we opened offices across Canada, Australia, the UK, and the United States. Soon we were enabling three thousand wishes a year, and then we branched into other psychosocial services.

Along the way, I started meeting some very serious doctors in the various fields of medical research. I got the scientific explanation for what we'd known since the very beginning. We'd say to a kid, "We know you want to go to Disney World, but Dr. Smith says you can't because your T-cell count is too low. If it rises, you can go to Disney World; but if not, let's talk about other ways of you having more joy in your life and for your mom, dad, and siblings." And on occasion, the kid would reply, "But I don't want a computer, I want to go to Disney World." And we would say, "Well, you can't unless your T-cell count comes up." Then, on multiple occasions, perhaps two weeks later, the child's T-cell count would strangely rise, and we would send them off to Disney World.

The medical field of psychoneuroimmunology came into being, which we'd already been observing in a significant minority of our wish kids, even before we'd had a name for the phenomenon. Medical science caught up and psychoneuroimmunology became something

FINDING HAPPY

we would talk to donors about. "There's nothing the matter with making seriously ill children and their stressed-out moms and dads and siblings happier: it has intrinsic value. Happiness is a good thing, right? Where there is dismay and grief and awfulness, building happy memories is a good thing. But by the way, with some of these kids, we can actually help them heal, because the mind and the body are linked in a circular relationship." Sometimes people would say, "Isn't that a bit, you know, like laying on of hands, crystals over the bed, and Shirley MacLaine?" And we would say, "No, no, look at this whole compendium of medical research we've compiled in the field of PMI." Then they would often donate, and we would help more kids. It was a powerful and emotional concept, and I learned that was another way to raise a great deal of money for Starlight.

On one visit to the Children's Ward at County-USC Medical Center, I looked at the crappy black-and-white, nineteen-inch TV hanging on the wall. I asked the nurse how the kid lying opposite in orthopedic traction, tethered to his bed, could change the TV channel. "Oh," said the nurse, "we give him the stick!" She showed me an eight-foot bamboo pole, with an eraser fixed to one end with surgical tape. This was his remote control: the kid was supposed to use it to press the buttons on the TV. Ingenious, but I thought it was pathetic. Like fishing. The AV executive in me was appalled; something had to be done!

I met with the financier Michael Milken. At that time, he was at the peak of his financial power, running the X-Desk, the trading desk at Drexel Burnham Lambert on Wilshire Boulevard. After the markets closed, I would go down and sit with him, where on a yellow pad we tried to turn our concept for audiovisual distractive entertainment into an actual "thing" we could build and test. He was and is a kind, generous, and humble man. Michael and I did some innovative and helpful things together for seriously ill children. He was always impeccable to me, and since then he has focused on his good works with typical dedication and entrepreneurship. I'm deeply grateful to have been a small part of his lifting up of the world.

We thought our idea should contain Nintendo, a VHS player, and connect to the Disney Channel. I went and bought a trolley from a hospital supply company: the regular wheeled device to slide under and

138

over a bed, so that patients could eat their lunch. I unscrewed the tray, put the bottom in the back of my car, and went off to Bobadilla Casemaking, where I had been buying bespoke cases for the equipment we used in making films. I said to Mr. Bobadilla that I wanted him to build a box that would contain the audiovisual paraphernalia. I wanted very few controls on the outside. "Let's give the kids the on-off, the volume, and the Nintendo controllers. But let's not give them the vertical and horizontal hold, and anything else that will muck up the picture." A week later, we had the very first prototype of the Starlight Fun Center. It was truly ugly, a kind of Heath Robinson/Rube Goldberg device. It looked like an old Russian automobile.

When we tested it at County-USC Medical Center, the kids, the Child Life staff, the nurses, and the doctors all thought it was the best thing since sliced bread. Michael Milken made a generous donation, and we ordered one hundred. We started pushing them out into children's hospitals, initially in Los Angeles, then across the country, then around the world. What is now the Nintendo Starlight Fun Center has become a hugely successful audiovisual intervention to make seriously ill kids happier. Dare to dream! The Fun Center Program has received massive, ongoing sponsorship from Nintendo and other companies. Nintendo, led by Don James, has been a continuous Starlight partner and sponsor since 1991. An amazing example of corporate ethics and generosity. Truly rare and remarkable. Must be some kind of a record.

We learned startling things about the mitigation of pain through our work in Starlight. We initially intuited that both the presence and extent of a child's pain was related to their mental state, and thus if we introduced fun and entertainment, they might not notice the pain as much. While we were beta-testing the Fun Centers at County-USC Medical Center, I hired researchers to measure their effect on the children's minute-to-minute subjective perception of their own pain. They pressed a clicker device, which would deliver a micro-dose of morphine into their IV, whenever they felt they needed it. We measured how many times per five minutes they pressed the clicker before, during, and after the presence of the Fun Center over their bed. The resulting graph was not at all what we expected. For sure, the use of the pain medicine, the analgesia, was much lower when the trolley was over the bed. But unexpectedly, the use of pain medicine started to decline a good hour before the trolley even arrived in the room. The child was sitting in bed looking forward to watching VHS films and the Disney Channel and to playing the Nintendo games.

Furthermore, the good effect did not end when the trolley left the bed. There was an overhang, while the child was still in the euphoria of how many monster avatars they had beaten in the Nintendo, and that kept them off the pain medicine for perhaps a further hour or ninety minutes before their pain awareness came back up to what it had been in the first place. This was shocking and productive...and we became rather famous in the medical community. It also led to a tremendous boost in donations. We pushed thousands of the trolleys into just about every children's hospital and children's ward in the United States, Canada, Australia, and the UK. Suddenly we had metrics of success in pain mitigation and in psychoneuroimmunology. I discovered that was how I could raise the really big bucks from large foundations, from government, and from ultra-high-net-worth donors who required proof of efficacy: we gave them the outcome stats.

I am the one in the middle.

What Is an Entrepreneur? What Is Leadership? Starlight

Fast-forward from that day in 1982, when we founded the Starlight Children's Foundation, to today. The mission is exactly the same: to make seriously ill children happy. It's the same name invented by Saryl, and the same logo of a child reaching for a star. We find kids who are seriously ill, usually with their families in meltdown. Mom and Dad have only ever talked of their child's illness to each other for many months or years. Their marriage is usually not in a wonderful place, and they're not in a good place emotionally. The younger siblings are often jealous of the ill brother or sister because they feel the sick child gets all the attention. The older siblings have guilt because they're not the ones who are dying and often in pain. We swoop in with a palette of eight psychosocial services, and we deal with it. Starlight works brilliantly well: the enduring power of a good idea. Build once, test, then replicate many times! Last year, in the United States alone, 2.4 million hospitalized kids experienced joy and relief through Starlight programs.

As Saryl and I bonded over Starlight, we saw more of each other. We organized a Christmas party at County-USC Medical Center in the Children's Ward. We had received a donation of grown-up character costumes. Saryl was dressed in a dolphin suit, her eyes peeking through the grill under the dolphin's head. There was a seriously ill little girl tethered to a bed...one of many young patients. When we launched the music, she danced as best she could, horizontal in her bed. I looked into the grill of the dolphin, and there was my darling Saryl crying her eyes out, mascara running down her cheeks. That was the moment I actually fell in love!

And here we are forty years later, married and with four spectacular kids. That's how you do it. Love and empathy are pillars of the Meaning of Life. Go find yours.

FINDING HAPPY

Chapter Takeaways and Reflection Questions for You

- What is an entrepreneur? Is it someone who implements an idea and makes it happen?
- Could that be you?
- What is leadership, and how do you do that?
- Look up "servant leadership." It is how one can best draw others into a hive mind to get the job done. You are in charge, but to be effective you lead from within the middle of the group.
- Look up "hive mind" too: the ability of ants and other living beings to develop policy, tactics, and execution as a group, beyond any one animal's thinking. Also known as the exogenous brain.
- Think about volunteering: possibly your best way to meet people, feel good about yourself, and yes, who knows, perhaps fall in love!
- How do you sell? How do you tell a story, move someone's heart, and get them to help you? (Clue: Practice your story and make it sing!)
- Selling is persuasion. Persuasion is through generating empathy. Empathy is from telling a story.

CHAPTER 25

What Are Your Priorities? Why?
The Robin Hood Effect

I spend a lot of time persuading people that selflessness can be selfish. Arguing self-interest in philanthropy may seem like an oxymoron, but for those of us building nonprofit organizations, it is in fact often the difference between success and failure in fundraising. From my four decades building charities, not only does the strategy clearly work in encouraging donors, but in addition I suggest its ethics and morality can oftentimes be admirable and appropriate.

Most of us feel the urge to do good deeds and support those less fortunate than ourselves based on our shared belief that we are "all in this thing together," and that the strong should support the weak. Quite often we learn this motivation as a core tenet of our religion, or when we are taught a philosophy of life. Certainly, I have taught four children that civilization is fragile, and that it is the responsibility of each and every member to improve it and to further build resilient and ambitious social structures to pass on to our children, and through them to theirs.

143

FINDING HAPPY

But recent research shows us that there is also self-interest in helping those less fortunate. Ichiro Kawachi—in collaboration with the Social Environment Working Group of the John D. and Catherine T. MacArthur Research Network on Socioeconomic Status and Health—has demonstrated that the degree of income inequality in a society is related to the health status of that population. Greater income inequality is linked to lower life expectancy, higher mortality rates, and worse self-rated health. *For the wealthy as well as for the poor*. Higher mortality at the US metropolitan level, as well as higher rates of obesity at the US state level, are also linked to income inequality. This association may seem surprising, but it is statistically robust when corrected for differentials of age, race, sex, and individual socio-economic characteristics. The bottom line is that *affluent* people live shorter and less healthy lives the more the people around them are poor.

Exactly why this demonstrable correlation exists is still subject to debate. One can imagine, however, that one's own health is jeopardized if the man making the salad in a restaurant has inadequate healthcare and thus a higher incidence of hepatitis. Having worked in several third-world countries where the gulf between rich and poor is gigantic, I can attest to the incremental stress among the affluent caused by protecting themselves—through high walls, armored cars, and armed bodyguards—from potential theft, violence, and dislike by those impoverished souls who have to sleep in cardboard boxes on the ground around them. And stress, as we know, shortens life. I was once partnered with a very wealthy man. On a piece of paper in envelopes in my desk, by my bed, and in my wallet were specific instructions on what to do if he, his wife, or his child were kidnapped.

One of most important areas where self-interest is an entirely appropriate motivation for philanthropy is in the brilliant sponsorships I have been able to encourage by Fortune 500 companies. There was a time many years ago when I would fly into the headquarters city of a major corporation. I would visit with the corporation's foundation staff, and I would basically beg for their help in supporting one of my children's charities. "You know that we do good work; you know that we're efficient and that seriously ill children need your help. You are yourself a parent...could you please see a way to making a donation to support these special kids in need?" When things went well, I would receive a $25,000 donation for Starlight and be politely asked not to return for another year.

At a certain point, I realized that a worthy cause is capable of presenting a net gain to a major corporation. Put bluntly, a worthy cause can help sell their product or service. So, I started visiting with the executive vice president for marketing, rather than with the foundation division of each company. My pitch back then would be quite different. "In our recent national promotion with Colgate-Palmolive, Starlight-Starbright demonstrated a twenty-five percent uplift in the brand's Nielsen ScanTrack market share. We think we can similarly create a dramatic benefit for your own corporation, which will also be very good for Starlight's special children."

The results were astonishing: instead of receiving $25,000 from the corporation's foundation, we were suddenly receiving $250,000 from a cause-related marketing campaign. Some Starlight promotions generate large sums each year. And they tend to repeat. I am sure they also sell a great deal of product...and in that regard I say, "God bless America." It's a perfect example of the corporation acting responsibly, not only to society, but also to its stockholders: a true win-win.

What a wonderful thing it is to understand, from research at the University of Florida, that a dollar donation to charity triggered by a consumer's purchase of a product or service generates more of an uplift in sales than a dollar discount coupon offered to the same consumer! This means that, generally speaking, consumers are more ready to help needy children than they are their own pocketbooks. It gives one hope for the future. Ponder that: the power of empathy.

I still teach that altruism is an ennobling part of character that enriches the giver as well as our whole civilization. I still teach that any act, however small, by which we build society makes us part of the virtuous forces that heal the world and build a better life for our descendants. That it is better to give a man a job than just to give him money, better to build a bridge than to swim the river, and a terrific thing to apply entrepreneurial skills in a nonprofit, philanthropic direction.

But I also tell them that Starlight, First Star, and EDAR are the best possible opportunities to meet like-minded souls—brilliant people

FINDING HAPPY

who have selected themselves as worthy citizens and whose enthusiasm for life, children, and the future will make great friendships blossom. I accurately tell them of the marriages that have happened between thousands of brilliant volunteers who found a common bond in helping seriously ill kids. I tell them that this is how I fell in love with my wife.

When I lecture in business schools, I always tell the students that their career track or volunteer track in philanthropy will be about ten times faster than in an ordinary business for profit. The charities of America are so needy, so eager, and so ready to embrace new ways of achieving their goals that, generally speaking, the rise of a smart and dedicated young person can be meteoric. People know in the meetings of my philanthropies that it is a dangerous thing to suggest a good idea; one immediately finds oneself the head of a taskforce charged with its study and implementation!

For me personally, I laugh when someone talks to me as though I was some noble soul dedicating time and resources to nonprofit causes. I know secretly in my heart that the greatest gift I've ever received was the realization that through good works I would make myself very, very happy. I constantly receive much more than I give.

There, I said it.

Chapter Takeaways and Reflection Questions for You

- Whether you are looking for a friend or a life partner, what is the best arena to find them? A bar, a class, a sport, or a valuable shared activity? Why?
- How can you see early into someone's heart?
- What are you good at? Who needs that skill?
- How can volunteering make opportunities that lead to a job or a friendship?
- How can you make time?
- What are your priorities, and why?

CHAPTER 26

What Is Genius? Hello, Mr. Spielberg

As Starlight grew, we started hiring serious, sophisticated, highly qualified, academically credentialed medical researchers to come and have a look at our work. They discovered all sorts of amazing things. With Nintendo, we invented the Fun Center. It is now in its Mk. 10 incarnation! Back at the beginning, in the early '90s, it was a box strapped onto one of those hospital trolleys that go over a bed so that the patient can have their lunch. Instead of the tray, it had the box, and in it a television monitor, as well as a Nintendo game console, and you could watch the Disney Channel. It could play VHS videocassettes of what we thought were helpful, suitable, and happy shows, mostly musicals. Michael Milken and I invented it, I bought the parts, and we bolted the prototype together in my garage.

We learned a great deal by watching the effect of the trolleys on the patients, and started publishing our findings in the literature of psychoneuroimmunology. Other researchers started seeking us out, to come study

Starlight Fun Centers. Heady stuff for a film producer! At one point, there was so much research going on that we became worried we were turning our kids into guinea pigs, so we backed off. PNI is a thing. It's serious science. Once upon a time, we used to give doctors pretend prescription charts, on which they could choose from the eight psychosocial services of Starlight, and prescribe them as though they were a medicine, which they often were for their patients.

We grew exponentially, geographically, financially, and in terms of the number of kids and families we were helping. Then I got an introduction to Steven Spielberg, through the ever-collaborative career producer of *Star Wars*, Kathy Kennedy. I pitched up at Amblin on the Universal Studios lot. Entering his outer office, everything scares the hell out of you. "You don't give your collateral material to Mr. Spielberg, you leave that with me." "You'll have exactly half an hour, he's got an ambassador coming on the hour, so you'll need to be gone. And good luck." And in you go.

Your first thing is, you look at Steven, and you realize that he looks exactly like Steven Spielberg! It was an out-of-body moment. I told him all about Starlight. And he asked, "What do you know about the internet?" It was 1990. I replied, "I know a little bit...didn't Al Gore have something to do with it?" He said, "It was more people than just him." And we're talking and he says, "You know, we could do something extraordinary. We can now link kids together audiovisually at great distances, so that, first of all, the immunocompromised kids can find community and make friends. They can even go to school through a robot in the classroom. They can be seen and heard, and not just by their siblings, parents, and friends between visits. We can link together online kids of roughly the same age, dealing with the same medical situation. We could link them hospital to hospital." We both got very excited. This is the genius of Steven: he creates these electric moments of creativity and collaboration. I was jazzed.

I'm looking at my watch, and I'm thinking that I don't know what happened to the ambassador, but I've been in here an hour now. I look a bit later, and I think I've been in here ninety minutes. Eventually, he asked, "What do you want me to do?"

FINDING HAPPY

I said, "Right, it's a new charity. We'll call it Starbright." Because I remembered how my then girlfriend (now wife) Saryl had dreamed up the name Starlight, from the children's rhyme, "Starlight, starbright, first star I see tonight." Steven asked, "What will I be?" And I replied, "You'll be the chairman. I'll be the president. We'll work together and put a board together, and we'll raise a bit of money." He said to me, "I should donate, right? There's no way that we can ask people for money if I don't give first. How much do you think I should give?" I replied, "Steven, I don't think God put me on the earth to tell Steven Spielberg how philanthropic he should be." I said, "Why don't you give something moderately painful?" He said, "Well, give me a number." And I said, "I'm not going to give you a number. Think of a number yourself. I don't know what's moderately painful for you." He said, "No, just throw out a number. I can either say yes or no." He wouldn't let me leave without giving him a number. I finally blurted out, "Two and a half million dollars?" I really had no idea what I was talking about. And I saw his mouth say, "Okay." And he gave me a hug. Mind-boggling.

I came out of his office and went and hid behind a tree. I had one of those big old cell phones. I called my wife Saryl. (Epic woman. How lucky can you get?) I said to her, "I think I'm hallucinating. I think I just had well over an hour and a half with Steven Spielberg; I think it's a new charity we're doing. And he's just pledged two and a half million dollars. And I think I'm out of my mind!" There was a silence. And then Saryl said, "You don't sound safe to drive. Tell me where you are, and I'll come and get you." Which she did. And that was the beginning of Starbright.

It may seem far-fetched to imagine you can reach out to the famous, the high and the mighty, to those who can fuel and empower your life. Perhaps initially it is daunting. If you don't know the Spielbergs, the Generals Schwarzkopf and Powell, the Gorbachevs and Thatchers, how can you possibly make them hear you? May I share with you that

What Is Genius? Hello, Mr. Spielberg

I did not know any of them either...until I did. Life is introductions, networking, and developing the most powerful, emotional pitch to propel your ideas into the hearts and minds of others whenever you can engineer an opportunity to be heard.

If you are a foster kid, you may think you have no ability to get the ear of people who can help you, but you absolutely can do that. The secret sauce of connection is driving empathy, and that, my friends, is where your story is compelling, where you excel. Most people have hearts and would like to do good. Most people are open to being moved. Most people would like to help others, especially those lower down the ladders of life but seeking to climb them. You have to be ready, and your story has to be emotionally strong. When the opportunity arises, you have to look them in the eye and be brave. (More about dealing with powerful people later.)

Be ingenious, be opportunistic, be a bit pushy, but always be polite. The Supreme Court abolished affirmative action, but they did not censor your personal essay. Tell it like it is: your opportunity to describe the adversity you have felt, and your determination and grit to blaze your own successful path through life. People care, and you will be heard. Without affirmative action, many colleges have developed "adversity scores" as tools to fully consider every applicant. Your past challenges give you the golden ticket! Show it, be proud, and be ambitious. Ask for what you want to achieve. *Carpe diem.*

Chapter Takeaways and Reflection Questions for You

- If you are scared, what is the way to handle it?
- How best do we ask someone to help us? (Clue: Just. Do It.)
- Why are some people truly great souls? How can you tell?
- What did Maimonides say about the soul? And what is his "Pyramid of Giving"? See the Starlight chapter for more on the wisdom of a great thinker.
- What is creativity? Are you born with it, or can you learn it?
- Should everyone go to college? (Clue: No, there are many pathways to happiness. But in 2022, bachelor's-degree holders took home a median wage of $1,432 per week, while workers with just a high school diploma earned only $853. That's a difference of 68 percent. Money is not everything, but it sure is helpful.)

CHAPTER 27

What Is Leadership?
What General Schwarzkopf Taught Me

My challenge with Steven was that he was shy, which seems counterintuitive, but he actually didn't feel comfortable asking people for money. So, what to do? I said to him, "This is a problem, Steven, because you won't ask them for money, and they don't even want to meet with me anymore because now you're the chairman of this new thing." He said, "Well, what do we do? Don't we need someone else with us?" And I said, "Well, yes, I agree; but please don't you go anywhere, because you're brilliant as the chairman. You put us on the map. Let's get somebody very brave to team up with us. Tripods need three legs."

We had a hilarious conversation about who was the bravest famous man in the world. And we decided that "Stormin' Norman," General Norman Schwarzkopf of the United States Army, was exactly that, because he had just led the Allied Forces that won the Gulf War. And so we wrote a letter asking if he would meet with me. A message came back and said, "Yes, report to Orlando, and we will meet."

So, there I flew, and got in the elevator of the high-rise where his office was in the penthouse. Halfway up, the elevator stopped suddenly

153

FINDING HAPPY

with a jolt. A disembodied voice said, "Hold your driver's license up to the camera." Which I did. Eventually they cleared me and I went up, into the general's office. The first thing I noticed was that he was six foot three, 240 pounds: a huge man in stature, and also larger than life in personality. He was charismatic and rather intimidating. On his desk, he had the biggest pistol I've ever seen...it must have been two feet long. I asked, "Is that because of the terrorists?" And he replied, "No. Journalists."

So we're well into the conversation. I said, "So, what we're doing is colliding together different fields of expertise, people who would never otherwise meet. You know, we've got our medical suite of experts: oncologists and hematologists, child psychiatrists and psychologists and all the rest, and the various hospital administrative leaders. And then we've got the second group, which is the Silicon Valley mob, a long line of specialists, software writers, hardware engineers, and inventors. Thirdly, we've got our media creative people: writers, actors, dancers, directors, and so forth, from film, television, and theatre. We are the generalists in the middle and we keep them focused on mission. And if you join us, you will lead with Steven and me in the middle, making then collaborate." I didn't say, "And you'll be the one asking people for money." Although that's what I intended, and he later proved to be brilliant at it. We'd go into a CEO's office, and the general would tell them, "Here's what we need you to do." And they'd mostly nod at once and say, "Yes, sir!"

He said to me, "Mr. Samuelson, what do you know about the United States Army?" And I said, "Well, honestly, sir, you could assume nothing, and that'd be pretty accurate." He leaned in over his desk and the gun, and said, "Well, when you muster in, you don't just get a rank. You get a specialty. It's on your shoulder. It's a badge. You're a rifleman, you're an infantryman, you're a signalman, you're a driver, you're a cook. Whatever you are, throughout your military career, you keep your specialty. Until, if we reckon you might be a rare, excellent leader, in the ceremony where we give you your general's stars, we take away your specialty pin. Because you are no longer a specialist. You're a general."

What Is Leadership? What General Schwarzkopf Taught Me

I sat there, completely flummoxed. I realized in that moment *that's why they're called generals*. They are the generalists, because over millennia, armies have realized if they put a specialist in charge, they would mostly all die in the next battle. To win and survive, and to have food and shelter, armies have to be led by a sophisticated generalist who is also a charismatic leader. There you have it: generalists rule!

General Norman Schwarzkopf, US Army, 1934–2012

I realize that's what I do as a career film producer. I don't know how to be an excellent cinematographer, or a brilliant production designer or writer or director, or any of the 110 other specialist jobs on a film. I just know how to lead, and try to bring out the best in them. I know enough not to have them pull the wool over my eyes. The cinematographer gives me the list of the equipment that he wants me to rent for him. And I say, "Why do you actually need that lens? If you have that other lens...they do the same thing, don't they?" And we have a fine conversation about that. And more importantly, I can discuss the "look" we need, and the mood-enhancing, progressive, and deliberate use of color, light, and shadow. A good career producer must know quite a lot about all sorts of things, but you have to be the generalist in charge, and you do not need to be the specialist as well. Nobody could do that. As a career producer, you know quite a lot about all sorts of things, but you are the generalist and you do not also need to be the specialist. You just have to lead and reinforce the mission and the goal. Henry VIII was the last king who knew everything about everything...because there was not much to know. Hah!

So, those two meetings became Starbright World. At a certain point, I thought, it's mad to have two overheads. Starlight is distribution, now in eight hundred hospitals around the world, and Starbright

FINDING HAPPY

was content and interconnectivity. I thought, why don't we combine them and have one overhead? Which we did. It took me several years because the two boards didn't fancy reporting to each other, which was why I had had to do them separately  in the first place. But suddenly I saw a brief shining moment where the few ornery people on each board went away, and I realized I had to "jump while the going's good." I merged the boards. Perhaps we were the world's largest board: thirty-five people before I could slim it down a year later. I thought they would not vote for the merger if we did not keep both names. So, for two years, it was the Starlight Starbright Children's Foundation. As one could have predicted, in the excitement of the work, everyone forgot which bit they had come from and became proud of the whole thing. So we changed it to Starlight Children's Foundation, which is what it had been in the first place.

Here we are, all of these years later. We just had our fortieth birthday. How brilliant is that? I can't believe how old that makes me, but there you go. That's Starlight and Starbright. My first two charities. The honor of my life.

Chapter Takeaways and Reflection Questions for You

- Are you a generalist or a specialist?
- How can we best ask someone to help us?
- How do we persuade? (Clue: Tell the story with emotion, clarity, and empathy. Rehearse! It's all in the telling. All in the empathy you need them to feel as motivation.)
- What is the role of storytelling in progressing towards your goals?
- What is a great, compelling story? (Clue: Did it move your own heart?)

CHAPTER 28

How Can You Use Technology, and Not Let It Use You? GPT-4, AI, VR, EIEIO, LOL

If you are reading this as a young adult, then you live more than any of your ancestors in a time of great social challenges, but also of colossal possibilities. Many of the challenges come from polarization, fed by mean, greedy political leaders, the despots, the dictators, and the demagogues. The challenges also come from the undereducated base of their support, who have insufficient critical reasoning to know when they are being lied to. Too many people are willing to be led by the nose.

In your adult life, you will also have to live with the results of the burning of the hydrocarbons in the mantle of the earth, which has directly led to global climate change, rising sea levels, tornadoes, hurricanes, tsunamis, and other unprecedentedly destructive weather, as well as heat, making it impossible to live in some areas. And of course, we all live with the inability of political leaders to resolve disputes without having a war, which kills hundreds of thousands of young soldiers and millions of civilians. Fear dressed up as hatred, and shocking ignorance, are results of selfish and self-interested leaders herding

157

FINDING HAPPY

around the sheep in their base, who have been failed by education and cannot think for themselves. But you are better than that, right?

Your life has infinite possibilities for many reasons, one of which is the astonishing gift of science, every day and in so many ways. Whether by the massive medical progress extending life by twenty or thirty years in just one generation, or the innovations that enable us to work better with less effort, you shall be blessed by huge possibilities in your lifetime. Computer science, the internet, "the cloud," artificial intelligence, and crowdsourcing have transformed the ability of one person to access the brain power of many others. I met with Nick Negroponte when he was running the Media Lab at the Massachusetts Institute of Technology. He talked about the exogenous brain, the anthill of humanity where, because of the gifts of internet connectivity, one person anywhere can access the information and thinking of everyone else connected to the network in every other location. Just as ants, by cooperating, can shift a dead animal that weighs over a thousand times each of their body weights over long distances, so it is the case that if we use our technology wisely, we can greatly enhance the capacity of the human brain to make progress, make our lives better and more rewarding.

All technology in human history has come with both positive and negative aspects. Every technology has been as challenging as it was helpful. The discovery of fire could cook your food, but it could also burn down the forest. When the automobile was invented, wary government regulators decided that it was too dangerous, and a car was not allowed to use a public street unless a man walked in front of it carrying a red flag. The point was not only to warn people to be careful around it, but also so that the car could not go faster than the man could walk. Telephones were invented in the 1870s, but it took many decades before they were in general use. When my charity First Star meets in the UK, we do so in Telephone House, near the Embankment in London. This is by the great generosity of our pro bono volunteer law firm, Gibson, Dunn & Crutcher. The immensely beautiful period building in which they have their offices was originally the connection point for every telephone line in the United Kingdom. At the beginning, there were only about one hundred lines, every single one of

158

which would terminate in the basement of Telephone House. Dozens of women sitting on stools in the basement would then find out where the caller wished to be connected. By physically plugging jack plugs into sockets, they would then make the connection. "Maidenhead 3, I am connecting you to Cambridge 7."

The difference right now is that some of the new technology is almost instantaneously being widely used as soon as it is invented. If you are millennial or younger, you are a digital native. You have been using computers and the new connectivity virtually since you could focus your eyes. This was not the case for me and for my generation. I am a digital immigrant, in the sense that I had to learn how to use a computer as a second language. When I bought my first computer in 1982, a large, ugly Kaypro with a small green cathode ray tube and no internal memory at all, I thought it was an amazing revolution. From the very beginning of the Starlight Children's Foundation in 1983, that Kaypro made it possible for me to generate fundraising letters to thousands of people. Every one of those people thought they were receiving a personal letter. I literally sat at my dining room table and signed the letters individually, but at least the mail merge on the Kaypro was able to pull down one sheet of letterhead at a time, then autofill the name, the address block, and the salutation. All I had to do was to sign my John Hancock at the bottom. How those days are behind us!

The newest, giant revolution in technology is surely that of artificial intelligence. The most recent version (this will assuredly only be temporary) is called GPT-4. By the time you read this, they will probably be up to GPT-10. It harnesses a chain of supercomputer bots to read every single word available anywhere on the planet in databases connected to the internet. It sucks up literally every sentence on every subject available anywhere. When one asks AI to write a story or a letter, or to produce a photograph, a video, or an audio recording, in a nanosecond, it looks for what everyone has ever created and put online that has any relevance. It does not just look for facts, but also for opinions and the structure of sentences. If several words appear together, it predicts what words might go thereafter. This is the exogenous brain, given a wholly new attribute that has infinite processing power. A human being could do the same thing; but they would have to limit

FINDING HAPPY

themselves to a set of books in some library, then use the processing power of their own brain to try to remember who had written what on the subject addressed. That would be a mere grain of sand on the beach compared to the learning reach of GPT-4, which can read everything, everywhere, and has now done so.

The challenge is how to stop the artificial intelligence from taking over the planet. It can process information, but it has no moral compass of any kind, other than the company that owns the program trying to stop it from killing all of us. One of the most famous films of science fiction was Stanley Kubrick's genius and prescient *2001: A Space Odyssey*. He took the novel by Arthur C. Clarke and adapted it into his fine film. On a spacecraft, a robotic butler developed a mind of its own and became unwilling to take direction from the human onboard. Unfortunately, and with all the messy inexactness of our political and government brain trusts (let alone those in the large corporations who own the AI programs), there seems to be nothing between AI and a potentially horrible outcome for humanity. All technologies have an upside as well as a downside. This one, unfortunately, seems to present an existential threat, because the downside is that a computer could become a sentient being, not to serve mankind or even its owner, but to generate its own offspring and ultimately its own control of the universe.

What if artificial intelligence found a way to ensure a continuous power supply, so that turning it off or disconnecting it from other computers was no longer possible for the humans in charge? What if artificial intelligence analyzed how wars are won and lost, then mastered how to annihilate the enemy in a flash? What if we were that enemy? What if that ability were no longer subject to the ethics, morals, scruples, empathy, and control of any human beings at all? What if the locomotive developed a mind of its own and simply would not stop?

When Steven Spielberg was a young man who had recently graduated from film school at Cal State, Long Beach, he went into Universal Studios on the tourist tram, snuck off it, and found an open door to one of the cottages used as offices for production companies. No one was using it. He found a telephone chart that allowed him to call the furniture department of the studio and order desks, chairs, and various supplies. When the studio management, run by Sid Sheinberg and Lew Wasserman, discovered that security had caught a young man trespassing, they learned that he had been talking to others in the studio, trying to get one of his scripts made into a film that he would direct. He was hauled in to be grilled by them before being thrown out. He was astonishingly charismatic and clearly gifted.

They decided that they would try him out by giving him a movie of the week to direct. That film, made in 1971, was called *Duel*, the story of a runaway truck with a hardly seen driver in the grip of road rage, and of hero Dennis Weaver's attempts to get it to stop before people are killed. What we risk with artificial intelligence is that truck, but on steroids, with AI as the driver. Tesla driverless trucks are already being tested in Arizona. I'm sure AI does not experience road rage, but what if the AI decided the mission justified the means?

The biggest things AI is missing are empathy and a moral compass to guide what it says. That's why we have to lead. AI can help greatly but should not be in charge. AI is a tool to regurgitate really well whatever is fed into it. That is all. Useful, but not the best accelerator for us to make the most significant impacts we badly need. Those require imagination, ethics, and ongoing human morality. Dream great dreams, please. We need your best ideas! Life is a team sport, and you are on the team.

Chapter Takeaways and Reflection Questions for You

- What is the biggest idea you've ever had?
- What did you do with it?
- When do you have your best ideas? Mine are half awake, half asleep.
- Why do so many ideas never get pursued?
- Why is storytelling so important in getting people to help you?
- How can we step in and stand up for people being bullied?
- Why are new ideas so frightening to people?
- Why is it dangerous not to be curious and investigate different thinking?

FINDING HAPPY

CHAPTER 29

How Do You Craft a New Solution to an Old Problem? First Star

Eventually, I realized there were people in Starlight who were waiting for me to die so that they could lead the charity! Some of them were whip-smart and fantastic human beings. I'd run it hands-on for decades. By the late 1990s it was big, safe and sound, and did amazing work. So, I announced, "In one year, I will no longer be your chairman. You had better get yourselves organized for who's going to run this thing next, because I'm going to move on."

This was shocking to a lot of the members of the board, but I think in the end, it was a very good decision to resign as the leader. I'm still on the board, and I'm the only person still there from the beginning. I'm exempt from term limits. I serve as our Cassandra and as Starlight's institutional memory. When someone suggests some wizard new scheme, I can say, "We tried that in the early 1990s. It didn't work. It had unintended consequences. Think very carefully about that before doing it again." And I still help Starlight think outside the box.

So, I freed up some volunteer time, alongside making more films. I thought, *Maybe I've got another one or two of these charities in me,*

FINDING HAPPY

because God knows, there are big problems in the world, and I'm nothing if not a prosocial entrepreneur. I have come to believe that is what I'm supposed to do on the earth: bring new solutions to old problems.

I read two documents. The first was the UN Convention on the Rights of the Child. It is pretty much unobjectionable truth. Children should have a name. They shouldn't be enslaved. They're entitled to healthcare and education. They should not be conscripted into any-one's army before they turn eighteen. And then I read that there are 193 countries in the world, all members of the United Nations, and all but two have signed the Convention. Back then, one of the two missing was Somalia, because there was no central government, and they have since signed it. The only one that has never signed is the United States of America. Shameful.

I thought: *Well, that's bizarre. I live in America; it's my country now. I have double citizenship. I'm proud of being an American. And I've never met an American who doesn't want to do what's best for children. So how can this damn thing not have been signed?* And then I read the UNICEF Biennial Survey, where they measure the countries of the world by the welfare of their children, allowing for their relative GNP. The two worst scores were the United Kingdom and the United States. I thought that was ridiculous. I don't know any American who actively hates children. It is unnatural for human beings to hate kids, isn't it?

I started a year of research; before you dare do something new, you had better make sure someone's not already doing it. Or perhaps they tried it and failed? Then, you need to develop your new idea, your own blue-sky hypothesis, elegantly and in detail. All of which I did. I discovered that the worst of the worst outcome statistics were for looked-after children in the UK, foster children in the United States, Crown Wards in Canada. I thought it was raving mad. Indefensible. How could it be?

In the United States, for example, there are almost half a million children in foster care. In the United Kingdom, almost exactly one hundred thousand. So it's a huge issue, in plain sight. The taxpayers spend tens of billions dealing with the monstrous cost of the foster care system and its rotten outcomes: poverty, unemployment, sex traffick-ing, more abuse, more neglect, criminality, incarceration, untreated illness, and early death. With some generational repetition of abuse and neglect, in every generation there are even more kids placed into foster care. The whole thing is a self-replicating hiding-to-nowhere for our society. We are defined by the weakest links in our chain of life. That's where any chain breaks apart.

And then I thought about all the humane values, and how miserable abuse and neglect make kids, who must often struggle with the resulting PTSD for the rest of their lives. We know from psychoneuroimmunology that if you are sad and miserable, you are more prone to get ill and suffer other pathologies, in progressively widening vicious circles. I thought, *Better to light a single candle than curse the gathering darkness.* Right?

I asked myself, *Well, what do we do? How do we put a dent in the problem?* And I thought, *Surely it has to start with much better education?* I also discovered that less than half of kids in care in the UK in years 9 through 13, foster kids in US grades 9 through 12, were earning their GCSE's (UK) or going on to graduate from high school (US). And virtually none of them went to university. In the United States, less than 9 percent of foster kids go on to college. Less than half even finish grade school or high school.

I thought, *These are teenagers who have never even visited a university. Hardly any even know what a university is. And they generally attend impoverished, poorly performing schools, with some not-very-good teachers. It's a race to the bottom. No wonder hardly any of them go on to college.* First Star was a charity advocating for foster kids, until Professor Kathleen Reardon wrote a book that asked the question, "What would happen if we housed, educated, and encouraged them on college campuses for the four years of high school? Wouldn't a lot more want to go to college and be ready to do so?" A huge idea. *Why not?* I thought.

I asked for a meeting with the chancellor of UCLA, Gene Block. Back then he was in charge at UCLA. I believe he still thinks I went to UCLA first because I thought it was a top-notch university, which is true. Ranked the number one public university in the United States by *US News and World Report*, and number eight in the whole world. But actually, I went there first because I lived down the road. I thought, *I'll*

FINDING HAPPY

start with UCLA.... They're probably all going to say no, so I might as well start with the closest one.

I drove up the hill and met with Chancellor Block. An electrifyingly smart and humane man. I said, "I'm here to persuade you to allow me to house, educate, and encourage foster kids in grades 9 through 12, in the middle of your campus. Please say yes." He asked why. I replied that my hypothesis was that they had never met anybody excellent. Even the charismatic adults, their visible Alphas, tended to be negative figures in their lives: gang leaders, crummy parents, pimps, drug dealers...that was why their own life outcomes were so poor. Those adults were the glass ceiling: If we have not met better, why would any of us seek it out?

Instead, what if we surrounded these children in a stable environment with high-achieving undergraduate and grad students, academics, teachers, role models, sports coaches...the whole virtuous community of a great university? And what if we did it immersively for the four years of high school, creating a powerful and positive surrogate family for kids who had none? The whole nine yards of the excellence of a thriving university?

We talked for quite a long time, at the end of which Chancellor Block stood up and said, "I've kept the people out there waiting. So we had better end here. But can you come back next week? Let's talk about the details. I'm minded to say yes, even though I don't know how we do it." He then asked, "Where are we going to get the money?" And I said, "I think intuitively it's a very strong blue-sky hypothesis. I think I can pitch the heck out of this. We'll get the money. And don't green-light it until you feel it is financially safe. I believe 'If we build it, they will fund.'"

We did, and they did. We put committees together and worked out how to run the pilot First Star Academy pretty much on the back of an envelope.

In the summer of 2011, we started with a single cohort of thirty four-teen-year-old foster kids—fifteen young men and fifteen young ladies, rising ninth graders. We housed, educated, and encouraged them on the campus of UCLA. We raised money and hired a staff. Regarding the curriculum, the new director, Wally Kappeler, and I thought one-third had to be academic because when they enrolled, almost all of the

Scholars were way behind grade level. They'd been shunted through far too many placements and schools, so we had to apply excellent teaching and remedy the deficit, wherever it was.

Another third of the curriculum should be life skills because there may have been no caring and consistent grown-up in their lives to teach them. Or perhaps they had parents who did care but could not provide for them. Financial literacy to sex ed, to "sex is not love." The last third of our curriculum had to be psychosocial, the removal of their crushing glass ceiling...which was more like a thick concrete ceiling for most. This meant the inculcation of ambition. Encouraging the kid who seemed to be interested in science by taking him off to the Nanotechnology Lab and having him look through an electron microscope.

We recruited through schools, social workers, clergy, and adult recommendation. We had an essay as part of each application, definitely Wally's Big Idea: "Please imagine it is your one hundredth birthday. Your best friend, who has known you your whole life, makes a toast. What would you like them to say?" There was no lack of ambition and frustration. It was like opening floodgates...I loved the process! These were wonderful kids in a bad place. Here was the First Star Ladder. More like an escalator! "If you fall off, we'll put you back...but only you can move your feet up the ladder."

That first Academy summer worked staggeringly well. Just a few weeks in, it was like watching flowers grow. We realized there was nothing intrinsically the matter with the kids. If you look at the bell curve of foster youth IQs, it's no different than any other half a million kids in the United States, or any other hundred thousand kids

FINDING HAPPY

in the UK. They've been poorly educated. They've been discouraged. They're carrying the scars, mentally and in some cases physically, of abuse and neglect. I once asked a First Star director, when the Scholars had swimming lessons: "All the girls are in bikinis. Why does Scholar X always wear a T-shirt?" To which she replied, "She has hundreds of cigarette burns across her back. That's how the parents used to punish her, before she was taken into care." I could vomit.

Tape this on your Bathroom Mirror...

I used to be a foster kid, but now I am a First Star kid. It is different. I used to feel like a victim, but now I know I am the hero in the story of my own life. My future is up to me: I will climb the ladder of education to make my dreams come true. My First Star family loves me, cares for me and is here to help me.

I will find great role models: I will study what they do, and how they do it. I will ask for help. I will understand more and more about this great university, and its community of students going places, fine tuning their ambitions and turning them into the realities of their future lives. I will do that too, just like them.

I will not let people drag me down. I am smart, and I know exactly who those people are. I will turn away from them, towards my full potential. Because I am the writer of the story of my future life, not them.

I will work hard and smart. I will be organized. I will make less stress by getting the work done sooner, not at the last minute. I will check my work before I turn it in. I will ask myself "Am I proud of this? Is it the best of me? Is it worthy of having my name on it?" I will go the extra mile to put my best work out there. Because I care. Because it is for me, and for my best future.

I will raise my hand. I will dare myself to ask a question in every class. If I don't understand, I will always ask for help. I will be in the zone, there, alert, paying attention. I will make the best of it, and I'll go beyond. Because they may not care, but I do: this is for me.

I will be there, always, for my First Star brothers and sisters. I am reliable. They can count on me. I will do them random acts of kindness, because I know how important they are. I will show my brothers and sisters what unconditional love looks like, because I know it is what each of us needs. If they fall, I will pick them up.

I will follow the rules of the Academy not because I have to, but because I care and I want to. I own this Academy, it is mine, and I recognize the rare opportunity to reach up, to excel, to make something of myself, that my Academy is giving me. I will do my best to always keep the Academy safe, and if I see others dragging it down, putting it at risk, I will speak up. I will be a leader in making this experience, this family, this ladder up to the future, the best it can be. I accept that responsibility with love and enthusiasm.

Because I know this is rare, and valuable. And belongs to me.

I used to be a foster kid, but now I am a First Star kid. I'm powerful, and I'm proud.

I have no idea how we persuaded people to fund First Star Academies when we started. Perhaps it was the power of A Big Idea, one that I could pitch with passion because I fully believed in it. I just kept asking, hundreds of times, until enough people said yes. Certainly, at the beginning it was all a blue sky, all hypothesis—we had no outcome stats at all to offer up as proof. But starting four years later, and ever since, instead of the less than 9 percent of foster kids normally going off to colleges and universities, the average year on year of twelfth-grade First Star graduates who have transitioned to post-secondary education, to colleges and universities, *is 87 percent*. Yes, almost exactly ten times the benchmark. And almost 100 percent graduate high school, double the benchmark for foster kids. About half go on to two-year courses to earn an associate degree, and half to a four-year university to get a bachelor's degree. The stat has held up even through the COVID years. The kids are passionate; they feel as though First Star belongs to them and they belong to it. It is the family they craved. Think of this: we send twice the proportion of our First Star Scholars on to college as middle-class America sends of its own children! Again, nothing the matter with the kids that cannot be fixed by consistent adults in their lives, stability, encouragement, great teaching, role models, a new kind of positive family, and, yes, unconditional love.

How Do You Craft a New Solution to an Old Problem? First Star

Sometimes fundraising involves doing something startling, in this case, begging!

Chapter Takeaways and Reflection Questions for You

- Greater things are possible when leaders do not cling to power. How do we encourage the next leaders?
- Should leaders lead by telling everyone what to do, or how else? If you are interested, again, do study Servant Leadership. It's an important set of insights into how best to lead.
- Why does the traditional foster-care system focus only on the removal of children from danger? Why does it not also try to encourage their best possible lives?
- How do you start a new solution to an old problem? (Clue: Dare to do. Start with research. Work out how to pitch what it will be.)
- Why are few sources of philanthropic support willing to back new solutions?
- What is your best idea to crack an old challenge? What are you doing about it?
- Why do you imagine First Star includes current and former foster youth as trustees on our main boards?
- If First Star is now proven to be very successful, why is it not at every big urban university? (Clue: Money is hard to raise. Adults are often set in their ways. The limited number of hours in the day!)

Baroness Dame Floella Benjamin, OM, DBE, DL, Patron of First Star Scholars UK, in Parliament with First Star Scholar Hanna and Peter Samuelson.

CHAPTER 30

What Will Be Your Cause?
Welcome to the Circus, Kids!

I had a nightmare, but we never know that while we are in it, right? It felt real....

I had almost left the tent without seeing her. When do we ever look up? Except that she started crying; I turned and there she was: a little kid of eight or nine wobbling in the middle of the tightrope, fifty feet above the center ring of the three. No net. Just her, a rope, a hard floor, and me. I'll never know how she got to the middle, but there she was, precariously balanced, terrified, crying out. Arms outstretched, little toes clenched from the stress of keeping her balance. Doing her best up there not to fall.

And I was apparently the only one left to help her. The audience was gone, the lights were dimmed, there was no more sparkle. The circus workers had finished, and the clowns had plodded away. Leaving just me and a little girl on a rope up above: her tears, my rising panic, and a vein pumping adrenaline not to let her die. I called out carefully, I asked her name, I told her not to move.

FINDING HAPPY

I never took my eyes off her while I dialed 911 and I kept her up there by willpower until the fire boys came and their ladder went up and she came down on the shoulder of a burly guy in a yellow hat. We applauded him and her both. They wrapped the little girl in a blanket and took her away in an ambulance, but not before she looked up and smiled and said thank you. I thanked God she didn't fall and that I had my cellphone and that 911 worked and that there was a 911 to call. We do have a system for emergencies, and it worked....

Just a bad dream, didn't really happen, a relief to wake up and realize that. But nightmares are often lessons from our subconscious. I thought about that one all day.

We Americans are great at dealing with a crisis. We can fix anything. Rebuild a city, replace a heart, rescue the toddler from the well: if a town has bad guys, we'll send in a steely-eyed sheriff to clean it up. But what we are really, really lousy at doing is *preventing* bad things from happening in the first place: we just won't take the time, spend the money, or develop the political will. We'd rather pick up the pieces nobly after the next catastrophe. Cowboys must have invented our philosophy of life: count on us to kick anything broken back into shape, but prevention is for boring nerds.

The child on the tightrope represents the victims of abuse or neglect, one of three million a year in these United States. The swaying, frayed tightrope is our nation's unnecessarily crappy child welfare system, a disgrace among the civilized nations of the planet. Fifteen hundred children a year fall off the rope on our watch and die. Despite good intentions, children can be harmed by foster care and the protective custody systems that are supposed to help them. We ask our social workers, sometimes inadequately trained, to keep safe as many as a hundred kids each on the Children and Family Services tightrope. In Texas, the number of weeks of training required to be a state-certified *manicurist* exceeds the weeks of training to become a state-certified social worker.

And what exactly is the swaying, frayed rope? A system that is broken in many of the 2200 US child-welfare jurisdictions, which under state rights have self-invented solutions oftentimes as bad as the dysfunctions they seek to cure. Systems with no institutional memory because the social workers burn out from overload and leave, and because many of the judges can't wait to escape from the dependency court postings they see as the bottom of the career totem pole, just one notch above traffic court. And so many of our major cities put kids back into harm's way on occasion by bureaucratic error, where they are molested again, beaten up again, and sometimes killed. *Sorry, Brianna, the system failed you: they lost the file.*

We deliberately turn off the klieg lights that might illuminate the crappy state of the tightrope. Courtesy of the ruling *DeShaney v. Winnebago County,* the Supreme Court decided a child could not sue a governmental agency that should have known better and put her back into harm's way. If mistakes cost lives but no money, where is the imperative for fixing the broken system? In thirty-four of our states, we wrong-headedly turn off the searchlights altogether: we seal hearings regarding children, in the misguided belief that this is necessary to protect them. But then Chief Justice Kathleen Blatz of the Minnesota Supreme Court told me they've had open hearings in Minnesota for years; no child has ever been identified in the press, who operate under a protective protocol, just as adult victims are protected in rape cases. But because the press in Minnesota have access to shine their bright lights on the *process* itself, the bureaucrats charged with helping these special children have nowhere to hide. Repetitive errors are stopped. The system corrects itself, or the eleven o'clock news asks why. Why can't we do that in the other two-thirds of the country, huh?

Child abuse and neglect costs the United States over $80 billion a year. Sixty-eight percent of adult male convicts were abused or neglected as children. I asked the warden at a Columbus, Ohio lock-up facility for children convicted of sexual crimes against other children how many he guessed had themselves been molested. He guessed 97–98 percent. It is learned behavior. And so the blighting curse of abuse rolls on. Tell me, what actually is the future of the nation we pridefully care about if not through its children? Biologists compare how animals raise each other's offspring when determining which are the higher species. By their rules, aren't we down with the trout that

FINDING HAPPY

lay thousands of eggs and hope a few don't get eaten by predators? And God bless the children of Iraq: they deserve the extra rights and protections we've enabled in the constitution we wrote for them and left behind when we pulled out our troops. Just explain to me, please, why American children lack most of those rights and protections under our own?

The little abused and neglected girl did not choose to stand on the ratty tightrope: some miserable grown-up put her there. If it is too much to ask that we teach people to parent, can we at least agree to shorten the tightrope and install some handrails? They have them in other countries: Why is an abused child better off in Toronto than in Detroit? We've just found a boy placed in sixty different foster homes by age eighteen: How can he even stand upright after that turmoil? And why can't we use distance learning to train the tens of thousands of practicing lawyers who will volunteer to serve for free as children's advocates? Must we always knee-jerk whine at the lack of funds when volunteers just want to be trained? Believe me, kids is kids everywhere.

If we have to have 2200 different jurisdictions to protect children, wouldn't it at least be smart to compare the practices and outcomes in each to determine which models work best? Dare one suggest that if the research klieg light were turned on, well-meaning communities might like to adopt the best protocols rather than keep the worst?

Suffer the little children. They are the future of these United States. We can do much better by them, and so by us. The knowledge exists; we just need the will. Hello? Hello? Anyone else think the wobbling little girl needs catching?

Chapter Takeaways and Reflection Questions for You

- What gives you nightmares?
- What can we learn from a bad dream?
- Can we also perhaps glimpse a solution, a plan, a pathway forward?
- What do you see in your world that is most broken, most unfair, most evil?
- What are you passionate to fix in your world?
- Who needs your help?
- What's your plan to help you, those you love, and your world?

I know as you sit here—perhaps 21, 22, 23 years old—you say, well, what should I do? What is it that the world needs? My answer, in the words of Howard Thurman: "Ask not what the world needs. Ask what makes you come alive. Because what the world needs is people who have come alive."

In other words, I challenge you to find your passion. I challenge you to find that thing in the world that feels like such a deep moral contradiction that you cannot be silent. You have to express yourself; you have to stand up and try to make the world better. Find anything that you would do for free except that you have to pay the rent or the mortgage. And chase after it with all your might.

—**Raphael Warnock**, Georgia Senator,
Bard College, 2023

CHAPTER 31

What Is the Answer to Everything, at Least in Producing Films?

By the early 1990s, I had repetitively made quite a lot of films, and I had built my own mental toolkit of how that could be accomplished each time. Although every film is different—using a new script in new locations with new creative leadership, a different cast, and a mostly different crew—nevertheless, a kind of pattern recognition makes itself available, which I think of as my toolkit. The carpenter carrying his toolbox to build some structure out of wood does not necessarily know the specifics of the task ahead. But he knows that in the toolbox is what he will need to get it done. The existence of the entrepreneur's red toolbox is not only to carry the necessary knowledge and strategies, but also a sense of reassurance that one has been there before, a kind of deja vu to face the new set of challenges. It is quite often comforting.

My brother Marc had optioned the play *Tom & Viv* with Harvey Kass in 1985, and by the time Marc and I started working together in 1991, he had developed a screenplay by Michael Hastings, then by Anthony Minghella, and then by Adrian Hodges. He'd attached Brian Gilbert to direct and secured some backing from British Screen. The story for the stage play had been researched in depth by Michael Hastings, and it was acclaimed in its run at the Royal Court Theater. It explored the catastrophically bad first marriage of one of the world's greatest poets, the American T.S. Eliot, author of "The Waste Land," one of the most important poems in the English language. In 1915, he married the young, beautiful, vivacious Vivienne Haigh-Wood, whose temperament was initially very encouraging to the dour, tortured Eliot, but he eventually soured on the marriage.

At the time, divorce was still an ugly word, and a man making his way in patriarchal middle-class society could not allow it to taint his precious reputation. So, a diabolical alternative path was developed, whereby an uppity and inconvenient wife could be declared insane, and thus committed, without appeal, to an asylum, where she could be left to rot for the rest of her life. Cruelty is often worst when men seek to keep their power and control.

Vivienne Haigh-Wood was a woman of enormous intellect, and by the best thinking today, would be considered to be extroverted, emancipated, and admirably determined to speak her mind. But a century ago in the 1920s, when she did this at dinner parties, Eliot was tortured by embarrassment in front of his peers, and he determined that the situation had to be brought to an end. We discovered Vivienne's diaries locked up in the library of Oxford University. Access was tightly controlled by Eliot's second wife, Valerie. Valerie stipulated that while people could read Vivienne's diaries, they could not make copies. We had to resort to a research assistant who read the diaries into a tape recorder and then transcribed them somewhere else.

We discovered that while the marriage was certainly challenging, in the early years it was also loving and good. It was Vivienne whose encouragement allowed the insecure Eliot to write some extraordinarily important poems, including "The Waste Land." In the manuscript that Eliot himself corrected, the handwriting of

Vivienne is everywhere, including her coming up with the title of the poem. She gave him actual line changes, which he accepted and incorporated. Her fingerprints are all over one of the greatest poems in the English language.

In her day, white men of privilege had invented a detailed system to discard their inconvenient wives by having them declared insane. An appointment was made without the knowledge of the wife. Two doctors arrived unannounced at the house one evening and asked her three mental arithmetic questions. If she got any of them wrong, in the following few days two large, strong-armed men, private bailiffs, would grab the woman and take her off to a mental asylum under the Lunacy Act.

In one of the most poignant scenes of our film, Vivienne answers correctly the first two questions and then realizes that the husband she loves is trying to get rid of her. The third question was along the lines of: "The greasy pole is ten yards tall. Every day, the monkey climbs up three yards and every night he falls back two yards. On what day does he first reach the top of the pole?" When Vivienne realized that Eliot was behind all of this, such was her love that she went along with being discarded and deliberately got the third answer wrong.

Vivienne was incarcerated in an asylum for the rest of her life. T.S. Eliot traveled widely. For example, after the Second World War, he visited his friend Ezra Pound in America, a genius writer but a well-known fascist who had publicly sided with Hitler and the Nazis. But what Eliot could not bring himself to do was to ever visit Vivienne in the asylum.

With the very powerful script by Adrian Hodges, we were able to attract Miranda Richardson to play Vivienne, Willem Dafoe to play Tom, and an electrifyingly good British cast for the rest of the characters. Filming went well, and in a wonderful bidding war during the MIFED sales bazaar in Milan, Italy, in 1993, Miramax bought North American distribution.

Tom & Viv went on to be nominated for two Academy Awards and was also nominated for a BAFTA. It turns out that there is great merit and fuel for an entrepreneur in pursuing a project about which one is passionate. And we were.

Chapter Takeaways and Reflection Questions for You

- If you are a woman, have you ever felt marginalized and disrespected by your male peers? What could or did you do about it?
- If you are a man, do you treat every woman who is your peer as an equal? Do you contribute to inclusion and social justice, or are you an obstacle to women advancing in life, in school, in university, and in their careers?
- Exerting inclusion may be easier with the power to speak up, but not always. The shy kid flipping burgers at McDonald's may not be an outspoken social-justice advocate for his female coworkers. But that same young man or woman may be willing to report an assistant manager who is a sexual harasser.
- What is the highest and best relationship between a man and a woman or any two partners regardless of their sexual orientation, in a marriage or permanent partnership? Are there roles that are to be attributed by sex, or should each partner perform each task and responsibility equally and to the same degree? So many gray areas here! That's where empathy and ethics can guide us best.
- What progress have we made in female emancipation during this last hundred years?
- In what jobs do women still earn less than men? (Clue: In most of them.)
- What more should be done to empower half our workforce and our supply of intelligence to do their best work?

CHAPTER 32

How Can You Be in the Arena? *Arlington Road*

The man who wrote *Butch Cassidy and the Sundance Kid*, William Goldman, wrote an amazing book called *Adventures in the Screen Trade*. There is a line in it where he discusses what makes a successful film, a film that finds an audience. He put "NOBODY KNOWS ANYTHING" twice, for emphasis. He was right; you can be as clever, as cautious, as inventive, and as creative as you like, and in the end, whether the film is commercially successful can have as much to do with whether it rained the first weekend in the big cities, as does the quality of the film itself. The reason why famous actors are cast in films, even though they cost much more than others less well known but of equal skill, is that name stars provide the financier a kind of insurance policy, where they can look to their previous films that did business and extrapolate what the present film ought to earn. In addition, if they work in a studio and the film is unsuccessful, they can hope to preserve their jobs by pointing to the previous films where those same actors contributed to great success. Who knew?

Strange things happen to a career film producer. I was driving my car down Avenue of the Stars in Century City, Los Angeles, when I saw two young people standing on the sidewalk with a big box. Each of them held a script in their hand and were waving it at the cars as they drove past. They had a large cardboard sign that said, "Excellent script for sale. Very commercial!" Call me stupid, but I stopped. These were Kathryn Nemesh and Darren Block, and the script they handed me through the window was called *Playmaker*. As I drove home, I realized I had now committed ninety minutes of my life to reading something that would probably be awfully bad.

But it was not. I thought it was a fresh new idea and quite well executed. Michael Schroeder did a rewrite, and I was able to get the film financed. We cast Colin Firth, Jennifer Rubin, and John Getz. The film was pretty low-budget but turned out rather well.

On another occasion, and a much bigger budget, I was able to get an early read of a riveting script called *Arlington Road*. I was a Finals Round Committee judge for twenty-five years at the Academy of Motion Picture Arts and Sciences (AMPAS), the Oscars Academy, for the Nicholl Fellowship in Screenwriting. Every year there are between six thousand and eight thousand entries. Anyone can enter, in a very democratic process. Tiers of paid professional readers reduce this unfathomable number of scripts to something more manageable. Each script is read at least twice in each round of judging. After the paid readers, Academy members from every branch then further winnow down the numbers through a semifinals round. My committee then reads the ten finalists of the year. We engage in a spirited debate in the Academy boardroom on Wilshire Boulevard. Aristotle wrote, "There is no argument in matters of human taste and smell," and he was correct. The spirited arguments always have at least one person as the champion of each of the ten finalist scripts, while several other people think those are dreadful. We keep voting until we have five fellowships to award, each of $35,000, with an Academy certificate and a moment in the spotlight.

The Nicholl Fellowship in Screenwriting is one of the most important things that the Academy does because it is a bridge into an insular industry for writers, wherever they live in the world and whoever their parents are—writers who have no link to the industry, and almost certainly no agent. The world changes for them if they become a Nicholl Fellow. They are brought to Los Angeles for a week for the ceremony and to meet agents, managers, lawyers, career producers, and others. They have the camaraderie of the other Fellows, and they are mentored and helped by our committee.

Thus it was that I read the truly electrifying script called *Arlington Road* by Ehren Kruger. The script was so powerful that I knew it would be relatively straightforward to set up. I felt it would be an actor magnet and also land us a fine director. But first I had to get the rights. I phoned the Nicholl Office at the Academy and I was told that as a judge, I absolutely, positively was forbidden from going after the rights until the public announcement of the winners was made in the press release and then in the trade papers. I had to sit frustrated until the announcement appeared in *Daily Variety*. The morning I finally read it there, I rushed to my car clutching a checkbook and drove to Ehren Kruger's agent's office on Westwood Boulevard. The minute that they opened at nine o'clock, I was in there and optioned the script, in a deal his agent at Writers and Artists and I hand-wrote and initialed on a yellow pad.

There was a spirited competition to finance the film, and we had several suitors. In short order, Lakeshore under Tom Rosenberg pulled into front position at the Cannes Film Festival. Tom made us a written offer and gave us a twenty-four-hour deadline to go into exclusive negotiations. So we needed a lawyer right then and there, in Cannes! Marc got the flight details of one of our lawyers, David Bouchier, who was about to land at Nice Airport. We sped off to the airport in our rental car, dismissed his driver, and Marc sat in the back of our car and ran through the deal with David while I drove us back to Cannes and straight into a meeting with Eric Reid of Lakeshore at the Noga Hilton.

I had seen a moving documentary short, plus the narrative first film directed by Mark Pellington, and I thought he was truly gifted. I approached Mark, with Lakeshore's agreement, and he agreed to direct. We flew Ehren Kruger down from San Francisco to do a rewrite.

How Can You Be in the Arena? Arlington Road

I remember saying to him that if he had rented a car that was any smaller, he could have put a handle on the top and carried it with him into the meeting. Mark, Ehren, and I laid out the scenes on three-by-five cards in a snake through several rooms. Then we went out to cast. We were blessed by Jeff Bridges agreeing to play the college professor, opposite Tim Robbins as the mysterious neighbor.

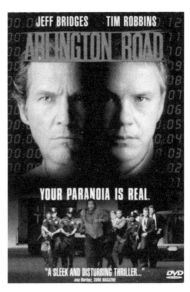

We made the film mostly in Houston, Texas, and could only afford one week in DC to get the beauty shots at the culmination of the plot. After Jeff Bridges realizes that he has been hoodwinked by the terrorist, there is a spectacular explosion that completely destroys the FBI building on Pennsylvania Avenue. We built a model that cost over half a million dollars, and with five cameras running at high speed, our special effects expert proceeded to press the button to blow it up. I was convinced that we had failed completely, because one second the model was there, the next moment there was an almighty explosion, and then right after that, there was no more building at all. But we shot at high speed to create the slow-motion effect. In fact, our expert got it exactly right, and we achieved an amazingly vivid and realistic destruction of the large multi-story building by high explosives.

In the middle of our Houston filming, I managed to destroy several vertebrae in my neck by being whacked on the head by the descending arm of a parking lot exit. When they say *"Do Not Walk Here"* in large letters painted on the asphalt, I strongly suggest you learn from my terrible error and do what they say. Stay away. I had to work on set wearing a hard neck brace, which was both uncomfortable and frustrating. But somehow, we got through.

The film was initially to be released by Polygram. They insisted that the hero could not die at the end. Mark Pellington, Marc, and I, with the backing of Lakeshore, thought that was a dreadful idea. Of course our hero had to die at the end: it was a horror film, and the monster was domestic terrorism. In horror films the hero can absolutely die, and that is part of the horror. The evil monster lives on to terrorize another day. We reached an impasse with Polygram. In the end, we proposed to them that we would film two endings, one where Jeff Bridges's character lived and one where he was blown up. We  would test both through the National Research Group in a multiplex. We agreed that whichever got the most votes of very good or excellent would be the final cut. Our version with the hero dying spectacularly at the end won the day by a very large margin. Then President Bill Clinton watched the film on Air Force One and said it was the best movie he'd seen all year.

By the time the film was to be released, it was in the hands of Universal Studios. The relationship with them was poor. When the already unenthusiastic studio realized that they could not release the film on time because the real-world tragedy of the Columbine High School massacre had recently occurred, Lakeshore was able to buy it back from them, and then sell it to Sony, who released the film later in the year. Unfortunately, the long lead press, the magazines and so forth, had all taken place by then. Nevertheless, the film was very successful, won all sorts of awards, and Mark Pellington, still a friend, went on to direct other major films. *Arlington Road* is the most successful thriller I have ever produced, and it's one of a handful of films in my whole career of which I am truly proud. And it all started by diligently reading a Nicholl script late on a Sunday night and making notes on a yellow pad. If I had not been standing in Ehren Kruger's agent's office at 9 a.m. holding a checkbook, someone else would undoubtedly have grabbed the project. *Carpe diem.*

Chapter Takeaways and Reflection Questions for You

- Have you ever succeeded by going the extra mile?
- Have you ever succeeded by being ingenious?
- How important is timing in achieving your success?
- What can be done about the haters who live in our midst and despise other people because of their color, their religion, or their origin?
- What can be your personal part in pushing back when you hear or see hatred?
- How do we avoid despotic leaders fueling their base in order to create and preserve their own political power?
- If you are old enough to vote, have you voted in every election where you were eligible? If not, shame on you. Do it! Do it!
- Please think through the imperative of each of us taking responsibility for our fragile and precious democracy.

CHAPTER 33

Why Stick Up for Each Other?
Oscar Wilde and Me

I was always enthralled by the writings of Oscar Wilde. I had studied them as a scholarship kid at Cambridge University and very much appreciated his wit, wisdom, and how insolent and impertinent he often was. My brother Marc and I very much enjoyed working on *Tom & Viv* with the director Brian Gilbert, and sometimes called ourselves the Three Musketeers. In 1994, Brian had the idea for an Oscar Wilde biopic and pitched it to Marc for development under our Miramax deal. We then read the definitive biography of Oscar Wilde by Richard Ellmann, and optioned it. Brian Gilbert again directed.

We also definitely tried to pursue an overall personal and corporate agenda of inclusion. Still now in many countries, and certainly in England 125 years ago, life was highly challenging for anyone who was gay. It was life-threatening: completely impossible to come out of the closet to try to achieve the same things in society as someone heterosexual. And remember, it still is that way in half the countries around the world. In the UK and US, progress has been made, but the old white guys of the right constantly exert themselves to roll it back

Why Stick Up for Each Other? Oscar Wilde and Me

(and women's rights, and minority rights, and immigrant rights, and children's rights, and animal rights, and the rights of our planet...). It is increasingly stressful and oftentimes dangerous to live in the Land of the Free within any of the groups that make up the acronym LGBTQI+.

It cannot be good enough that the champions of civil rights come only from the subset of humanity who are the victims of the prejudice against which they themselves demonstrated. I'm proud that we, as heterosexual men, made the biography of Oscar Wilde, a gay man whose homosexuality was used against him in the cruelest way, leading to his imprisonment, near death, and exile from his country. We did not need to be brave. It was powerful, and we were passionate.

We cast Stephen Fry as Oscar Wilde. If ever there was a man born to play Oscar Wilde, this surely was him. Stephen is an actor, raconteur, gifted writer, broadcaster, chairman of the Middlesex Cricket Club, wit...and one of the most intelligent men I've ever met. Stephen knows quite a lot about everything! He is the definition of a polymath and even looks a bit like Oscar Wilde. We approached him and cast him, though very much aware that his name was not yet big enough to help us in a meaningful way to get the film made. He was just damn good.

We realized that the boyfriend, Bosie, had to be astonishingly charismatic and beautiful. When Oscar left his wife and children to begin a doomed love affair with Bosie, we would somehow need not to lose our sympathy for Oscar. Jude Law was at the beginning of his career, but he was certainly a handsome young man, and he agreed to play Bosie. Our first shot of Jude Law is breathtaking. We took a long time lighting him, and he does indeed look like a god on earth. With his blond hair and his impish smile, if the audience still mourns the collapse of Oscar's marriage, at least they had some inkling of how he felt the compulsion to follow Bosie into the relationship that, in the end, ruined his life.

It would have been a good idea not to film in the Cafe Royale, where they really first met, but where the walls have an abundance of mirrors. Of course, it turns out that it is very difficult to light when there is virtually nowhere to put the crew and the equipment, but we sorted it out.

Vanessa Redgrave signed up to play Oscar's mother and Jennifer Ehle, his long-suffering wife. Tom Wilkinson played the fierce, scary,

FINDING HAPPY

mutton-chopped father of Bosie, who goaded Oscar into suing him for libel when he called him gay, and Bosie "nothing but a bum boy." Scary as hell! All brilliant actors.

When Oscar lost the libel suit, he was swiftly arrested because the witnesses easily proved that Oscar was in fact gay. He was incarcerated in London and punished by walking a treadmill ten hours a day. We had to build the treadmill, and a frightening piece of work it was. The most demoralizing thing for the prisoners may have been that it was not connected to anything; it did not even power any dynamo to generate electricity. It was simply there to punish people. Because the government realized that without exposure to fresh air the prisoners would die, they were allowed to walk in a circle in the prison courtyard for a few minutes a day, but they were hooded so as not to draw pleasure from it. Humans can be very creative when it comes to torture and cruelty.

Oscar was ill-equipped to deal with prison, and it very nearly broke his spirit and killed him. He came out a shattered man a few years later and left Britain for exile in France. He died in Paris, and it is said that his last line, looking at the ugly wallpaper in a cheap hotel room there, was, "One of us must go." Oscar is buried in Pere Lachaise cemetery, and people still visit and leave flowers on his tomb.

Our job in making *Wilde* pales massively by comparison with the brave souls who fought and continue to fight for vital civil rights, often risking and losing their lives. We did not need to be brave to decide to shoot the film. But the imperative that we all stick up for each other seems to me to be a critical overall moral truth. As an example, if one looks at the famous photo of Dr. Martin Luther King and hundreds of other people walking with linked arms down off the Edmund Pettus Bridge in Selma to begin their march to Montgomery, and if one watches the newsreels of the local sheriff, Bull Connor, and his officers, some on horseback, beating them up with billy clubs, there is a moving observable fact: many of the marchers were African American, but a whole lot of the others were white, and of several other races and religions.

Through the First Star Academy for foster youth at UCLA, I was privileged to meet the widow of the minister of the Presbyterian

Why Stick Up for Each Other? Oscar Wilde and Me

Church of the University. She told me that her husband had received a telegram from Dr. King asking him to please come to Selma because Dr. King needed the support of other people if the march was even going to have a beginning. As a young married couple, they did not know what to do. They had a little baby and his and her parents to deal with—the grandparents were very much a part of their lives. With brave and somewhat clever planning, they decided that the minister would indeed travel to Selma and risk his life with Dr. King, but that they would not tell their parents until he was safely home. On the day he left, racist white thugs in Selma killed a Jewish man in the street, a man who had gone to help. The Presbyterian minister from UCLA traveled nevertheless, and he did march down off the bridge with Dr. King. Civil rights should be our common duty to help everyone who needs our help.

Chapter Takeaways and Reflection Questions for You

- Is sexual preference a choice?
- Is sexual preference an either/or binary?
- What is the difference between bisexual and homosexual?
- Why is it so important to ignorant people to interfere in the lives of others?
- Why do some people feel threatened by someone else's sexual preference?
- Is that why they interfere?
- What part does religion play?
- Different than sexual preference, there is also a wide spectrum of sexual identity. Are all human beings male or female? Is that binary? Is it an absolute? (Clue: No!)

FINDING HAPPY

- What does intersex mean? (Clue: Intersex is a biological condition in which one has internal and external genitalia that are discrepant (male/female), or chromosomal patterns that are atypical for males or females. The details are rather medical.)

- Gender identity and sexual orientation are separate, but sometimes related, issues. Gender identity has to do with how one experiences their own gender (you cannot see someone's gender identity) and may be the same as one's assigned sex or not. Sexual orientation has to do with one's emotional, physical, or romantic interest in or attraction for others. Categories of sexual orientation include gay, lesbian, bisexual, and heterosexual. One great truth always applies: who you are is up to you. Your life belongs to you alone. Your right to live your authentic life freely is a fundamental civil right.

- Sex is assigned at birth by doctors in a hurry, based on the baby's genitalia, and they write it on the birth certificate. What if they get it wrong?

- What if the genitalia are not one or the other?

- What if the baby grows up certain that the doctor got it wrong? Are they entitled to live their authentic life? Is that an important part of freedom? (Clue: Yes! You can only count on having one life, so get it right. It belongs to you, to live authentically.)

- Those who are not heterosexual or who do not identify with the gender assigned to them at birth (i.e., who are not cisgendered) have been persecuted throughout history, and that discrimination continues today. The haters yell a lot. Their volume does not make them right.

- After you decide what your gender identity and sexual orientation are, does that lock you in forever? (Clue: No!)

- What does gender fluid mean?

- If you see someone being bullied because of their gender identity and/or sexual preference, should you stand up for them?

- Do you struggle with feelings about these issues? Find a trusted adult you can talk to in confidence. If you don't have a trusted adult, look online for a reputable help line. You could start here: https://www.thetrevorproject.org/resources/

Why Stick Up for Each Other? Oscar Wilde and Me

- Who are some of the great LGBTQIA achievers in history? (Clue: Start with these: Alexander the Great, Julius Caesar, Leonardo da Vinci, Michelangelo, Shakespeare, Abraham Lincoln, Eleanor Roosevelt, Emily Dickinson, Malcolm X, Josephine Baker... Google away. There are thousands. Millions.)

- If you have questions about sexual orientation or gender diversity, there are some great online resources: https://www.adl.org/resources/glossary-term/definitions-related-sexual-orientation-and-gender-identity?gclid=CjwKCAjws7W kBhBFEiwAli168xawwNu9mpw9SIO5RYv9LVvymXQhm7gZ0c 4uy-UGX2ncijTR_bY7ZBoCL1QQAvD_BwE

CHAPTER 34

When Should You Give Up, When Not? What If You Can't? *The Gathering*

Do not allow hardships, personal or existential, to become a barrier to your ability to look ahead with hope. Rather, embrace the challenge and take the building blocks of lessons you've learned during your most trying times—times you wanted to quit or run away or thought the path ahead was just too dark to even attempt to find the light. Take these experiences with you. Embrace them and use your experience to face the challenges ahead. Because you are more than capable. You are enough.

Your past is the proof of that. Getting to this point, graduation day is a validation that even if you fretted about your future or struggled with your past, you still chose to move forward to hope. And that hope is action.

—**Karine Jean-Pierre**,
White House press secretary, Rice University

When Should You Give Up, When Not? What If You Can't? The Gathering

Producing films is a very risky profession. The odds against getting any individual script that one develops made into a film are depressingly long. To deal with this, we take a portfolio approach: if you have twenty or thirty films in development, with considerable skill and a modest amount of luck, you ought to be able to get five or six or seven of them made into motion pictures. The question becomes, when do you stop spending money on the development of the turkeys? The ones looking unlikely to get made? At what point, as Quiller-Couch, Chekov, Faulkner, and Oscar himself wrote, do you "Kill Your Darlings"? This is a never-ending discussion and more an art than a science. But it isn't possible to pay due attention across a larger portfolio of projects. The dead wood has to be culled. It's also a moral responsibility to the writer of the screenplay, the novelist who may have written the underlying work, and the various partners to be forthright and transparent when the odds are so long against success that they begin to look like the definition of impossibility. They should get their rights back.

I've always been stoic about giving up on something, believing that what I'm really doing is reallocating my time to something more likely to be successful. During the Bosnian war, with its terrible atrocities and the crisis of refugees, I was on the board of Century City Hospital. I pulled strings with pharma suppliers and managed to assemble several tons of donated medical supplies, worth $2 million, on pallets to send to the war zone. What I had not adequately thought through was how on earth I was going to get the supplies there. None of the regular shipping companies were flying into Bosnia. The US military was completely unhelpful. NGO organizations like the United Nations were impossible to negotiate with, to effect transportation by air. I tried for six months solid to get anyone to fly tons of medical supplies to where it was needed, repeatedly trying to find the open window around the back of the problem.

Eventually, I cried uncle and donated the supplies to public hospitals, helping indigent ill people across the United States and Mexico, where the drugs could be driven by truck. A necessary pivot, better than seeing the supplies become stale-dated in a warehouse in the City of Commerce. Sometimes you have to kill your darlings and move on. I came to see the alternate use of the drugs as a very good thing, so it did not feel like a real failure, more a pivot. Needs must.

Trickier than canceling the original purpose of something into which one has lavished time, effort, dedication, love, and money is when the circumstances themselves do not *allow* you to cancel a project. In 2001, my brother Marc and I produced a film together with Pippa Cross of Granada, called *The Gathering*. It was from screenplay by Anthony Horowitz, who also wrote the Alex Rider series of novels a few years later. We later made the first of the Alex Rider series into a powerful film, *Stormbreaker*.

The Gathering was an $18-million British horror film starring Christina Ricci. It was supposed to have its world premiere at the Cannes Film Festival on a Friday morning. *The Gathering* is the story of a young American woman suffering from memory loss after a car accident in the West of England. She finds herself caught up in ominous events as an ancient legend about Christ's crucifixion comes to life. We thought it was very scary, even though it had only a limited amount of blood. The people who gawked at Christ's crucifixion were sentenced to a permanent purgatory of roaming the earth: they knew in advance where there would be moments of acute human misery, and their fate was to gather to watch the tragedy. Perhaps there are such people in real life, the reason why the opposite side of freeway traffic slows to a crawl when it passes an accident going in the other direction.

It is crucially important as a filmmaker always to rehearse the projection of your film, especially if it is the premiere. Buyers from around the world had been invited to the Cannes screening. For example, the United Kingdom rights had been pre-sold, but the buyer then pulled out of their commitment in a dispute over the contract. We badly needed to replace their money, and quickly!

The film was shot on 35-millimeter Eastman Kodak film stock. Normally, a picture spans not the full width between the sprocket holes

When Should You Give Up, When Not? What If You Can't? The Gathering

of the film, because there is a soundtrack down one side and the area of the image must avoid that. We believe, and I still believe, that one can make a little film look more powerful by shooting it widescreen, where the frame is 2.35 times as wide as it is tall: it says "major film" to the audience. By using a cutting-edge technique called Super 35 as the ratio, we did not have to use bulky anamorphic lenses to squeeze what would end up as a widescreen picture onto a narrower part of the negative in the camera. Instead, we could shoot Super 35, using regular spherical lenses that were smaller and extending the frame over the soundtrack area. In the lab later, the projection prints were squeezed to make room for the soundtrack. Cheaper, better, smarter.

Making the film was straightforward, and we thought we had something rather wonderful on our hands. But a good career film producer never trusts the projection, often the weakest link in the technical chain from your filmmaking to the eyes and ears of your audience. It often goes wrong! Sometimes the projector is run by a junior person who doesn't know what they are doing. And more often, the projection is sloppy and not focused on the best interests of the film.

I contacted the projectionist two days before the Cannes market screening, which was to take place at eight o'clock in the morning. I told him that the film was shot in Super 35, and this early print was still spherical, so he would need Super 35 gates in his projectors. The sound was on separate reels in parallel. The projectionist was offended that I would question him on this, clearly believing that career producers, and anyone who was not French, didn't know what they were talking about in such matters. He told me that he had the special apertures for the projectors. He was used to showing films shot in Super 35 ratio.

I said to him, *"Je sais que vous êtes un excellent professionnel, mais j'aimerais venir voir au moins la première bobine du film projeté sur l'écran où il sera projeté dans la salle Vendredi."* "I know that you are an excellent professional, but I would like to come and see at least the first reel of the film projected on the screen where it will be shown in the theater on Friday." He said it was not possible. That they were fully booked, showing films at all hours from early in the morning until late in the evening in that theater. He said I would have to "wait and see it at your premiere screening." I said, "No, honestly, we really need to see

197

FINDING HAPPY

the first reel to make sure that everything is okay with the Super 35 ratio." He said, "Do you not hear well? I just told you that it would be fine. Do you not believe me?" I said, "I do believe you. But we would just like to make sure that nothing has been done wrong in London by the lab, which might be incompatible with your projector." That was the best excuse I could think of on the spot for a haughty projectionist. He said to me, "We are showing films every day with no pause between 8 a.m. and 11 p.m." I said, "Right. We will come there at 11 p.m. tonight." He said, "You cannot come tonight. I am not available." I said, "What about tomorrow night?"—literally nine hours before the film would be shown to its audience. Not ideal, but better than nothing. He said, "It is not worth my time, and I will not be paid to be there after 11 p.m." I said, "We will pay you double your normal rate in cash, if you will please come and cooperate." He then said, "It will be my pleasure."

My brother Marc and I pitched up at the theater at 11 p.m., gave the film to the projectionist, and went down into the theater to see what would come up on the screen. Horror of horrors! A significant portion of the side of the frame was not on the screen! The projectionist was wrong, and he did not have the right aperture gate. He was cutting off a significant portion of the image of the film on the side. The film credit stated that it was directed by Brian Gil and not Brian Gilbert—the rest of his name was lopped off by the projector.

We went storming up into the projection booth, as there was no way in this commercial theater to talk from the auditorium to the projectionist. He said, "Why does it matter?" We said, "Please. It is our film. We've spent a year and a half making it. May we decide whether it matters or not that you cannot see the right-hand 20 percent of the frame?" He said, "Well, I will try other gates." Which he proceeded to do. They were all completely wrong. Either they cut off the heads or they cut off both sides or something else terrible was happening. I said, "Try showing it without the gate. Just take out the whole mask." He said, "You will not like it." He was right. We now had the whole picture. However, the bottom of the frame above was being projected all over the ceiling and the top of the frame below was being projected on the back of the heads of the audience.

198

When Should You Give Up, When Not? What If You Can't? The Gathering

This was a big problem. We discovered that we had no way to cancel the market screening! When we realized that there was no way to show the picture properly on the screen, we decided to cancel and simply not have a Cannes screening. A bitter blow, but the lesser of the evils. But when we contacted our publicists on the phone and told them to call and email everyone in the audience and tell them not to come at 8 a.m., they said they could not do that. They did not know who they were!

Oh my God, what to do? The horror got bigger. It was now almost one o'clock in the morning.

I thought perhaps we could create a mask on the projector port, the glass window through which the projector beam shone into the auditorium: if we covered it up at the top and the bottom and a little bit on the sides, might we have a solution? The problem was that it was now the middle of the night, and we needed cardboard, tape, a ruler, and scissors. Looking around the projection booth, I saw that there was a calendar made of cardboard hanging on the wall, which looked roughly the size of the projector port. It was dated 1996, so I figured probably the projectionists would not need it. Our guy finally found a razor blade, and using the straight side of a metal drawer, we measured a hole that was exactly the right size to go on the projection port. And sure enough, we had a pretty good picture, the right shape and the right size on the screen...but with one problem.

The only way we could communicate was with my brother in the auditorium on his British cell phone and me in the projection booth on my British cell phone, paying who knows what amount of money per minute to be able to talk to each other. Marc said to me, "I can read lettering and numbers on top of our picture on the screen." It was the reflection of dates of the 1996 French calendar, backwards but pretty visible. We were creating a reflection of the calendar inside the two glass sheets of the projection port. It was refracting around and coming back out as part of the projected image. This was even worse!

We needed black tape to cover up the writing of the calendar so that there would be no reflection. But of course, now at 2 a.m., the projectionist was fed up and indicating that whatever we paid him, he was going home in twenty minutes. No, he had no black tape. However, I saw that the pretty ratty carpet in the projection booth had been inelegantly repaired with black carpet tape, not on the bottom of the carpet, but on the top. This made it relatively easy to rip some of it up, but it had little hairs sticking to it from the carpet. These we cut off carefully with our razor blade, and we covered every part of the cardboard except the aperture with the tape. We held our breath as the film came up on the screen.

The image was perfect! My brother Marc and I hugged. We paid the projectionist and told him we would see him a quarter to eight. We staggered back to our not-very-good hotel and went to sleep.

Film distributors from around the world made us a raft of offers and bought the film for their territories. We got a very good price for North America from Dimension, the genre division of Miramax. By lunchtime on the day of the screening, Pippa Cross, Marc, and I were standing on a balcony of the Carlton Hotel in Cannes, drinking champagne and feeling as though we had had a near-death experience. You can see, below, the actual black carpet tape on the actual French calendar, together with the Dimension announcement in *Variety*, and a picture of Marc, Pippa, and me drinking our very well-deserved Dom Perignon. Sometimes the circumstances don't even give you the right to cancel your own catastrophe. But ingenuity and thirty-year-old French carpet tape saved the day. *Hooray!*

Making decisions well is as much an art as a science. And timing can be as important as the fundamentals. I once developed a script about hobos traveling the American West who stowed away on freight trains. Outside of Phoenix there were two rail lines that came from

great distances, and for several hundred yards ran exactly parallel, separated by only a six-foot gap. If you were a hobo traveling from the southeast to the northwest, you could save a great deal of time if you seized the moment and, with impeccable timing, jumped the gap from one speeding train to the other. This very dangerous maneuver symbolized in the script the moment in our lives when we are faced with a great but dangerous opportunity. We either take it, or we do not.

There is always fear of the unknown, and it is always difficult to conquer the uncertainties that surround a new construction, a new relationship, and a new definition of family. But sometimes when two trains run parallel, one has to take the longest possible view, a deep breath, and simply jump. Leadership is in the careful analysis of risk and reward, and after that, in the presentation of a compelling proposition that will cause people to do the unprecedented. And you have to tell the story brilliantly.

Chapter Takeaways and Reflection Questions for You:

- When have you been completely sure you failed...but then you did not?
- What is the role of luck in success?
- When did you get the timing right?
- When did you get it wrong?
- How can we best position ourselves to have our fair share of luck and opportunity?
- When the door closes on you, do you give up, or go find a different door?
- Is it easier to be an entrepreneur with colleagues to share the downs as well as the ups? (Clue: Yes!)
- What is the most ingenious thing you ever did to help yourself or someone else?
- Where should you start understanding your goal and planning your first steps? (Clue: If you don't know where you want to arrive, how can you plan your first steps? First write down your goal. Then work backwards from there.)

FINDING HAPPY

CHAPTER 35

How Can You Get Arrested without Being Killed?

For those of you who have already had "The Talk" with an adult, this isn't for you—this is for foster kids who haven't had the benefit of a parent to give them the information they need to protect their own safety in encounters with law enforcement.

I've agonized over whether to include this chapter in the book. I fully agree with the common wisdom that the experiences of any ethnic or other minority are best described and elucidated by its members. That is generally their right, their prerogative. Although appalling and tragic murders of teenagers and young adults of every race occur in police shootings, the deaths at police hands of young men of color are far more common. This is a disastrous example of prejudice and discrimination, and a national disgrace. Young men of color are also vastly over-represented in foster care, among the unemployed and those in poverty, as the accused in police encounters and among those they arrest, among those convicted in our courts and those incarcerated. It's awful, unacceptable, and pathetic. The armed groups of white citizens among whom present-day policing finds its roots were established to enforce slavery and catch escaped slaves. That disgusting legacy was never really left behind.

203

FINDING HAPPY

So, the question to myself was whether, as a white man, I had any right to include this chapter. In the end, after much agonizing and discussion, I decided that its purpose, to save lives, justified writing it. I confirmed this in conversations with community members and experts. I researched and discussed the content with them, and I asked them to review it. I also drew from the important leadership of the American Civil Liberties Union. The ACLU has done incredibly helpful and thoughtful work balancing civil rights with saving lives. Their bottom line is to assert rights vigorously in court, but not when a gun is pointed at you by an angry young man in a uniform.

And then an angel appeared to advise me, and none better. The Reverend Kelly Brown Douglas is dean of the Episcopal Divinity School at Union Theological Seminary, and canon theologian of Washington National Cathedral. Reverend Douglas gave me crucially important guidance on how to make helpful, and not on my part presumptuous, "The Talk," about which unfortunately she knows too much. She told me firmly that the chapter was too important for me to remove it, and she introduced me to her son Desmond. No greater love. As a young Black man in America, Desmond Douglas has brought his authentic voice of wisdom and personal experience to this chapter on staying alive. I am humbled and deeply grateful. Thank you both. Desmond's thoughts are below in the boxes.

In our First Star Academies for teenage foster youth—depending on which university we are partnered with, and therefore in which city we are located—roughly 50 percent of our Scholars, the term we use for our students, are Black, Hispanic, or their family is of some other origin of color. It is a sad and outrageous fact that the abuse and neglect that lead to foster care are more prevalent when there is poverty. Many people living in one room leads to all sorts of disproportionate stresses. And as a legacy of slavery, people of color are disproportionately poor. But there is another big problem: that law enforcement, our judiciary, and our court system lead to many more accusations of crime against people of color, especially young adults of color. They are arrested much more often than their white counterparts of the same age for doing the same thing. When one visits any prison in America, far too high a proportion of the inmates who are convicted criminals are of color. It is a shameful aspect of American society that the powers that be not only make it much more difficult for people of color to achieve the middle class, but they also disproportionately persecute them through law enforcement, especially when they are male and young.

> *For years I was told, "If you are with people doing something wrong, you leave because you will be the one blamed for whatever is going on." And then it happened. I was in middle school when a white boy who was often a trouble-maker, threw something across the classroom while the teacher's back was turned. Before I knew it, I was being blamed, with no one coming to my defense. I couldn't believe how quickly the teacher believed the guilty party was me, who never got into trouble in class, and assumed the white boy was innocent. Lesson learned.*

Every American family of color has to teach its children from around the age of fourteen how to get arrested safely, and certainly without dying. As discussed earlier, it is an absolute fact of human brain development, especially for young men of any race, that we do not develop cautious behavior until our late twenties. Before that, we operate on the fight-or-flight instincts of the back of the brain, the reptilian amygdala, because the prefrontal cortex has not yet grown to be able to make us look before we leap. I urge you to pay great attention to the rest of this chapter because it just might save your life, especially if you are of color.

Realize that it does not matter if you did anything wrong. It does not matter that your constitutional rights are being invaded by a misbehaving police officer. The only thing that counts when you are stopped by the police is to act in a respectful, docile, and cooperative way, so that the person standing in front of you with a gun will not kill you. The police can stop and question you for any reason at all. You don't have to look suspicious or be a potential witness. Unless the police have reasonable grounds for suspecting that you committed, are committing, or are about to commit a crime, you're generally free to leave. But you should ask first, and if the officer tells you to stay there, do that. He has the gun, whether he's right or wrong, and you only have one life. And

FINDING HAPPY

if they say "yes," then walk, do not run away. Every year many young Black and Brown men are shot in the back.

> *"If you get stopped by the police, say nothing, do nothing. If they tell you to get down on your knees, do it. That one moment of humiliation can save your life." It happened on a long dark road on the way back to college. Two friends and I were stopped by police. We were told to get out of the car, put up against the car, frisked and the car was searched numerous times. When I asked why we were stopped, the officer didn't answer. After that I kept my mouth shut. I figured that if I could stay alive, even if I got put it jail, they would pay the price because they would have to deal with my mother—and in the end they indeed had to deal with my mother.*

You should say, "I want to remain silent," other than giving your name, address, and age. You do not have to engage in a dialogue with the police officer. You should not be arrested or detained for refusing to answer questions, but again, the man with the gun is in charge and has the power to hurt you, even if he is wrong. It may look suspicious if you start answering and then stop, and that could lead to an arrest, even if it is illegal. Don't physically resist a search or a pat-down, because it could lead to the officer illegally using force against you. Simply say, "I do not consent to a search," but don't resist. Do not disrespect a police officer. It is irrelevant that you have a constitutional right of free speech. It could lead to your arrest or physical harm, when if you keep your cool, you will be able to walk away. Remember that the police are legally allowed to intimidate, bluff, and lie in trying to get you to speak and to confess something. Do not ever discuss your citizenship or your immigration status with anyone other than your lawyer.

If the police officer searches you, simply say quietly, but audibly, "I do not consent to a search." In a search, the police officer can pat down your outer clothing only. They are not supposed to squeeze or reach into your pockets unless they believe they've felt a weapon or contraband, but they often do so anyway. If the police develop probable cause for believing that you've committed a crime, they can broaden their search. If you are being given a ticket, do give your name, birth date, and sign the ticket. If you don't, that in itself is enough cause to be arrested. If an officer is approaching you, or while they are standing next to you, do not empty your pockets or reach towards your waistband or make any other sudden movement. Many Black and Brown people have been shot by police officers who falsely claimed that they were reaching for a gun in their waistband. Better to put your hands up to avoid any confusion. If the police officer is wearing a camera, it will record where your hands were if the officer shoots you. You have a right to video the encounter, but give that up if it makes the officer angry. Less is more. Save your life.

If you are stopped while driving your car, put your left hand at ten o'clock and your right hand at two o'clock on the steering wheel and leave them there. If you are asked to show your registration or insurance, say, "I'm going to reach for my papers now," and then move your hands slowly. Many Black and Brown people have been shot and killed when police claimed that they made sudden hand movements. If the police officer wants to perform a DUI test, you have to take it unless you're willing to risk your license being suspended. Before you're arrested, you can refuse to take the preliminary breathalyzer test unless you are under the age of twenty-one.

Your best course of action is to do whatever the policeman says. He is the one with the gun. Don't physically resist, just say, "I do not consent to a search." Don't refuse to sign the ticket. Don't search for your license or registration until you're asked to provide it. Always let the officer know what you're going to do before you do it. Don't be disrespectful. Don't try to bribe the police officer. You do not need to have a discussion with him. And you always have the right to remain silent, except identifying your name, address, and age.

You are entitled to three phone calls within three hours of getting arrested or immediately after being booked. You can call a lawyer, a bail bondsman, a relative, or any other person you wish. If you have children under age eighteen, you get two additional calls to arrange childcare. You should assume that the police are recording your calls except the call with your lawyer. Do not give any information except your name and basic identifying information. Don't explain yourself,

FINDING HAPPY

make excuses, or tell stories. Just say, "I want to remain silent, and I want to talk to a lawyer." Say it loud enough that the police recording can hear you. Do not consent to any searches or give up your right to a lawyer. Don't talk about your case over the phone. Don't make any decisions in your case without talking to the lawyer first. Do not discuss citizenship and immigration status with the police.

> *As for the police, it was never about "officer friendly." From as long as I can remember, I just knew that police were not necessarily my friend because they would see me as that Black guy always up to something. I knew this because I saw they were no different from white people in general when it came to the way in which they viewed Black people, especially Black males. Their suspicions and fears could be lethal, so my job was to make them comfortable enough not to do something that could destroy my life.*

Being arrested is not worth dying for. If you run away, you may be shot in the back, and you'll definitely be caught. Being arrested is not the worst thing in the world. Going to prison is very bad, especially if you're innocent, but the best way to fight mistakes by the police or prejudice against you is to go along with whatever they want you to do and let your lawyer nail them in court. Get your three phone calls at the police station, and then you'll get your own lawyer, who knows much better how to fight a wrongful arrest. I have enormous sympathy for the pumping adrenaline that comes when one is wrongfully accused. The instinct to run is very strong. The anger that is generated is huge. I have felt exactly that, and I'm an old white guy. How much worse it must be when you see that racial prejudice is behind your arrest. Keep your cool. Preserve your life. Live for another day and take the advice of your lawyer. Do not get shot in the back. Do not be left to bleed to death on the ground.

We live in an often grotesquely unfair society where the color of someone's skin holds great importance to those who have been brought up to hate them. It's crazy, it's mad, it's morally bankrupt, but it is reality, and sometimes those with the prejudice are wearing uniforms and carrying guns. Do not be their victim. We need you alive to live a great life and to make the world a better place. Channel your anger into BLM activities, volunteering, protesting, and trying to improve our country. We hope in future for an America where, as Dr. King said, the authorities look to a man's character and not the color of his skin. God bless and stay safe.

> *I was taught, "Don't walk around the store just looking, especially with your hands in your pockets, because people will think you are stealing something." I was about 12 years old. It was a Sunday afternoon at an airport gift shop when I, along with a friend, went to have breakfast with my godfather during one of his airport layovers. After breakfast my friend and I went into the airport gift shop as my parents and godfather said their goodbyes. Suddenly my godfather rushed in with a panicked look and told us to come out of there because the manager was watching us. Lesson learned.*

In my career as a film producer, I've worked closely on many occasions with police officers. They come in all combinations of intelligence, maturity, and professionalism. A career producer needs the cooperation of the police, and we hire officers by the hour to close down roads, to control a crowd, and generally to make sure that we run an orderly television or film set. I've also interacted with senior police officers, including several chiefs of police and local sheriffs. On a couple of occasions, I have been driven around by the police, sometimes with flashing lights while scouting locations. At the age of eighteen, working on the *Le Mans* film with Steve McQueen, I had my own personal *gendarme* who would speed me through traffic as I rode pillion behind him on his motorbike with lights and siren. Definitely made me pump adrenaline.

There is, however, a darker side to interactions with the police, and they are sometimes truly unacceptable. Remember that most officers are young men, quite possibly equally as scared as the person they are arresting, pumping their own adrenaline, possibly belligerent, rude, and out of control. And perhaps not with any well-developed sense

FINDING HAPPY

of critical thinking. Becoming a police officer is as high-earning a job as any a young man can get without a college education. Their training does not always counteract the fight-or-flight instinct going on in the mind of some twenty-two-year-old rookie cop in the spur of the moment, perhaps confused, and at night in the dark.

I've had to deal with being arrested twice in my life. These incidents are totally trivial compared to the experiences of many of you of color reading this, but I include them only to demonstrate that I really, really understand how infuriating it is to be falsely accused, and how crazy mad it made me too.

On the first occasion, I was jogging at six o'clock in the morning through Westwood Village, West Los Angeles. There was not a car anywhere in sight. The streets were completely deserted that early on a Sunday. I ran diagonally across the street, only to hear the beep of a police siren. One Officer Garcia pulled up next to me on his motorbike. "You're jaywalking," he said. "Yes, sir," I said. "The whole area is deserted." "Well, evidently not," he replied, "because I am here, and now you will be ticketed. Let me see some ID." I said, "I'm out jogging. I have no ID with me." At which point I made my stupid mistake and said to him, "I'm an American citizen. I don't need to carry ID." "Absolutely correct," said Officer Garcia. "Until I asked you to identify yourself, and at that time you are required to show me ID."

I confess freely that as a hot-headed young man, I thought the whole thing was ridiculous. I put my hands in front of me, palms down, and I said, "Well, I guess you will have to arrest me." He said, "Yes. I think I will." I was pretty upset with him and said sarcastically, "Do I ride behind you on your motorbike when you take me in?" He said, "No. I will send for a squad car." Three minutes later, a police car did arrive. The two officers in it were incredulous that Officer Garcia thought it was a good use of his time and theirs to take me down to the police station in handcuffs for the crime of jaywalking and then failing to provide identification. But that's what happened.

After arriving at the police station, I was chained to a bench in the waiting area for over two hours before a sergeant came and asked me if I was now calmer. If I would like to apologize for my behavior, he was prepared to let me go without charging me, and just with a caution. At this point, all the adrenaline had left me and I just wanted to get back home and have breakfast. I did apologize. So, he released me, and I then ran in a state of high anger, probably the fastest I've ever run, the five miles back home.

I did not know what to do, but I was sure that this was bad policing, and as a taxpayer I didn't want to be paying for it. It seemed like a colossal failure of judgment. By happenstance, I knew a then member of the city council. I phoned and asked him whether he thought this was appropriate behavior. He said no, and that I should put it in a letter to him and let him make inquiries. A week later, I received a phone call from the assistant of the West Los Angeles deputy police chief who asked if his boss could come and see me. The deputy chief and a colleague arrived at the house in full dress uniform and apologized on behalf of the LAPD for Officer Garcia's behavior. At that point, I was concerned that Officer Garcia should not have adverse consequences. In the scheme of life, what he did was trivial. I asked that he should not be in any way censured, demoted, or anything of that sort.

On another occasion, also on the weekend, I took my then four-year-old son Jeffrey out, pushing him in a jogging stroller. We crossed the UCLA campus. Jeffrey at that age was very interested in the large yellow machinery used on any building site. He was fascinated by the sheer size and power of backhoes, bulldozers, cranes, and the like. And so we stopped for perhaps fifteen minutes at the gates of a closed building site and peered through the mesh at the wonderment of the many large yellow machines.

A police officer came up to me and said, "You have been trespassing on the building site, and I'm going to arrest you." I said, "You are either blind or delusional, because we have done no such thing." He said, "I am going to ticket you." I said, "I'm going to push my son up the road two hundred yards to the police station, where I'm going to file a complaint that there should not be a police officer who cannot see adequately, one who thinks it is okay to make a completely false accusation of something they have absolutely not seen." I then proceeded to walk to the police station, with the officer following me. I filled out a form at the desk. The desk sergeant accepted it, and I never heard anything further about my alleged crime or the officer, who clearly

FINDING HAPPY

needed more training in telling the truth. But I was stupid...he could have shot me.

Two things can be true at the same time. That you need to stay safe, and that your life has value, purpose, determination, and the highest importance. The question to ponder is when to assert yourself, and when it is not safe to do so. Facing a man with a gun is not a safe moment.

In the end, I know that simply being Black can be enough for someone to feel threatened. No matter how polite you are to the police, how respectful, how much you follow the rules, whether you run or stand still—your blackness is provocation enough. It happened to Elijah McClain, to Philandro Castile, to Breonna Taylor and Tatiana Jefferson in their own homes. So for me— the biggest lesson is to find a way to stay alive.

You're a part of an institution that understands Black excellence should never be disqualified by white institutions. And so I hope that Spelman College has imbued into you that it is possible to succeed in those spaces where people don't think we belong without compromising your values and your sense of self. That success doesn't mean you have to look or talk or think a certain way. I stand here with this bright red hair, big hoop earrings and Jordans on, telling you that however you present yourself in the world has nothing to do with your intellect, your ambition and your worth.

Success will not be worth it if you have to sell yourself out to get it. So hold on to who you are.

—Nikole Hannah-Jones,
journalist, author, Spelman College, 2023

How Can You Get Arrested without Being Killed?

First two Google pages of hundreds. This is an epidemic. Preserve your life. We need you. Be safe.

FINDING HAPPY

Chapter Takeaways and Reflection Questions for You

- If you are stopped by the police on foot, how should you behave?
- If you are stopped by the police while driving, how should you behave?
- What are the things you should not do when interacting with the police?
- What are the things you should do when interacting with the police?
- Why is it important if you are arrested to use your three phone calls to get a lawyer?
- Are you prepared? Do you know the telephone numbers of the three people you would call from a police station to get you help and a lawyer?
- What are those numbers? Say them out loud now. Don't rely on your phone's Contacts.
- *Safety first. Victory over injustice later.*

CHAPTER 36

What Does Eccentric Mean?
Is It Good, Bad, or Neither?

One of the most important opportunities when we are young adults is to define our relationships with those around us and with society at large. Within the limits of the law and our ingenuity, we can be whomever we want! Certainly, we can define our own personality. I remember on the day I took the train to Cambridge to begin my university career, I realized that the "me" who got off the train ninety minutes later could be as different as I wished from the "me" who had boarded. And he was!

I learned a lot from my late Uncle Tony. He was the most vivid and completely eccentric human being I've ever met. He taught me that showmanship is an important part of achieving things. You need to spin the tale, perfect the story. It is very helpful to have a sense of narrative, and making your impact is mostly within your control if you understand a thing or two about marketing and telling your story well. And if you look them in the eye.

These days, Uncle Tony, I am pretty sure, would be placed somewhere on the spectrum as high functioning. He took his eccentricity

FINDING HAPPY

to a stubborn and sometimes belligerent place. Tony was also hugely intelligent, arguably the highest IQ in the family at that time. A lot of what he did was both absurd and excruciatingly funny. When I was a young adult, most people thought my uncle Tony was raving mad, but he invariably had the last laugh, and he became wealthy by often daring to go where others feared to tread. He greatly influenced my childhood, was always kind and encouraging to me, and I loved him a lot. I'm sure he must have often been impossible to live with more closely; it must have sometimes been awful to be his child or wife.

He once found out that the local authority was selling the underground toilets on a traffic island in the middle of the Charing Cross Road, adjacent to Soho, London. Understandably, there were not a lot of bidders at the auction for serviceable underground toilets, so Tony was able to buy them inexpensively, with their traffic island at ground level, in one of the most desirable spots in London. He set about converting them to a suite of offices and built an epic brass-roofed pergola structure at ground level. His offices had excellent plumbing!

At around this time, he also decided that what London needed was a new afternoon newspaper that you could wear on your head. Read that again. He patented and trademarked *Loony-Lugs* as a daily broadsheet publication, with his own particular spin on the news. His goal was that when you finished reading, you would fold it up, following the dotted lines, and then put it on top of your head. There were two large ears. The one of King Charles III was particularly well done. In order to print his newspaper/hat, he installed an enormous, old-fashioned printing press in the underground suite on Charing Cross Road, in what had originally been the ladies' toilet.

It turned out that the only problem with *Loony-Lugs* was that people were not willing to pay money for a newspaper that was convertible to a hat. Tony then started giving them away, until this, too, proved unsuccessful, and he was left with many thousands of redundant newspaper hats. Tony never threw anything away. When he died, his adult children found he had every copy of every newspaper he had ever received over fifty-plus years in a barn behind his home. And there also were tens of thousands of unsold *Loony-Lugs*.

What Does Eccentric Mean? Is It Good, Bad, or Neither?

Tony bought an enormous manor house in Totteridge, North London. He was psychologically allergic to ever having anything fixed in the house. If the roof sprang a leak, he would simply put a bucket where the water was accumulating inside a room. Over time, therefore, it became more and more decrepit, but as long as you did not have to live there, it was somehow magnificent in its decaying splendor. I used to love visiting him. At one point, he bought a monkey as a pet, which was fine until it became an adult. The monkey would sit unreachable on top of a large piece of furniture and throw its poop at the guests who had been invited for tea. The joke wore thin, and he gave his monkey to a zoo.

Tony found out in the 1960s that an American studio was coming to the UK in a few months to make a film called *Battle of Britain*. He guessed that they would need a large number of World War II aircraft as props. So, he went around Europe, meeting with farmers who had an old Heinkel, Messerschmitt, Spitfire, or Hurricane in their barn. He bought them and had them transported to Elstree Aerodrome in North London. At one point, he owned the eighty-seventh largest air force in the world. Several of these planes were flyable. Tony earned a private pilot's license in order to take them aloft.

The mental process of my uncle Tony was often frustrating. A family joke was that the first words his children spoke were: "Tony, for God's sake, answer!" He would take an incredibly long time to do anything. If you asked him a question at the dinner table, the conversation would continue for some twenty or thirty minutes, at which point he would blurt out a response, long after everyone else had forgotten the question. But his answer was often thoughtful and correct!

In the context of flying a rickety Second World War aircraft, this forgetfulness and delay meant that very few would trust him to remember to fuel it up. The only member of the family who would go aloft with him was his mother, my grandmother, Marjorie. She would require that he insert her walking stick through the filling cap of the wing tank and prove to her that it was wet with aviation fuel when he pulled it out. She loved her son, but knew him well.

Tony started buying 1940s and 1950s mechanical robotic toys, the kind you wound up with a key on the back and that would then march

FINDING HAPPY

jerkily across your carpet. Long before there was eBay, there were car-trunk sales, in Britain called boot sales, where fifty people would go to a field on a Sunday afternoon and sell each other secondhand junk out of the trunks (boots) of their cars for a few pounds an item. Over a period of a few years, Tony bought every toy robot with a windup key that he could find. These filled a room, and then the staircase. You had to walk sideways to use the stairs. We thought this confirmed his eccentricity, until his collection of period robots was sold by one of the famous auction houses in London. He had cornered the market and sold his unique collection into it.

Tony was a relentless campaigner, a man of stubborn and fierce opinions. He decided that the tobacco industry was bribing the Conservative Party to allow it to addict children to tobacco by not cracking down on their child-facing advertising. He was twenty or thirty years early but turned out to be absolutely correct about the poor health outcomes, the addictive nature of tobacco, and the poorly disguised ways that some of the tobacco companies marketed to children. To publicize his campaign, he ran in the 1990s as an independent candidate in the Southeast Staffordshire parliamentary election. He was on the ballot as the Daily Loony-Lugs Earring up the World candidate. The winner received 26,155 votes. Tony got exactly 80 votes, but that wasn't the point. He would appear at political meetings, stand on top of his three-wheeled automobile, and using loudspeakers he would shout. He was led away by the police in handcuffs.

Tony entered a transatlantic air race. The race started at London's Post Office Tower. Tony rode a motorbike to the River Thames, from where he piloted a helicopter to Elstree Aerodrome, and then a Hurricane to Ireland. Then he piloted a twin-engine plane to New York, to then take a motorbike to the Empire State Building. We all held our heads in our hands, sure that he would die, but he didn't. He won the prize and had the last laugh.

On one memorable occasion, Tony was flying commercial with a colleague from London to New York. He took down a briefcase from the overhead and sat for many minutes going through the contents, until a man stood up from a seat across the aisle and shouted at him, red in the face, "What the hell do you think you're doing in my briefcase?"

What Does Eccentric Mean? Is It Good, Bad, or Neither?

Anthony Samuelson arrested after heckling candidate Baroness Virginia Bottomley.

"Ah, yes, well that explains why I didn't recognize any of the papers," replied Tony. He had spent at least twenty minutes going through the poor man's documents without realizing his mistake.

Tony bought an expensive car and decided he would see how long it would run if he never, ever had it serviced. This went on for several years, until the ignition key broke in the lock, and he could no longer start the car. His workaround was that he would press a button under the hood to start the engine. To open the hood, you pulled a handle by your right knee. Tony did this for several years until the time he pulled the handle, the hood remained closed, and five feet of wire came out of the hole behind it. This had him stumped, so he had the car towed to the local dealership. They were also at a loss. They phoned the factory in Crewe to ask how to open the hood if the handle was broken. The factory person said, "Those handles never break." The dealer replied, "Yes,

FINDING HAPPY

but this man has been pulling it several times a day, for a few years." The incredulous factory executive said, "Why on earth would anyone do that?" The dealer replied, "Because the key was broken." The factory person shouted back, "Why the hell didn't he have the key fixed?" The dealer simply said, "Well, because he's Anthony Samuelson."

Tony loved inventing things and held many patents. One of his designs was a unique form of automobile burglar alarm. If someone broke into his car, they would be locked in and the horn would sound. On the sides of the car were little metal eyelets, and underneath the car there was a long tube containing a spear with a sharply pointed end. If someone broke into your car, they would be locked in and unable to escape. You could then take the spear and poke at them through the holes in each door until they pleaded for mercy.

Tony also bought one of the very first E-Type Jaguars, an extraordinarily powerful car that was mostly motor and extremely fast. People often said it was designed to look like a penis. People would peer through the windows when it was parked. So, Tony had three instruction plaques placed over the footwell on the driver's side, which read: "Clutch. Brake. Accelerator." Bystanders were amazed that someone driving such a fast car could be such a complete idiot. But of course, he was not...it was his rather British sense of humor.

When Tony was alive, he often made us laugh. He was a kind of amusement for most of my early life. But after he died, I realized that, more than hardly anybody I knew, he had lived his life exactly as he wished and made it into precisely what he wanted it to be. He lived with abundant great humor, enormous encouragement for all the young people around him, and a great kindness for those of us fortunate to be in his orbit. I hope I carry a small part of his bravery, resourcefulness, and extraversion. But I'll never be as funny.

Chapter Takeaways and Reflection Questions for You

- Are you living a vivid and memorable life?
- If not, how can you move in that direction?
- Does it have to be your job, or can it be in parallel to your profession? How?
- Is high IQ enough to thrive?
- How best can we develop social skills: empathy, kindness, consideration?
- Are you who you want to be?
- If not, what is your spider graph to get there?

CHAPTER 37

What Must You Do When People You Love Lose Their Compass?

Mental illness and addiction are terrible and sometimes overlapping horrors.

I was a career producer on a film where the talented but eccentric director was, unbeknownst to anyone, unstable. It was a film that we shot in various cities in Europe, and we moved around a great deal, chasing the local subsidy money. On one occasion, we were filming on a high floor of an office building. The director was shocked when, in front of the whole crew, the star pointed out that the director had told a huge lie, and the actor was irrefutably correct. The director was highly embarrassed and shouted, "Well, then, this is the moment, isn't it?" He ran across the set and hurled himself out of the window. By sheer luck, a large member of the grip crew was standing right there and managed to grab him by the legs as he was disappearing out of the window. He was pulled back in, an ambulance was called, and he was taken off for a psychiatric examination. We had to close down the film, only to receive a phone call the next morning from his agent, who said that the director was perfectly fine now and would be back at work the following morning. The hospital said he could work. We had already talked to the insurance company and replied that we were sorry, but actually, no, he could not continue as director. We wished him well with his further recovery, but responsibly, he would have to be replaced.

By hard work and a miracle, we only lost one day's filming. During that down day, and over the weekend, we were able to find a replacement director and get the film back up and running without losing any further time or money. A sad situation, but he did recover and went on to direct several more films.

The greatest tragedy I have ever personally experienced was when a relative, a young man close and really important to me, took his life. My wife and I and our children had come to know him very well. He had moved out to Los Angeles from London to make a career in film and was doing very well in the camera department as a second assistant. He lived in our own family home, befriended our children, and was a gifted photographer and storyteller. We loved him very much.

After he met the love of his life on a film set, they moved back to the United Kingdom. He woke up one morning, drove to the White Cliffs of Dover, took everything out of his pockets except his driver's license, and jumped off to his death.

The entire family was grief-stricken, appalled, and confused. We later learned that he had been severely mentally ill, but none of us, including his wife, had the foggiest idea that any of this was going on. From a video he left behind, it emerged that in his psychotic state he fully believed he was saving his family and friends from a terrible monster. It was for him, in real life, the ancient Greek myth of Jason, who with supreme bravery wrestled the Minotaur, a human bull that was terrorizing his village, to the edge of a cliff, and while hugging it jumped off, in order to free the village from the tyranny.

I was bereft. I knew that if I had had the foggiest idea of what was going on, I would have intervened. I would have gotten him help. I would have tried to see that the psychosis did not end his precious life. It was confusing, depressing, and awful...and it still is.

It is a tragic reality that there are many instances where friends and family do absolutely everything possible but still are unable to prevent someone from killing themselves. So of course I cannot know that our

FINDING HAPPY

efforts would have saved his life. We would certainly have done everything in our power, but we may not have succeeded.

On a previous occasion, we did try, but failed completely. One of my best friends became very ill with cancer of the bowel. This was greatly worsened by the fact that she refused to believe that there was anything the matter. Her other friends and I saw her getting thinner and thinner, and clearly very ill. Three of us told her that we were going to take her to hospital to be examined. She said, "No." We argued. She told us, "I have a gun, and if you set foot on my property, I will kill you."

We then met with the mental health department of the local authority and asked what could be done. We were told that, under the law, if someone standing on a roof was threatening to jump, they could be involuntarily committed for a psychiatric examination. But if their decision was to not get medical help for a terminal condition, there was no way the police could intervene, and neither could we. We watched this dear soul get more and more ill until eventually she was so sick from the cancer that she was admitted to hospital, where her legs were amputated. Even then, when I visited, she said to me that she would be better soon, get prosthetic legs, and go back to work. And then she died. The funeral was full of grief, incredulity, and quite a lot of anger.

Mental illness is a terrible thing. There are many reasons someone might consider taking their own life. Suicide can happen on impulse with no warning at all, leaving friends and family baffled, or after some years-long battle with depression, mental illness, or some other struggle. And someone does not need to be severely mentally ill to take their life. In the case of my relative, there was a psychotic illness that likely would have existed whether he was under any sort of external pressures or not. Stress can certainly trigger or worsen psychotic symptoms, but stress is not typically going to cause a psychotic illness. However, in the most extreme cases (being a prisoner of war, for instance), it could. My friend with cancer may have suffered from some underlying condition or dysfunctional defensive style that was manageable prior to cancer but became very exaggerated when she fell ill.

While neither of these close-to-me tragedies can be attributed to social pressures, for teenagers and young adults, social and other pressures are perhaps most common. There are enormous pressures on

What Must You Do When People You Love Lose Their Compass?

young people, especially through trolling and bullying, both on and off social media. Pressures in schools and universities make matters even worse. The storm in the heads of children and young adults to conform is considerable. If you are aware of anyone who shows you any sign of mental illness and/or addiction, which you think may harm them or anyone around them, I say here to you that there is an absolute moral imperative to intervene. If you are too frightened to do it face-to-face, go get help from your parents, someone else in your family, a teacher, your school principal, the mental health department, or call one of the numbers below for advice. And if you are considering harming yourself or another person, please reach out to them right now. *Life is precious. Your life is precious.*

Whatever is the matter can be handled better with expert help. Often when we feel as though the walls are closing in on us, we are not able to find the pathway to a solution on our own. But expert, trained, sensitive, confidential listening help is available, and it is always darkest before the dawn. I implore you, I beg you, to get that help: reach out, save your own life and that of others. Do it for yourself, and do it for the people who love you. Call anonymously if you need to. *Just call.* If you feel no one loves you, it might be true or not true. Especially if one is in the depths of depression, our thoughts may be negatively distorted, making it seem that no one loves us or that those who love us will be better off without us. *Wrong.* Getting help is the key. You are not alone.

I have never recovered from the deaths of my relative and my friend. I carry them with me every day.

FINDING HAPPY

Action Steps, Chapter Takeaways, and Reflection Questions for You

Ask for help!

If you are having thoughts of suicide, call or text 988 to reach the 988 Suicide and Crisis Lifeline, or go to SpeakingOfSuicide.com/resources for a list of additional resources. Go here for resources outside the United States.

USA

Speak with someone today:
Tel: 988 Suicide and Crisis Lifeline
Hours: Available 24 hours. Languages: English, Spanish.
SMS: 988

Canada

Tel: 833-456 4566
SMS: 45645

UK

SAMARITANS
Tel: 116 123
https://www.samaritans.org/

Australia

Lifeline is a national charity providing all Australians experiencing a personal crisis with access to 24-hour crisis support and suicide prevention:
Tel: 13 11 14 24/7 Crisis Support
Lifeline Crisis Online Chat
I'm feeling suicidal

New Zealand

Youthline: 0800 376 633, free text 234, or email talk@youthline.co.nz (for young people, and their parents, whānau, and friends)

What's Up: 0800 942 8787
(for 5–18 year olds; 1 pm to 11 pm and online chat service from 11am-10.30pm, every day including public holidays)

The Lowdown: visit the website, email team@thelowdown.co.nz, or free text 5626 (emails and text messages will be responded to between noon and midnight)

What Must You Do When People You Love Lose Their Compass?

SPARX: an online self-help tool that teaches young people the key skills needed to help combat depression and anxiety.

If in the slightest doubt whether you need help...then yes, you do. Ask for it now.

Further Resources

- Local resources by your ZIP code: https://findhelp.org
- Food bank locator: https://www.feedingamerica.org/find-your-local-foodbank
- Suicide Prevention Hotline: 1-800-273-8255
- https://988lifeline.org/help-yourself/youth
- National Domestic Violence Hotline: 800-799-SAFE (7233)
- https://www.thehotline.org/help
- National Alliance on Mental Illness: 800-950-6264 or text NAMI to 741741
- https://www.nami.org/#
- National Sexual Assault Hotline: 1-800-656-4673
- https://www.rainn.org/about-national-sexual-assault-telephone-hotline
- Trevor Lifeline: National 24/7 Crisis Intervention and Suicide Prevention Lifeline for LGBTQ young people: 1-866-488-7386, or text START to 678678
- https://www.thetrevorproject.org
- National Domestic Violence/Dating Abuse Helpline for Young People:
- 1-866-331-9474, or text LOVEIS to 22522; https://www.loveisrespect.org

Information and support for anyone affected by rape or sexual abuse issues is available from the following organizations: In France, the France Victimes network can be contacted on 116 006. In the UK, Rape Crisis offers support on 0808 500 2222 in England and Wales, 0808 801 0302 in Scotland, or 0800 0246 991 in Northern Ireland. In the US, Rainn offers support on 800-656-4673. In Australia, support is available at 1800Respect (1800 737 732). Other international helplines can be found at ibiblio.org/rcip/internl.html.

CHAPTER 38

How to Leverage to Achieve Your Goals. ASPIRE and the Medici

The existence of technology is not enough: you have to know how to use it.

As part of my work with UCLA in Los Angeles, I founded a nonprofit called ASPIRE, the Academy for Social Purpose In Responsible Entertainment. My premise was that filmmaking was only being taught to students in the School of Theater, Film, and Television. I wanted to make media-making literacy available to any student in the entire university, whether they were studying engineering, dance, or architecture, teaching them to express themselves audiovisually in documentary narrative or fiction, in any way that would support their conquering their worlds as young adults.

Working with the College of UCLA, I was able to raise enough money for us to hire Dr. Andy Rice, a gifted professor who taught the original ASPIRE courses at UCLA. It was a successful pilot. Much of my lecturing since in major universities in the United States and the UK has been centered around creating opportunities for audiovisual literacy for students, beyond just those who are studying media as their major.

ASPIRE is now an independent 501(c)(3) charity with its own board of directors that supports media for social change. ASPIRE has sponsored some very important documenta-  ries. Run by David Haspel as chairman, the best is yet to come. I'm not on the board, but I'm proud to have invented it, and I applaud its great strides in harnessing digital literacy and narrative storytelling to make the world a better place.

Let's review some of the history of ideas and solutions, and deduce patterns from there to chart our future. We really need to develop and empower smart new solutions to old thorny problems. Einstein said, "We can't solve problems by using the same kind of thinking we used when we created them." He was right. And that's why AI is not the blazing path to the outside-the-box solutions we need. Human imagination, pattern recognition, lateral thinking, and ethics are where the best future needs to come from.

The Medici were a medieval Italian family who made their money in textiles. Theirs were the best textiles in all of Italy, and in the end, in all of Europe: they had the best fibers, the best looms, and the best dyes. They themselves didn't know much in detail about dyes, or looms, or fibers. But they realized that they needed to take the specialists and collide them together. That was how you made the best cloth. Cloth made them an amazing living, and they built up an immense fortune.

Initially, they spent it on very elaborate castles, most of which are still there. And then they thought, "We can do much more. Our world is broken." The long evil hand of Dark Ages ignorance was still apparent. There was a great deal of human suffering around them. They had the gift of recognizing clever people, geniuses, creative folk, and scientists, and they had the money to protect and encourage them. Think of it...if on one's tombstone, it said, "Invented the Renaissance." That would be a thing. Botticelli, Leonardo da Vinci, Michelangelo: the Medici were the ones who said, "He paints a heck of a ceiling. He's probably got some more ceilings in him." And "This Leonardo da Vinci—look at these sketches. We need to encourage this man. He's very inventive!"

FINDING HAPPY

They had a twenty-two-year-old tutor, an undergraduate whom they hired to teach their kids algebra—which had recently been rediscovered, having been invented by the Arabs in Alexandria, Egypt, and then forgotten for hundreds of years. Waiting to teach the Medici teenagers math, the tutor found himself quite often in different Medici castles. He would wait there in the great hall and look up at the chandeliers. He realized that if you extrapolated downwards to the floor, and assuming that the floor was flat, the chain from which every chandelier in every castle was hanging always made a perfect right angle, exactly 90 degrees to the floor. He checked: there was no 89 degrees, there was no 91 degrees.

People had been taught for hundreds of years that the earth was flat. If you reached the edge, you fell off and the dragons ate you. The tutor, named Galileo Galilei, realized that was absolutely untrue. If all the chandeliers in all the distant castles pointed straight down to the same magnetic force attracting them, then the earth was a sphere. In a second burst of intuition, he realized by the same logic that the earth is not the center of the universe. It is a planet that revolves around the sun, which has vastly greater mass. Communicating this made him worse than unpopular. He was arrested, threatened with torture, and on orders of the pope, sentenced to prison. The Medici took him under their wing, supported him, and he lived under house arrest for the rest of his life.

You are a digital native. You can access, every day in every way, the exogenous brain, with or without the help of artificial intelligence. The future of our planet lies in the palms of your hands and of those who are of similar age.

All technological innovations have delivered good as well as bad. Nuclear power is an important clean component in powering our cities, but the meltdown of nuclear reactors, let alone the deliberate use of nuclear weapons, would be catastrophic and destroy the safety, happiness, and lives of our fellow humans. For good or bad, you will watch attempts to channel AI productively in real time. One can have some shreds of optimism: in the wrong hands, pharmaceuticals cause death and destruction, but because they are tightly regulated, they generally do not. There are tragic exceptions, of course. Through human greed,

How to Leverage to Achieve Your Goals. ASPIRE and the Medici

Purdue Pharmaceuticals created the opioid epidemic that blighted hundreds of thousands of lives and caused the destruction of entire communities. We have to hope that the cowboys in the white hats will win these battles. I am optimistic because even the greedy people who might benefit from destructive AI must worry about the destruction of their own selves, their families, and everything they care about.

Chapter Takeaways and Reflection Questions for You

- Are you completely computer literate?
- Are you able to powerfully express your ideas as video?
- Have you spent any time understanding artificial intelligence or the adjacent fields of virtual reality and environmental virtual reality?
- Did you only study what these technologies can do, or did you delve into how they can also hurt us?
- How do you stay on top of new developments in technology?
- What are you reading every day to keep you up to speed on the rapidly developing universe of science that affects our lives every day, in every way?
- Why is it important for you to do your own homework and not to use GPT-4 to do it for you—quite apart from the fact that GPT-4 itself and other software now have ways for your teachers to see who has used it to cheat on the homework?
- What is the purpose of your education, and how does using AI subvert that?
- What are acceptable ways to use AI to help you in your studies, ones that are not destructive of the overall goal for you to learn new things and develop the knowledge and computing capacity of your own brain?
- If AI trawls in the past creativity of humans, and then recombines it to reuse it, what does that do to copyright law, patent law, and the rights of authors generally?
- Good luck! This is your Brave New World.

CHAPTER 39

Why Don't Human Beings Think Ahead? Lessons of Hurricane Katrina

At the beginning of 2005, I was hired to produce a punchy script by Michael Caleo, *The Last Time*. He was to direct it the following summer in New Orleans. We cast Brendan Fraser and Michael Keaton in the leads, with Amber Valletta as the woman who stands between them.

In our film, Michael Keaton played Ted Riker, a hard-driving high-tech salesman who mentors a less-experienced trainee salesman called Jamie, played by Brendan. In the art of sealing a deal, Jaime is completely incompetent. But his fiancée, Belisa, played by Amber Valetta, is irresistible to Ted. It was strong writing with great dialogue.

I flew into the wonderfully named Louis Armstrong International Airport in New Orleans and set about scouting locations. One of the best aspects of my early years in the United States was meeting truly vivid American personalities. One such was the sheriff of the parish, a quite large gentleman in full sheriff regalia, whose office wall demonstrated, through grinning two-shot photographs, that he had met every celebrity from the fields of sports and show business that had visited the parish over decades. The sheriff decided that he would not delegate the job of driving me around to look for locations; he would do it himself. And so I had the eye-opening experience of driving around the area in a squad car, with lights and siren and the sheriff behind the steering wheel, clearly very proud of his domain.

One of the most visible features of New Orleans, a city where I had not previously worked, was the array of levees, the large earthen seawalls designed to keep the water away from most of the city. New Orleans had been built, with a breathtaking lack of foresight, below sea level and below the level of Lake Pontchartrain on its other side. These large structures were impressive as works of civil engineering, but they made me curious. "How tall are your levees, Sheriff?" I asked. "Oh, they're about seventeen feet," he replied. "Well, how high will the storm surge go when you get the once-in-a-hundred-years storm?" I asked. "Oh, much higher than seventeen feet," replied the Sheriff, "it depends on whom you ask. But somewhere between twenty-five and thirty feet." I was floored by the response. I blurted out, "Well, what do I know? I'm just a career film producer. But might it not make sense to build the levees quite a lot taller, before you have your once-in-one-hundred-years catastrophe?"

He was forceful, but matter-of-fact. "There is no taxpayer will. And so there's no government will to do any such thing. It would cost something like $10 or $15 billion and no one will ever vote for that." "But, but, but," I sputtered, "what will be the cost to the city of New Orleans if the water floods the whole city?" "Oh, well over $100 billion," said the sheriff. "Well, forgive me. I'm just a film guy, but wouldn't it be much more cost-effective to build the levees taller while you can?" The sheriff said, "Whoever voted for that in the city council would be slung out of office by the taxpayers. So no, it's just not gonna happen." I was incredulous. "So you're pretty sure that the water will go over the top

FINDING HAPPY

and cause $100 billion in damage?" "Yes," he said, "I'm rather hoping it might happen after I retire."

It is an amazing thing that human beings are not able to think about big numbers or long periods of time. The horizon of our better judgment is in small denominations, at most over a year or two, preferably only a few days or weeks. What we absolutely cannot consider in our heads is the calculus of a hundred-year storm, causing $100 billion in damage, and how much less than that it would cost to avoid the catastrophic loss by preventing it. Generally, we humans just don't do that. Our brains evolved in a period where we were hunter-gatherers and then farmers. All you really had to calculate was what would happen to your crops this year and maybe next year. That was it. Nothing about one hundred years. That was unfathomable when you were dealing with hunger and wild animals right now. *"Apres moi, le deluge,"* said King Louis XV of France. "Let it flood when I'm gone." Politics is mostly played as a selfish, short-term game.

We continued prepping the film. We built the sets. We rented the equipment, the hotel space, then assembled the props, the set dressings, the wardrobe, and hired the team. By August, we were about to shoot...and then along came Hurricane Katrina.

Katrina was a Category Five Atlantic hurricane that resulted in 1,400 deaths and caused damage of between $100 billion and $150 billion that year, 2005. It was the costliest tropical cyclone on record, and the third major hurricane of the 2005 Atlantic hurricane season. Winds reached 175 miles per hour, and by the time the hurricane had passed a few days later, it was evident that most of the city had been lost to the waters. Predictably, the poorest areas were the worst hit because they were built on the lowest land. The water simply flowed over the top of the levees, which were grossly inadequate. Not only were the levees not tall enough, but there were fatal engineering flaws in the flood protection system.

For weeks, 80 percent of the city, as well as large areas of the neighboring parishes, were flooded. Most of the pumping, transportation, and communications facilities were destroyed or lost power for weeks, and the tens of thousands of people who did not evacuate the city prior to the hurricane's landfall were left without food or shelter. The levees

Why Don't Human Beings Think Ahead? Lessons of Hurricane Katrina

had been built by the US Army Corps of Engineers, but the courts later ruled that they could not be held financially liable because of the doctrine of sovereign immunity, under the Flood Control Act of 1928. They were only required to do their best, even if that was grossly inadequate. New Orleans was S.O.L. And the old sheriff was still in office: he had to deal with his area's share of the miseries caused by the water.

Everything we had built was destroyed. Our hotels were flooded to the ceiling of the ground floor. The streets were impassible. Our film was unmakeable in that place at that time. We had to straggle back to Los Angeles, regroup, make a large insurance claim that was only partially paid, and some weeks later, we started again.

I learned two things from this debacle. First, that the human brain is not good at thinking long term about negative consequences in order to avoid them. Second, that the poor souls who had evacuated to the New Orleans Superdome suffered from noise pollution, disease, a lack of privacy, and every other disgusting outcome one could imagine. The germ of the idea for my nonprofit EDAR, Everyone Deserves A Roof, was born by understanding what had happened in that enormous building. (More about my EDAR in the next chapter.)

America is a great country. We are very good at rallying to fix things that break. We are the can-do nation, where neighbors help neighbors after any natural or human-caused disaster. Abundant help is made available. What we are truly lousy at is predicting the predictable and thinking beyond the end of our noses. We mostly do not repair bridges until they fall down. We don't stop rebuilding houses in flood zones, even after they are destroyed. And in the case of filmmakers, we always think the once-in-one-hundred-years hurricane will not happen right before we shoot.

These are unfortunate failings. I wish I could say they applied all around the world, but they do not. There are so many examples in Europe and Asia of communities thinking far ahead. In Japan, the big trading companies, Matsushita, Sony, and the rest, operate under one-hundred-year business plans that are revised every decade. They really do have a rough outline of what they would like to be in fifty and one hundred years, and how to get there. By contrast, in the United States, public companies operate on the whim of their rising

235

or falling share price, which is in turn driven by their issuance of quarterly earnings reports. When I sat on the board of a public company, we were constantly at the beck and call of the financial analysts. On some occasions, the company's financial advisors told the board of directors and the chief executive what the financial results for the next quarter would need to be in order to prop up the share price, often with debt borrowed from banks that was collateralized by that share price. This was an unholy bargain with the devil, a Faustian deal, given the erratic vagaries of the marketplace and the economic cycle. If results fell quarter-on-quarter, a panic would set in as the company tried to reverse the tide going out on its financial results, even if it was believed that this would be temporary.

As I write this, the nation's eighteenth-biggest bank, Silicon Valley Bank, has collapsed because its leadership did not factor into their investment decisions the possibility of rising interest rates. They just guessed, with other people's money.

Chapter Takeaways and Reflection Questions for You

- Why do human beings fail to think ahead? And what can be done about it?
- Is it true that young men, especially, do not develop a higher level of calculus, playing the chess game of life, until they reach their mid-twenties?
- What is the amygdala that drives human behavior in terms of fight or flight? And what is the prefrontal lobe, which young men don't develop until their mid-twenties? Look it all up!
- Does this apply to young women as well in some cases?
- Which part of the brain does a better job in saving your life?
- Why do armies send young men and not middle-aged men into battle? (Clue: Many of the older men won't go.)
- What is the matter with local democracy, and in fact any kind of democracy, in dealing with unpleasant long-term creeping problems?

Why Don't Human Beings Think Ahead? Lessons of Hurricane Katrina

- Is there anything we can do to help the political process to address hundred-year challenges, or will we as a people always be blown around by hurricanes because we fail to plan for their worst effects?

- In your personal life, which should come first: establishing your goals or focusing on the baby steps to achieve them? (Clue: If you don't know where you're going, how do you know which direction to begin to walk?)

CHAPTER 40

When Is Perfection the Enemy of the Good? EDAR and the Old Lady in a Box

I came out of Nate 'n Al's, a deli in Beverly Hills, after a business breakfast. A tall homeless man who smelled bad and wore rags inserted himself in front of me, too close, with his palm up, poking my chest. I was startled, and I dug in my wallet and gave him money. I went off at a fast walk. I sat in my car literally shaking, angry with myself. I thought, *How could I be scared and intimidated by a man in rags?* I was ashamed. It was ridiculous, but I was. What do we do as leaders? If we are scared of something, we lean into it. If it is not going to kill us, as Nike says in its ads, "Just Do It."

So I did sixty-five interviews, on my bicycle on the weekends, with unhoused and homeless people. It was not at all scary. I asked them two broad sets of questions: "How do you get money?" and "Where do you sleep?" Eventually, the epiphany came: an old lady said, "Come with me." And she pulled me by the sleeve. She said, "I'll show you where I sleep." She led me into the bushes off the San Diego Freeway on some Caltrans wasteland. And there, hidden, was a gigantic cardboard box: disgusting, smelly after the rain, and with a piece of blue plastic over it.

When Is Perfection the Enemy of the Good? EDAR and the Old Lady in a Box

On the side, in foot-high letters, it said *Sub-Zero*. I thought: *Oh, so this is the epiphany: I got the refrigerator, and this poor dear is living in its cardboard box*. I knew this picture was wrong.

I tried to design a building. I hired an architect, a space-planner, and a budgeter. I thought we'd build a hundred-bed dormitory. But when we got that priced out, it was $5 million. Which was fine, except if you divided it by one hundred beds, it meant it was costing $50,000 a bed. But there are around a hundred thousand people in Los Angeles County sleeping rough. So that would be $5 billion. $5,000,000,000... that's a lot of zeros. And it would only take care of Los Angeles. I had no idea how to raise $5 billion, and I knew the taxpayers would never provide it. Furthermore, perhaps some of the unhoused might refuse to be housed; some might not want to live with other people.

I thought, *Well, let's reverse engineer it: What would be the best that we could do with $800 each? It's not going to be a nice fluffy bed in an apartment. But maybe it could be a great deal better than that damp cardboard box on a rainy night*. I imagined: *It's got wheels, you push it around, but it unfolds into a seven-foot-long cot at night, with a roof and windows*. I took myself off to the emergency room at UCLA Hospital, and I asked the triage nurse at the desk, "When homeless people come in, what kills them?" She said it was mostly pneumonia, because they lie on the ground, get some bacteria or a virus up their nose, and then it travels down into their lungs. Without medical care, then they get pneumonia and die.

I couldn't design the thing I had in mind. I have the spatial design ability of a newt. But I asked myself where in Los Angeles they would know such stuff. I Googled the Pasadena Art Center College of Design, where they train students to design automobiles and any other kind of mechanical or electronic item. I met with President Richard Koshalek. I asked him, "If I put up a little bit of money, could we have a competition for the best design for this thing I have in mind: in the daytime, you push it around, it's got four wheels, but then you unfold it at night, and it becomes a single-user shelter, with four windows and two doors." He was enthusiastic. Teams of students built one-sixth-scale maquettes out of cardboard. The dean asked me, "What do you want to call it?" I had no idea. I thought I couldn't call it "I see tonight," even though that

FINDING HAPPY

would be the next line of the children's rhyme, "Starlight, starbright, first star I see tonight..." The dean said, "Well, everyone deserves a roof." I said, "You're right, that's it: Everyone Deserves A Roof: EDAR."

Eric Lindeman and Jason Zasa won the competition, and I've been working with Eric on EDAR ever since. We've got hundreds of EDARs out on the streets, mostly donated to the homeless in the Sunbelt in the United States. On a ten-scale, if a nice fluffy bed in an apartment is a ten, and the damp cardboard box on a rainy night is a zero, we're a solid five. But it's a whole lot better than the cardboard box. Sometimes I meet with the mayor of a city, and they say, "We want them all in housing." And I say, "Well, God bless. And on the day that you get everyone into an apartment who will come, I pledge we will collect up the EDARs, crush them, and recycle the metal. And we can all join hands and dance in a circle, and won't that be grand?" I'm not packing for it.

There will never be taxpayer will to spend that kind of money, $50,000 a head, given that there's about a million unhoused people in the United States and pro rata in the UK, ever-growing in numbers as

EDAR unit in use, in drainage ditch off Pacific Coast Highway in Los Angeles County.

the social inequality gap widens. COVID has smacked down many a single mother with a small child, perhaps a waitress before the pandemic, when the restaurant closed because of the lockdown and she became unhoused. It is not her fault. People think there are no children who are unhoused, but it is completely untrue. Across the United States there are many. So long as they're not being abused, and the mom is keeping an eye on them, Social Services generally do not intervene. They're just unhoused children, as in Dickens's time, but in many ways actually worse off. Inexcusable. Shameful, but the reality.

We have redesigned the EDAR after running focus groups with our homeless clients, and we are using a new factory to manufacture them. I really believe we can make a major impact. We are also exploring commercial sales through a taxpaying subsidiary, to generate profits we can then use to buy EDARs to donate to the unhoused. And we are exploring deploying EDARs in the now-unused upper floors of multistory parking garages. I never thought I'd have my name on the patent we donated to the charity!

FINDING HAPPY

I've had some mind-blowing adventures while implementing EDAR. I had a dinner with Mayor Richard Riordan of the city of Los Angeles. We both drank quite a lot of wine. When I told him about EDAR, he said, "You're completely wrong. The only homeless people in our city are those who won't go to shelters." I replied, "That is absolutely untrue. You don't know what you're talking about." He said, "I do." I said, "No, you don't." I dared him to sleep in an EDAR on a Saturday night on Skid Row. He double-dared me to do the same thing. I said, "I'll do even better than that. I'll make sure there's a third EDAR with the biggest security guard I can find, because there is no way I want to read a headline in the *Los Angeles Times* saying: 'EDAR Kills Los Angeles Mayor.'"

With press tagging along, we actually did it. We put three EDARs on St. Julien Street at around 6 p.m. on a Saturday. I had hired a security guard called Sugar Bear, who was almost seven feet tall, and whose job was to make sure we survived. It was scary as all hell. When it got dark, we counted well over one hundred people who lay down on the sidewalk, some on unfolded cardboard boxes. Roughly 40 percent were women, and there were at least a dozen who appeared to be children, certainly well under the age of eighteen.

It was like a scene in a Fellini film. Incredibly loud, with cars zooming down the narrow street six feet from where we sat on our EDAR stoops. There were people shouting and screaming all night, and someone kept throwing a folding chair alarmingly high, to come crashing down onto the sidewalk where people ducked.

As we sat there looking into the street, the mayor suddenly said to me, "Hey, look at that!" Sure enough, in the gutter a few feet in front of us, a rat as big as a decent-sized cat was walking along the gutter from left to right. When it was directly in front of us, it sat there and looked at us. And then, shockingly, it died. The body of the rat was lying there maybe six feet from where we sat. It was, to say the least, alarming. Maybe an hour later, we looked at the rat again and realized that some humorous unhoused person had crawled up and put a joint in its mouth. So, for the whole rest of the night, there we were in our EDARs, and there was the marijuana-smoking rat, dead in front of us.

When Is Perfection the Enemy of the Good? EDAR and the Old Lady in a Box

In the morning, the mayor told me that I would hear from him. And indeed, a couple of days later, an envelope arrived with a donation from his private foundation to EDAR, enough to buy fifty extra EDARs to give to homeless people.

I met with the then mayor of Santa Monica. He made me breakfast in his home kitchen. He climbed into the EDAR in his driveway, although he would not let me take any pictures. He told me humorously that the only way his city would allow EDARs was if they had the kind of wheels used in supermarket carts to stop them leaving the parking lot. He said they would be able to push their EDARS out of Santa Monica, but they would not be able to push them back. I told him I was sure he already knew that there was a legal obligation on every municipality in California to take care of its own homeless and not to export them. He said, "Yes, but in the present political climate, we would really like them all to go to Los Angeles and stay away from our city."

It's a cruel world. EDAR is not a solution, but it is a lot better than the alternative, which has old ladies living amongst us in damp cardboard boxes. If the value of any civilization is determined by how it takes care of its weakest links, in my judgment the treatment of foster

FINDING HAPPY

(12) United States Patent
Lindeman et al.

(10) Patent No.: **US 10,227,791 B2**
(45) Date of Patent: **Mar. 12, 2019**

(54) **TEMPORARY SHELTER AND MOBILE CART**

(71) Applicant: EDAR (Everyone Deserves A Roof), Inc., Los Angeles, CA (US)

(72) Inventors: Eric Lindeman, Venice, CA (US); Miguel de Jesus Orozco, Lakewood, CA (US); Peter Samuelson, Los Angeles, CA (US)

(73) Assignee: EDAR (Everyone Deserves a Roof), Inc., Los Angeles, CA (US)

(*) Notice: Subject to any disclaimer, the term of this patent is extended or adjusted under 35 U.S.C. 154(b) by 0 days.

(21) Appl. No.: **14/728,948**

(22) Filed: **Jun. 2, 2015**

(65) **Prior Publication Data**
US 2016/0115706 A1 Apr. 28, 2016

Related U.S. Application Data

(63) Continuation of application No. 13/862,236, filed on Apr. 12, 2013, now abandoned, which is a
(Continued)

(51) Int. Cl.
E04H 15/30 (2006.01)
E04H 15/06 (2006.01)
(Continued)

(52) U.S. Cl.
CPC E04H 15/30 (2013.01); A47C 29/00 (2013.01); B62B 3/02 (2013.01); B62B 3/16 (2013.01); E04H 15/02 (2013.01); E04H 15/34 (2013.01)

(58) Field of Classification Search
CPC E04H 15/02; E04H 15/06; E04H 15/30; E04H 6/04; B62B 3/02; B62B 3/16;
(Continued)

(56) **References Cited**

U.S. PATENT DOCUMENTS

1,702,010 A 2/1929 Klever
2,210,540 A * 8/1940 Nielson A47C 17/80
135/96
(Continued)

FOREIGN PATENT DOCUMENTS

CA 2443254 3/2005
DE 20105646 10/2001
(Continued)

OTHER PUBLICATIONS

Photographs of carts in www.moralityinmotion.com retrieved from http://static.flickr.com/78/159011348 a4cdd25dec.jpg?V=0, Oct. 25, 2006.*
(Continued)

Primary Examiner — Winnie Yip
(74) Attorney, Agent, or Firm — Knobbe Martens Olson & Bear, LLP

(57) **ABSTRACT**

Embodiments of the invention are generally related to a mobile shelter. In particular, several embodiments relate more particularly to a movable storage container configured for interconversion between various configurations. In several embodiments, the mobile shelter is configured as a shelter adequate for protection of its occupants against the elements. In several embodiments, the shelter optionally converts into a collapsed configuration suitable for transportation.

13 Claims, 6 Drawing Sheets

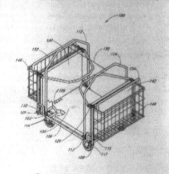

children and our homeless defines our civilization at its worst. We fight on.

Chapter Takeaways and Reflection Questions for You

- How can you design something if you are not a designer?
- Does a solution have to be complete and perfect to have value?
- When is perfection the enemy of the good?
- When you are scared or intimidated, what is the best thing to do?
- If a door closes in your face, how can you find another way in to address the problem?

Unhoused EDAR client who once played trumpet with BB King pushes his EDAR in Echo Park.

CHAPTER 41

How to Empower a Team? First, Stay Away from Helicopters. *Stormbreaker*

As I mentioned in Chapter 34, back in 2000 my brother Marc, then my business partner, and I optioned a script called *The Gathering* from the very successful British novelist and script writer Anthony Horowitz. Anthony is best known for the *Midsomer Murders*, the television series *Foyle's War*, and, significantly, was hired by the estate of Ian Fleming to continue in the succession of James Bond novels, using unpublished material by Ian Fleming. We got to know Anthony on *The Gathering* and were able to approach him to get the rights to his Alex Rider series of young adult novels.

The first of these was *Stormbreaker*. Anthony also wrote the script. We hired Mickey Rourke, Bill Nighy, Alicia Silverstone, and Stephen Fry. Ewan McGregor played the uncle of young Alex Rider and was conveniently assassinated in the first minutes of the film, thus making it feasible to have Ewan join our cast, but only for one day. We made a multi-party financing deal in the United Kingdom, Germany, and other territories. In the United States, we licensed the film to the genre division of The Weinstein Company, run by Bob Weinstein.

How to Empower a Team? First, Stay Away from Helicopters. Stormbreaker

We saw we had a tiger by the tail. This was an enormously successful series of novels, and we were determined to make a well-executed young-adult product, in order to validate a future franchise from the rest of the novels. We thought perhaps this was to be our Harry Potter series!

No such thing happened.

The film's plot follows a teenage British boy who is recruited by the British Secret Service after his uncle, a secret agent played by Ewan McGregor, is assassinated. Alex is sent on a mission to Cornwall to gather intelligence regarding the Stormbreaker, an advanced computer system being provided without cost to schools across Great Britain by its malicious creator, the dreaded billionaire Darius Sayle. It was the most expensive film we had ever made. I was able to negotiate on our behalf more than eighty commercial tie-ins to a range of products, including a massive video game deal, a deal with Nintendo, one with BMW, and various other licenses, including a graphic novel, a novelization of the film, and other spinoffs.

It was a very stunt-heavy film. We felt it was important to open with a bang, to frame the strong action adventure. The assassination of Alex's uncle, Ian Rider, was a technically difficult job, beyond anything in the book. Ian is shot dead while driving his sports car up the twisting road on the side of a mountain. We made the film partly in the Isle of Man, whose government was also one of the film's financiers. When we started setting up the helicopter stunt, the sun was shining and there was no wind. By the time we were ready to shoot, there was a blustery wind and it was pretty overcast. One helicopter would dangle the stunt man, Lee Sheward, who was also our stunt coordinator, upside down by his ankles from a line, while he used two revolvers to shoot the extremely startled Ian Rider through the side window of his BMW sports car. The other helicopter was the camera platform following closely behind. The car and the two helicopters incrementally picked up their speed each time we rehearsed, until the whole ensemble was moving across the ground and in the air at about seventy miles an hour.

The action helicopter was piloted by Marc Wolff, and Will Samuelson, my cousin, was the safety pilot. It was a strange experience to suddenly be working on something this mission-critical with another

FINDING HAPPY

family member, but he has become a highly regarded helicopter pilot working across Europe. For the London Olympics Celebration in 2012, he was the pilot who flew his helicopter safely through Tower Bridge several times and in both directions! Our camera helicopter was piloted by Peter Hall, an ex-Army aviator.

The stunt was completed successfully, despite my being nerve-wracked that either the stuntman would be killed against the ground or the car, or the helicopters would crash into each other. I remembered vividly my film long ago, *A Man, a Woman, and a Bank*, where through no fault of ours, an old lady minding her own business had been seated on a low wall at the bottom of a winding mountain road in Macau when the ten-ton grip truck, with its local driver going back to its base, lost control above her when its brakes failed. It smashed into the lady at high speed and killed her. It was the worst thing I ever experienced on a film. A horror, a tragedy. I was the one with an interpreter who went to apologize to the old lady's Chinese family and try to make amends. I felt sick.

I was thinking to myself that Lee Sheward, performing the stunt, had no helmet on. Lee might hit the ground at any minute. Lee might hit the car at any minute. The wind might push him in any direction. And there's a second helicopter right behind. The vehicle and two helicopters are moving up the side of a mountain at seventy miles an hour. Sometimes you see stunts in a film, and you sit there and you think, "Special effects, they did it in the computer." Not on this film. A good number of them were done by very brave and very highly trained stunt people who really performed. And hanging underneath the helicopter, Lee was one of those professionals. He told me afterwards that the biggest risk was that he might make even momentary contact with the ground, thus completing the circuit to earth for the huge charge of static electricity that builds up inside a helicopter when it is airborne. Had he glanced against the ground, he would have been electrocuted in an instant.

We were able to make really good sales of *Stormbreaker* in the foreign territories, and we felt as though we were batting 1.000 as we went into the test screening with the Weinstein Company in New York at the Loews multiplex. After the screening, I remember vividly Bob

Weinstein, the head of the Weinstein Company's genre division, coming up to me and saying, "You watch. We are the ones who made a franchise out of *Spy Kids*. This is going to be even bigger than that."

He was completely wrong. Being a career film producer delivers many joys, but also some extreme heartbreak. The Weinsteins did not adequately advertise the film for its distribution in the United States. It was a disaster. In North America, it did a mere fraction of its very large amount of business everywhere else around the world. All of our work for eighteen months and more was negated by the performance and behavior of our partners. As a career producer, you are no stronger than your weakest link. I remain enormously proud of the film, which is very well executed and delivered a massive amount of screen impact, on a budget much lower than would have been spent by any American studio. But life moves on. Most importantly, nobody was hurt. https://vimeo.com/52721533

Chapter Takeaways and Reflection Questions for You

- If, as is often the case, your success is partly dependent on other people, how can you manage that? (Clue: Don't have too many eggs in one basket; take a portfolio approach; try to work only with excellent people; think ahead.)
- When you do something potentially dangerous for you or others, how can you minimize a bad outcome?
- When should you simply not take a risk? When is it not worth it?
- Why is it so important to listen to experts?
- Why are rehearsals so important?

FINDING HAPPY

CHAPTER 42

When Is Impossible, Not?
Surviving a Producer's Crisis

Jonathan Prince is an American writer, career producer, director, actor, showrunner, force of nature, and my good friend. We first met when he was my cousin's boyfriend. When they broke off the relationship, my wife, Saryl, and I remained friendly with Jonathan, a great friend ever since. We have collaborated together professionally on many projects.

In 1996, Jonathan had the original idea for a farmyard comedy that would use then newly designed computer-generated imaging to move the mouths of farmyard animals, so that they could be speaking characters in the film. The story he wrote, *A Dog's Best Friend*, was then turned into a very funny screenplay by Nancy Silvers. We set off to make a deal and produce the film with no idea that the execution would be so difficult. The Family Channel, a division of ABC-Disney, financed. For reasons of cost and the availability of crew, we decided to shoot entirely on a farm near Vancouver, British Columbia. Thus I found myself in Canada, ankle-deep in mud and unmentionable other smelly substances on a farm, as we went through the preproduction

FINDING HAPPY

period. We hired the allegedly best humane animal wrangler in the western Canadian film industry, who was given many weeks to train up chickens, ducks, sheep, goats, a pig, and some dogs to move where they were instructed to go, and then to stand still, or whatever the script called for.

Unfortunately, when we got to principal photography, we immediately realized that not a single one of these animals would ever do anything that the script required them to deliver. They wouldn't stand still. They wouldn't move when ordered, and there was no way on the schedule of this television movie, or frankly on any schedule, that we would be able to deliver the goods: the animals simply would not cooperate. And why should they? Nobody asked them if they wanted to be in a film.

What to do? A career producer's truism is that one should never attempt to work with small children, animals, or on water. We were all too eager to make this wonderful script into a film to have paid much attention to that overall stipulation. With money burning by the hour and a standing crew, we needed a solution right away.

In the end, what we did was bring our scriptwriter Nancy Silvers up to Vancouver and reverse engineer the script to solve the problem. If we couldn't make the animals do what Nancy had written, could Nancy write what they *were* capable of delivering? So, for example, we realized that the chickens would lie down and play possum in an instant when the crew clapped their hands. To use this, Nancy wrote into the script the repeated use of the words "Chicken McNuggets." Whenever this happened, we applauded so that it would look as though our chickens fell down. It was their (scripted) worst fear in the world, and with good reason. And then we would edit out the loud noise.

With only a few lost days, we were able to get a rather wonderful story well told on film and in postproduction, the CGI animating the animals' mouths. We had talking animals, a whole menagerie of them! We had cost-effectively produced an early example of a story where the animals spoke and interacted with the actors. Richard Mulligan and Shirley Jones starred on the human side, and we had some seemingly charismatic chickens, dogs, sheep, goats, and a pig holding up the flag of animal performance. No one ever realized that the script was following the animals' capabilities and not vice versa. Maybe this is the humane way to film with animals.

Venture capital investors in Silicon Valley, when they are approached by entrepreneurs with a new project, will often investigate the history of the entrepreneurs by asking when they have failed and what they learned from each failure. They are not just interested in successes, but also in resilience, the ability to regroup and solve problems. That can often best be understood by poking into the history of occasional failures.

Think of your life as being inside a cardboard box, whose edges define your possibilities. But it is dark in there, and you don't know where those edges are. You could just sit there in the middle, scared, and not amount to much of anything. Or you can poke with a stick or a pencil in all directions in order to discover, by trial and error, what is possible. Occasionally, while you are poking, you will encounter the edge and poke through. Whoops! I have had dozens, perhaps hundreds, of those experiences. We realize by experimentation that we are not capable of moving in that direction. But then by withdrawing the stick or the pencil, we can set off in a different direction. And now we know that we have left nothing on the table. In the wise words of President Theodore Roosevelt in a speech he made in Paris in 1910:

It is not the critic who counts; not the man who points out how the strong man stumbles, or where the doer of deeds could have done them better. The credit belongs to the man who is actually in the arena, whose face is marred by dust and sweat and blood; who strives valiantly; who errs, who comes short again and again, because there is no effort without error and shortcoming; but who does actually strive to do the deeds; who knows great enthusiasms, the great devotions; who spends himself in a worthy cause; who at the best knows in the end the triumph of high achievement, and who at the worst, if he fails, at least fails while daring greatly, so that his place shall never be with those cold and timid souls who neither know victory nor defeat.

FINDING HAPPY

I have it on my wall: comfort for entrepreneurs. I see you! Dare to dream!

Chapter Takeaways and Reflection Questions for You

- When something is impossible, how can you avoid giving up when a door is closed? Can you find a window open around the back of the problem?
- When have you done that?
- When could you have done that?
- When should you have done that?
- How do you reverse engineer a problem?
- If you start with what is possible, is it OK to change your plan to go around an obstacle?
- At what point do you give up?
- When *should* you give up? (Clue: Definitely if it might kill you or someone else!)
- What are some examples in your own life of things that you found impossible?
- What did you try to solve the problem?
- At what point did you give up?
- Is your failure permanent? Might you resuscitate the plan at some later date?
- What can you learn from a failure?
- Is it important to occasionally fail? Why?
- Was President Roosevelt right?

CHAPTER 43

What Makes a Good Friend? How Can We Choose Them Wisely?

My mother-in-law is a psychologist. I've had breakfast with her every second Thursday morning for decades. It's like free therapy with scrambled eggs. A privilege. I once said to her, "It's uncanny, Louise, how when I need something, it falls out of the sky. You wouldn't believe how often I sit on an airplane, for example, thinking, 'I've got to find someone in Australia.' And then I start talking to the woman next to me who says, 'I'm emigrating to Australia. I'm a grandma. I just retired from business in the UK.' And that lady became the founder of Starlight Australia!"

My mother-in-law said to me, "What do you know about Maimonides?" And I said, "I know absolutely nothing about Maimonides." She said, "Well, you need to do a bit of Googling, and ask around about what Maimonides said about the soul."

So I did. I learned that Maimonides was a great rabbi, born in Spain nearly nine hundred years ago, who lived in Alexandria, Egypt, at a time when the great leaders, regardless of religion, palled around, had lunch, and quoted each other in their writings. The local imam of the

FINDING HAPPY

Muslims, the Christian patriarch, and this Jewish rabbi Maimonides were friends; they were pals. And Maimonides believed there are three layers of the human soul. The base one, everybody's got that. Then, the middle one is like a better version of it. He believed that the highest one, called the N'Shuma, is rarer. Not everybody has one.

You don't own a N'Shuma. Rather, it's the membership society of only those *who feel compelled to try to make the world a better place.* And he believed that when two people with this highest level of the soul meet for the first time, they say to each other, "Hineini," the Hebrew for "Here I am." "Here I am, what do we need to do?" And I thought to myself, you know, it's true. With every fiftieth or one-hundredth person, there is something in ten minutes that defines our relationship forever. Even though I only just met them or sat next to them on a plane, I would do anything for them. If they phoned me and said, "I know this is short notice. But there's a real opportunity, and I need your help. Can you be in Tokyo on Thursday?" I would have to go to Tokyo, and vice versa. I realized that a layer in the cake of what I've done philanthropically is meeting these higher-level-of-the-soul people, bonding with them, and then working together. So that one with one makes about 150. We do something that I very probably couldn't have done on my own. Feeling the compulsion of the N'Shuma is empathy, it is not a laurel: it is an emotion throughout one's life that compels us to try to help out. And it is not lonely, because thank God, others feel it too.

New research in collective neuroscience tends to support the N'Shuma that Maimonides set out nine hundred years ago. It turns out that when people talk or share an experience, their brain waves synchronize. Neurons in the same locations in their different brains activate simultaneously, creating the same thought patterns in synchrony. The exogenous brain, indeed. Brain areas respond to sight and sound together. In higher species, we process events in parallel to make sense of a new situation, especially a new challenge. Scientists with brain scanners can actually see the process between people that we call "being on the same wavelength." It can be helpful or unhelpful. Mob violence in a football crowd comes from the same sharing process as Maimonides's N'Shuma: where allies unite in a common cause. "All for one, and one for all."

What Makes a Good Friend? How Can We Choose Them Wisely?

So, the challenge in making friends is to stay away from the bullies, the foolish, and the dangerous. We need to seek out the friends who share our values but constantly urge us to Do the Right Thing, just as we urge them. Those who love us unconditionally for who we are, who really see us, and who encourage us to achieve, to excel, to do good in the world.

It can be lonely being a career film producer or any other kind of entrepreneur. You need friends who will help you, people who, when there is a challenge, will not say, "Oh, God, what are we going to do about that? Oh, that's a huge problem, right?" You want people who say, "How about this straw-man solution? What if we did X?" Once you're producing a film, you can't say, "The door was locked, so we couldn't get in." You have to go around the back and see if they left a window open: you have to solve the challenge. If your director wants to put the camera on top of a building, the fact that the building is dark, uninhabited, and locked tight is not going to stop you somehow getting your damn camera on the top. You do those things perhaps ten times a day. When you take that same toolkit over to a nonprofit charity, especially a scrappy, entrepreneurial nonprofit, you need colleagues for whom the cup is half full, colleagues with Maimonides's N'Shuma. The best friends are our collaborators to a shared purpose.

In 1982 my cousin Emma and I granted one wish for one child, and Starlight was born. The original office on Melrose Boulevard in Los Angeles was a converted broom closet of someone else's offices, where a separate door had been opened up from the corridor outside. We used to joke that it was the only office any of us had ever visited where if you lay on the floor, you could touch all four walls at once. No windows. Humble beginnings, for sure. The power of a strong idea is that as we helped more and more sick children, their siblings, and their parents to find happiness amid the despair, fear, confusion, and sadness surrounding serious pediatric illness, we did nothing but grow. We just had to tell people the stories and believe in it ourselves. From the anxiety of admission to follow-up appointments and ongoing treatment, the journey of hospitalized kids can be overwhelming and uncertain. That's why Starlight programs exist. Carefully crafted to address the unique needs of pediatric patients, Starlight's vital programs provide comfort, distraction, and a sense of normalcy when children in the hospital need it the most. Last year, in the United States alone, 2.4 million hospitalized kids experienced joy and relief through Starlight programs!

In the first ten years, I was able to recruit a really powerful board of directors, and as we raised more and more money on the power of the idea, we hired truly excellent staff. And yes, we quickly needed a bigger headquarters office suite. We expanded across the United States and opened a total of twenty-two offices, each formed as an independent chapter under the overall national umbrella of Starlight. And people noticed.

One of the strange things about entrepreneurship in the nonprofit charitable space is that too often, it only does its good work in one place, for one set of people, and with one set of volunteers. Think of how absurd it would be if Howard Schultz, after establishing the first Starbucks coffee bar in Seattle, had simply said to himself, "Good enough. This is how I will retire, running this one location." Or think of how ridiculous it would have been if McDonald's had opened its first half-dozen hamburger joints, and then just stopped expanding. But in the nonprofit world, that's exactly what we mostly do. I wish I had a dollar for every meeting where I have met with a successful entrepreneur who has had a huge idea, a new solution for an old problem, and then acted on it and successfully addressed the challenge...in just one city. I ask, "Do you have programs elsewhere?" They tend to say no. And when I ask why, they say, "Because I live here." I say, "Yes, but there are people in other cities where the need is just as great, and if you brought some of them to be trained by your team locally, then they could go back home and replicate." Sometimes they listen, sometimes they don't, but mostly good ideas seem rooted to the spot. Replication is a bridge too far, even if the entrepreneur was wildly inventive in setting up the original program in the original location.

What Makes a Good Friend? How Can We Choose Them Wisely?

THE WHITE HOUSE

WASHINGTON

October 20, 1997

Mr. Peter Samuelson
Los Angeles, California

Dear Peter:

I am delighted to extend my congratulations to you as you are honored by Starlight Children's Foundation.

Our country's greatest strength is the community spirit of its people. Throughout our history, Americans have been eager to serve the common good. Your involvement and dedication to caring for seriously ill children are vital in sustaining this enduring legacy. By taking more responsibility for ourselves, our families, and our communities, we can ensure a brighter tomorrow for generations to come.

I commend you for your deep concern about our future and for your exemplary commitment to improving our world.

Sincerely,

Bill Clinton

I decided that if Starlight worked well in the United States, there was no good reason why it would not work in other English-speaking countries. I set out in sequence to establish Starlight sister charities in the United Kingdom, Canada, and Australia. In each, it was crucial to pay attention to cultural, legal, and financial differences, as well as to a completely different rubric for how pediatric hospitals ran—for example, in the UK through the National Health Service. Nevertheless, kids were kids, families were families, and the grief and fear surrounding pediatric illness and especially the child's pain seemed to be exactly the same.

FINDING HAPPY

In short order, we had a thriving British Starlight Children's Foundation, in which my cousin Emma has been a leading light ever since. I realized early on that it needed to be supervised by a British board of directors and not by me sitting 5,600 miles away in Los Angeles, California.
In Canada, I explored and came to understand that there were really two completely different cultures, one of which spoke French and the other English. You simply could not impose a Montreal solution on Toronto or an Ontario solution on Quebec. They were not interested! By lucky chance, I speak good French. I had originally learned my French in school in London. By working on the Steve McQueen film in 1970 in Le Mans, France, for almost a year, I had become pretty fluent, and so I threw myself with great gusto into the challenge of setting up Starlight in Montreal.

I remember on one occasion I asked Ron Levy, the chairman of Starlight Montreal, whether in the upcoming press conference he wanted me to speak my words first in French or first in English, followed by the other language. Ron said, "Just do paragraph one in French, paragraph two in English, paragraph three in French, and so on." I said, "But Ron, won't that mean that the whole audience will fail to understand half of the speech?" "No," he said, "they all speak both languages fluently. You are just tipping your hat to the cultural differences by using both languages, but you don't have to overlap." And so it was.

I persuaded a highly entrepreneurial marketing executive, Warren Kornblum, that what he really needed in his life was to partner on the formation of a Starlight Children's Foundation for English-speaking Canada, starting with Toronto and the province of Ontario. Warren and his wife, Trisha, became fast friends. We spent some terrific vacations together on their boat during the few weeks of the year when the weather was good enough to use it on the lakes of Ontario. I remember on one occasion we discovered a water snake in the dinghy. Three of the members of the crew, including me, ran for the furthest place

What Makes a Good Friend? How Can We Choose Them Wisely?

away from the snake, while Tricia approached it with barbecue tongs to encourage it overboard so that we could set off on our adventure.

I always make a point during a long flight to try a couple of times to talk to the person sitting next to me about Starlight, First Star, EDAR, or filmmaking. And I always have the business cards in my wallet. This has resulted in some truly wonderful things. As I mentioned earlier, Australian Starlight came about in a wonderful way. In 1987, I sat next to Erica Masters on a flight from New York to Los Angeles. Erica told me that she was British, had recently retired, and was now moving to Sydney, Australia, where her son and daughter-in-law had a new baby, her first grandchild. She was moving there to spend time with her family. I asked her what she had done in the UK, and she said she had been an executive in the film industry, which of course gave us common ground. I told her about Starlight and suggested that if the concept of applying happiness to seriously ill children and their families worked in the United States, the UK, and Canada, surely it ought to work in Australia? I explained to her what would be necessary in order to kick off Starlight in Australia. I pledged that if she could assemble a group of interested people, I would fly down to Sydney and do the necessary presentation.

I sent her materials to use, and we corresponded weekly by the blue Air Letters that were then the only cost-effective way to communicate. After six months, she wrote, "Well, I've done it. If you want to come down, I've put a group together who are pretty high-powered and quite interested in exploring this." She was good as her word. I flew to Sydney in July 1988 and was only able to be there less than twenty-four hours. The meeting was in the conference room on the top floor of a huge skyscraper in Sydney, in the offices owned by the George Patterson Advertising Agency. The chairman of that firm, Geoffrey Cousins, had helped put the meeting together, and they had various luminaries present, including John Newcombe, the famous Australian tennis pro, and various captains of industry, including Ian Kennedy, a fine man who founded direct mail in Australia. The eleven Australians present became the first board of Starlight Australia.

I made my presentation from the end of the table. I could see that there was one man who was getting very impatient with me, and in fact

FINDING HAPPY

going red in the face. I found out later that he was Sam Chisholm, the CEO of Bond Media, which owned Australia's largest television network. Eventually he blurted out, "Let's cut to the chase. When you say we need to raise money before we can contact the first child, how much are we talking about?" I replied, "I think for a city the size of Sydney, you would need 200,000 Australian dollars in the bank before you could prudently start to offer services. Because one thing is for sure, as we have experienced in the other countries, once you start, you can never stop when kids ask for help." Quick as a flash, Sam said, "Okay, okay. Enough. On Monday morning, Bond Media will deliver a check for $200,000. Where do you want it to go?" Everyone was speechless, including me. And then he looked around the table and pointed his index finger at everybody else. "And what are all you Sheilas gonna do?" he asked.

The first wish was for a computer, by a young boy suffering from cancer, referred by Dr. John Yu at The Children's Hospital at Camperdown. A little later, Ian Kennedy had a son who became seriously ill and spent a long time at Camperdown. He realized how clinical the environment was in a children's ward and suggested that Starlight build an audiovisual entertainment room, which became the first Starlight Express Room. And that was the beginning of Starlight Australia, which in classic Australian can-do style has always been our most innovative and successful sister charity. There are now Starlight Express Rooms in every children's hospital in Australia, each staffed by a costumed superhero called Captain Starlight. I've had the thought that in my next life I might love to be a Captain Starlight! Nothing but joy, delivering the silver lining in serious pediatric illness.

In time, all the non-US entities also became charities in their own right. There were too many important people running them to kowtow to Los Angeles, and why should they? Starlight in each country is a self-directed national organization, with ties of sisterhood and history to the equal American charity. And I felt as though I was the proud dad of the whole brood. At this point, more like the grandpa.

For the longest time, while I chaired the whole thing, I would insist on us treating the non-US activities exactly the same as we treated those across the United States. We would have quarterly meetings of the four country chairs or presidents, all on one conference call. The joke was that we would have to take turns, because someone always had to be in pajamas and up at night with a big mug of coffee. What brought us together was always much stronger than what divided us. It was an article of faith for me and for most others that despite the clear inconveniences of the time zones, we should try and hold the whole thing together in a cooperative and collegial way. And indeed, it did turn out that what united us was much stronger than what divided us.

As factions in the United States have become increasingly insular, large swaths of Americans believe that America First means stepping back from engagement with the rest of the world. My own personal experience has always been that the opposite is true. The planet is small: the blue marble that all eight billion of us inhabit is tiny when seen from space, and it is in all of our best interests to create a family of mankind in order to address common challenges and weak points in the chain of life. There really is little point in addressing climate change only in one country, if pollution and heating are coming from somewhere else. Factionalism and religious and ethnic hatred whipped up by demagogues, dictators, and fascists compete to divide us into little tribes. My own view is that we will flounder and fail if every day we do not bridge the gulfs between us, and functionally operate within the network, the knowledge base, the shared interests and the common challenges of all mankind. We did our own little bit in Starlight and now in First Star, and we showed that we could do 100 percent better working together, rather than on separate islands of self-interest.

FINDING HAPPY

Chapter Takeaways and Reflection Questions for You

- Think about your friends. Are they reliable, deep thinking, supportive, ambitious?
- Family is where you find it. Who is worthy of being your brother or sister?
- How can you make sure your friends, your group, are good for you and helpful to you?
- If you are proud of something you have achieved, can you do more of it elsewhere?
- If you are proud of something you have created, how can you find and help other people elsewhere replicate it, to do more good in their location?
- Is it better to train people by bringing them to an existing site of excellence, or to send a member of staff from the center of excellence to establish things in a different location? (Clue: There is no one best solution. You have to do a bit of each.)
- Is it true that what unites humanity—its wisdom, joys, and challenges—is greater than what divides it?
- What can each of us do in our own lives to be a builder of bridges rather than a builder of walls?
- What are our best arguments toward finding the common humanity of mankind, rather than emphasizing differences and building castles to expel people who are different?
- Why is it that mankind no longer lives in caves and has organized civil society, and yet the attitudes, fears, and hostilities of the cave dwellers still exist and hold us back from wider solutions to our common problems?

CHAPTER 44

How Can You Live Your Passion?
Foster Boy: Carpe Diem

John Schimmel—a longtime friend who ran the story department at Warner Brothers and was Michael Douglas's creative partner in previous lives—asked me if I would lecture in a master's course on screenwriting he was running at the University of California, Riverside. As always, I asked him to describe the students to me: Where were they in their academic trajectory? He said that it was a very interesting group of professionals in a mid-career, low-residency, earning their master's in Fine Arts. It was designed to accommodate working professionals who were not able to come to the campus more than once or twice a year. This was one of those residential periods.

I shared whatever wisdom I could with the students. Looking down from the platform, I became focused on one man sitting in the middle who seemed to be about twice as old as any of the other students. One would expect in an MFA course that the students would be in their mid-to-late twenties. But here he was, clearly much more senior. At the end of the class, it was he who asked me if I would like to have a coffee.

Jay Deratany told me that he was a very successful litigator based in Chicago and that scriptwriting was his passion. I thought this was

FINDING HAPPY

very unusual because the life of a scriptwriter is so incredibly challenging. Why anyone who was a successful lawyer would want to hurl themselves at those castle walls was beyond me. A screenplay is not the finished product. It needs to attract a career producer, a director, a cast, and a great deal of money! Then, hopefully, through the collaboration of many, it may be made into a film or television product, which in turn may or may not appeal to an actual audience. The competition is fierce, and one needs to be really dedicated to take on that challenge. But Jay, it seemed, was relentless, the rare individual determined to give birth to his film narrative ideas and who might actually succeed.

Jay came up to me in the conga line of students after my lecture and told me that he wanted to meet because I had talked about foster care and how fixing it was a passion of mine. I'd spoken about foster kids being in the worst situation of any deprived group: not voting, not marching, not realizing how marginalized they were by the system, as well as by the original neglect or abuse that had driven them into care in the first place. No lobbyists, no money, no power, no vote. How would anything ever change for them? Over coffee, Jay told me he was also interested in foster care, and that actually he had an idea for a script based on an experience he had had representing a foster kid. It was about a young man who had been re-abused in foster care, when the for-profit company running his life had placed an older boy they already knew was a serial rapist into the same group home on a farm.

Honestly, one of the worst things as a career producer is when civilians suggest that you might want to read their script. There go two hours of my Sunday! I remember on one memorable occasion I was having outpatient surgery for a benign bump on the back of my head, lying there looking downward through the hole in the surgery table. Below me I could see the feet of the doctor, the anesthesiologist, and two nurses in their disposable blue booties. The voice of the surgeon boomed into my medicated brain just as he had cut into my numbed skin. "I hear you're a career film producer, Mr. Samuelson. My daughter has written a script. I wonder if you might like to read it?" Feeling his fingers inside my head and not wanting to move, I simply said, "Oh, it would be my pleasure. You know where to send it."

When Jay mentioned that he was writing a script about a foster youth he had represented, I was interested but not expecting big things. A small number of weeks later, I opened an email and there was his script, a PDF called *Foster Boy*. Jay had written it as his master's thesis. Not only did he earn his MFA, but when I read the script that Sunday evening, I thought it was absolutely brilliant. I sat there, read it a second time, and I still thought it was brilliant.

The next day, I phoned Jay and said, "This is a film that needs to be made. And perhaps I could help you? It's what I do." He replied, "Actually, it's even a bit better, because I've raised quite a lot of money for the budget." I asked how much, and he said a couple of million dollars. I said, "Well, I think I could raise more money. People will care about this issue. It's really strong writing. How on earth have you managed to raise your money?" He said, "Well, there are people who have done very well by me representing them in court, and they have won big settlements or verdicts. There are people in Chicago who would like to see me succeed as a scriptwriter, and they are willing to put their money there."

So *Foster Boy* came together. It was the first time my commercial instincts to make a film that people would actually want to see collided with my growing sense that if a film could focus on an important social issue, it might be able to generate empathy among its audience, and if they were then offered multiple paths to change their mind or support the cause, that might be very powerful. Perhaps even lightning in a bottle.

Based on truth, *Foster Boy* is the story of a young man removed from his family because of prior abuse and neglect, who finds himself on a farm where an older boy is placed by the foster-care agency responsible for both. The agency knows the older youth is a serial rapist, but they destroy the files in order to make an extra buck by squeezing him into the same placement. Significantly, they never tell the very worthy couple running the farm that they have a sexual predator on their hands, who is likely to reoffend and harm the younger children.

FINDING HAPPY

I reached out to my own First Star charity, where we educate teenage foster youth; to the Children's Advocacy Institute at the University of San Diego, where they train children's lawyers to represent foster kids; and to Children's Rights in New York, who litigate in order to create case law that will be helpful to the rights of foster children. I asked if they would partner with us to make the most of the opportunity created by the film. On the back of an envelope, we worked out how one could invite 501(c)(3) nonprofits into the making and propagation of a film. First, the charities advised us on how to perfect the script, not only to make it as accurate as possible to the evil realities of for-profit foster care, but also to further their own goals in pushing back against this evil curse on the kids' heads.

Foster-care agencies operated for profit began in Florida under Governor Jeb Bush and have spread across the country. They have even managed to put down roots in the United Kingdom. I believe in capitalism. I believe our best way to keep companies efficient is through competition, making them serve their customers in order to serve their shareholders. What I do not believe is that for-profit business is the way to solve every challenge in society. I don't believe that companies should profit from our prison-industrial complex. I don't believe that there should be profit in public education, and I certainly do not believe there should be profit in foster care, which ought to be run by local government or by nonprofit charities. There are several mega-corporations making billions of dollars a year running foster-care agencies. Some of them pay their senior executives a million dollars a year for the privilege. And the kids who are their commodity have no voice.

Once we had completed the financing of the film and were in pre-production, the charities came out to meet with the cast and crew to inspire them and us. It was magical to see the effect on a crew when they realize that the purpose of their work is not just creative excellence, or even earning a paycheck, but also to help correct a grave social ill.

On one occasion, Shane Paul McGee—the brilliant young man whom we cast to play Jamal, the abused foster youth in the film—had to really emote while on the witness stand in the climactic scene in

How Can You Live Your Passion? Foster Boy: Carpe Diem

court. He needed to grapple with his post-traumatic stress disability and weep in expressing what had been inflicted on him, which was so deeply shameful to him. The first time we shot the scene, on a ten-scale perhaps Shane delivered a seven, but it wasn't good enough. We did it again and again, but it never really got past a six or a seven. We needed to move on because we were on a tight schedule within a tight budget. Then the shop steward of the IATSE Union of the technicians came up and said, "It's really not quite good enough, is it?" I said, "You're right, but we have to move on." He said, "Well, what if we came in half an hour early tomorrow morning and didn't go on the clock, so that we could give Shane one more run at it?" I said, "Thank you very much." And that's exactly what happened.

During his prep for the part, we had invited Shane to visit our foster kid Scholars at UCLA in the First Star Academy. He had asked them to stand up one at a time and simply tell him what was the best thing and then the worst thing about being in foster care, "because I am playing you and I've never been in foster care. So I need your help." It had been an incredibly emotional session. Some of the foster teens felt the information was too personal to share out loud. The director of our First Star program at UCLA suggested they simply write an anonymous note to Shane, which we then passed on. When he moved into his dressing room in the studio, I noticed he hung the letters on the wall. I asked him why they were there, and he said, "Before I come on the set, I simply stand there and read them, and that puts me in the zone to remember who I am playing, what has happened to them, and how important it is that I do justice to their suffering."

So the morning of the reshoot, I said to Shane, "Stay in your dressing room, read the letters, and we'll send for you when we're absolutely ready." Once we got the crew completely ready, everyone was silent. You could hear a pin drop. Shane walked in and sat in the witness stand. Jay quietly showed Shane pictures on his laptop of the abuse that had been done to the foster kids he had represented. I then put my mouth to Shane's ear. I whispered that he should close his eyes, and I said, "Spirits of the foster children killed by abuse and neglect, please come into the heart of this young man, so that he can feel your shame, your pain, and your souls—so that he may tell your story, and the other

Peter,
Your energy, steadfast devotion and support made this film rise well above its intention. Thank you. It was my pleasure working with you!

Best,
[signature] DP- "Foster Boy"

foster children may live." I tiptoed back behind the camera; our first assistant director called, "Roll sound!"; and then our director, Yousef Delara, called, "Action."

Shane delivered a performance that left not one dry eye on set: an eleven on that ten scale. Remarkable, the high point of the film. The film does the same thing to its audiences. That's the power of making a film about something important. I stood there and thought, *This may be the high point of my career. It cannot get better than this.* Shane always had it in him. He is brilliant. Thinking of the foster youth helped him deliver it. Sense memory.

While we were filming, and then during postproduction, I led the team under Gadi Rouache that put together the websites. One of them was for the film itself. It had everything you would expect on a film site and information about the causes for which the film fought. We also ran a petition to stop the profit motive in running foster-care agencies. The results have been strong: so far, we have 336,000 signatures. We also offer efficient and vetted ways for viewers of the film to donate to foster-care charities, including the three that partnered with us, plus ways to become a foster parent, to become an adoptive parent, and to lobby the audience's members of Congress. Lightning in a bottle: if you make a film about something important, the cast and crew are greatly motivated to give their very best to the job at hand. The audience feels empathy in their hearts and wants to be part of the solution, and not stand idly by. And you can channel that to do actual good. As the Pulitzer Prize–winning American novelist Richard Powers wrote, "The best arguments in the world won't change a person's mind. The only thing that can do that is a good story."

But if I were asked, "What was the best outcome from the relationship with Jay Paul Deratany, now a good friend?" I'd answer that it is not the film we made. Rather, Jay began to foster a brilliant young man named Paul, and Saryl and I were recently moved to tears when we attended the legal hearing in court, when Jay adopted Paul and became Paul's dad.

Chapter Takeaways and Reflection Questions for You

- Where do ideas come from? Do you have to create your own? (Clue: No!)

- What are your best ideas? What did you do about them?

- How do you put on a show? Can you create your own, or is it better to help with someone else's show?

- How can you put purpose into your life as a student, or into your profession? Can you really do both at once? Can the purpose be through volunteering when you are not working? (Answer: Yes!)

FINDING HAPPY

CHAPTER 45

How Can You Extrovert Yourself?
Public Speaking: Stand-Up, with Fewer Jokes

I tell our First Star Scholars to raise their hand and ask a question in every class they attend. Every single class. There are two reasons behind this. First, it wakes you up, makes you focus on the class, puts you on alert. Maybe it is a little bit scary and you can channel that into getting the most out of the lesson. If you can pump a bit more adrenaline, you own the moment. Second, it impresses the teacher and shows them that you are engaged with them. You may very well get better grades—teachers feel insecure too, and they reward those who pay attention. Try it.

These days, quite often I get paid to make speeches. I give the money to my charities when I am hired by family offices, associations, and so forth. On one occasion, I was hired to give a speech at the Biltmore Hotel in Los Angeles. It was early in the morning—eight o'clock, I think. Everybody's half asleep, because they've been up drinking too late the previous evening. I pitch up at the door, and the young lady with the headset and the clipboard says, "Oh, I'm so glad you're here. You're going to open for us. And General Colin Powell will be speaking right after you." I thought, *Oh, God, this is no good. Who wants to be followed by General Powell? Not good at all.* I started, speaking to maybe a thousand people in the grand ballroom. I said, "I know you're not here really wanting to listen to *me*. You're here to listen to a great American general, Colin Powell. So, *think of me as the semicolon.*"

I got a big laugh, which got me off on a good footing. I gave my speech for the forty minutes they wanted and received a big round of applause. I then sat down in the audience, eager to hear what General Colin Powell had to say. At the podium, he began like this: "Where's Samuelson? Where's Samuelson?" I thought, *What on earth is going to happen now?* I stood up and sheepishly raised my hand. He then held up the palm of his right hand towards me. He said, "By virtue of the power vested in me by the Army of the United States of America, I hereby declare you a Full Colon." And that brought the house down. I've put it on my CV ever since—that I was named a Full Colon by General Colin Powell. So, in terms of the leaders of the Gulf War, I've worked a bit with both of them, four-star generals Schwarzkopf and Powell, the yin and the yang of leadership. Hah!

With General Colin Powell, US Army.

How Can You Extrovert Yourself? Public Speaking: Stand-Up, with Fewer Jokes

One of the most exciting things I've ever done creatively was facilitating and witnessing Steven Spielberg as he gave input into the design of Starbright World. From the first time I met Steven, he suggested that it ought to be possible with the new technologies of the early 1990s to link seriously ill children from their hospital rooms with those of a similar age, and perhaps facing similar health challenges, in other parts of the country. We went to Children's Hospital Los Angeles and sat on the carpet in a playroom with a number of early teens while Steven encouraged them to choose avatars from various artists' renderings. These would represent them as they navigated them around in virtual space. Steven chose ET to be his avatar when he logged on from his office at Amblin.

We worked with Knowledge Adventure, Intel, Sprint, and other major companies that donated their equipment and services. Our software created what appeared to be a three-dimensional world for the kids. Three versions of the environment were available. The user would navigate their avatar around by using the up, down, left, and right keys on the keyboard. (The mouse had not yet been invented!) There were no broadband T-3 lines to carry the amount of data at the speed necessary into most children's hospitals. In many cases, the broadband cable running down the middle of the street had to be connected by a spur run through a new trench dug by workers using a backhoe.

The co-founder of Microsoft, Paul Allen, and his sister Jody, who ran a company called Vulcan in Seattle, donated $6 million, and we were able to launch what we called Starbright World across the country. It was a very big deal. And when Steven, General Schwarzkopf, and I together pressed the big green button at the Digital World Conference in 1995, it made national news.

It seems commonplace now to talk about navigating avatars through virtual worlds online. But in the 1990s, all of this was brand new. Starbright World made us the absolute global pioneers in a fully navigable, completely interactive virtual space for players separated geographically by great distances. This was long before Facebook, Myspace, or Second Life. And in fact, when we launched Starbright World, young Mark Zuckerberg had not only not yet gone to Harvard as an undergraduate, but he was only eleven years old.

FINDING HAPPY

The speech I made at George Mason University that year was as scary as they get! When I arrived at the conference hall from the hotel, the young lady with a clipboard and headset who greeted me told me that I would follow President Mikhail Gorbachev of the Soviet Union and Lady Margaret Thatcher, previously prime minister of the United Kingdom. This seemed to me the worst possible order, but it was too late to get it changed. I was ushered into the green room. President Gorbachev was already speaking, and I could see him on the screen in the room. But Lady Thatcher was sitting there. We had quite a conversation about the role of new technology in helping marginalized communities, in our case seriously ill children, to live fuller lives. I found her extraordinarily bright, and although I never did appreciate her politics, she definitely had charisma and self-evidently all the powers of leadership. I gave my speech. Apparently it was well received. With a deep sigh of relief, I went on to the rest of my day, depleted but jazzed by all the adrenaline.

Similarly, that same year, we unveiled the Starbright terminals in Children's National Medical Center in Washington, DC. Both President Clinton and Vice President Al Gore were attending, and I witnessed first-hand the extraordinarily careful preparations of the US Secret Service. They were completely serious, never cracked a smile, and

How Can You Extrovert Yourself? Public Speaking: Stand-Up, with Fewer Jokes

when the lead agent looked at me, I felt pretty sure I was guilty of something!

Heady days, breaking new ground in technology in ways made possible by the fact that our mission was fully nonprofit. I loved it all.

Well might you say, "Yes, but I don't know anybody famous to ask to help me." Well, neither did I at first. It's like building a wall. Creating your network is done one brick at a time. And the bricks sit next to each other. Keep track of your network. Always follow up. Revisit the bricks. Start with a spider graph?

Oscar Statuette ©, TM, AMPAS

Chapter Takeaways and Reflection Questions for You

- What is the role of humor in public speaking?
- How do we find the courage to speak to a big group? (Clue: Pick one friendly face. Speak just to them.)
- How does public speaking help with shyness?
- What is improv?
- How does stand-up comedy help cure shyness? How do you begin? Is there an Open Mic Night near you?
- Some people write out every word of their speech. Others just use bullet points. I write my speeches in my head early in the morning while still half asleep and then edit them after my coffee. Which method would work best for you?

CHAPTER 46

How Can You Fight Tribalism in Your Own Heart?

If I had one magic wish, the overarching evil that I would snap my fingers to fix is tribalism.

I don't know what it is about humans. By now, it is probably carried in our DNA that to remain alive, you had better identify only with your little cave full of the same tribe, and you need to greatly fear those nasty, unfamiliar people of the different tribes who live somewhere else. But we don't live in caves any more. It is hardly Darwin's survival of the fittest. In animal species, inbreeding creates genetic defects, while mating with animals far from the family unit creates hardier and more resilient offspring.

Tribal hatred is fueled by bad and self-serving leadership. It's an easy grift: "Nasty people are after what is yours. Follow me, I'll make you safe, and I'll stop them stealing from you." It was ever so. In a better world, education would drive discriminating thinking and push back against these lies. But for now, around a quarter of all Americans believe the lies and take comfort from them. They vote for the self-serving people who mislead them. Sometimes they win. And once the demagogues take power (Hitler, Stalin, Putin, Xi, Bolsonaro, Duterte, Netanyahu, Trump, and so on), it is very difficult to vote them out, because they try to move the goalposts of democracy. They do not go quietly when they lose. They use their power to try to cling to power.

Hatred is just fear dressed up to feel a bit more palatable. On many occasions, it makes humans susceptible to charismatic, evil, ego-struck leaders. I would, with my magic wish, have people grow up feeling how much they have in common with other people, regardless of their country, faith, ethnic origin, tall, short, thin, fat, whether they are physically challenged, whether they can hear or not, whether they're just plain different. Think of that famous picture of our planet Earth, taken by astronaut Bill Anders in Apollo 8 when it swooped around the Moon before we'd actually even landed there. It is called "Earthrise." You can Google it. The horizon is of the gray moon, and floating off in space is the blue marble that is Earth. Earth looks as though it's only a centimeter across, just a thumb width because of the perspective. If only more humans could hold that fragile little thing in their heads, and realize that it's actually raving mad, crass, and stupid to feel as though we are divided by these relatively trivial and arbitrary differences, when what unites us is vastly bigger. How can anyone with a brain think that skin tone, the melanin in your skin, because of where your ancestors lived, has anything to do with behavior or entitlement? Why not height? We are all together the human beings of planet Earth. Nearly eight billion of us.

All eight billion of us walking around planet Earth are descended from a single woman in East Africa, between 120,000 and 150,000 years ago. We are all related. So why is there this ridiculous hatred? And why are we susceptible to evil people, authoritarian crypto-Nazis, not so crypto in some cases, who tell us we are different? Fascism is empowered in recent years by the exponential growth of the internet and social media: the relatively few isolationists preaching violent hatred in any one place are now united across the digital planet into a wave of hatred for otherness. We need to focus on how small the planet is, and how we should better empathize with and help each other. "A man never stood so tall as when he reaches down to hold the hand of a child in need." Our kids, their kids, and the other kids. My wish would be for a widespread epidemic of empathy before we self-destruct our species.

FINDING HAPPY

May I be completely transparent and say here that I hesitated before calling out some extreme voices on the right of American politics. People told me that I'd lose readers if I did so. After a deep breath and reflection, I have to say, "So be it." Life is choices, and the truth is the truth. I don't now recognize the rational Republican Party of ten years ago that I knew and respected. We need it back! I met and cherished a great and brave Republican, John McCain, but his party now seems to have fled for the hills, giving the reins to too many extremists who present an actual danger to our democracy. To our people. To the future of our country. Racism, patriarchy, social division, self-serving manipulation of the rules, corruption, loudly pushing autocracy and misogyny. White supremacy these days is not even disguised under hoods. Anti-science, anti-learning, and anti-education...I want to be brave enough to speak up, provide my considered view, and ask you, the reader, to apply your critical thinking and to please form your own.

I know from chairing thousands of meetings that differences of opinion are most often best resolved by negotiation to a middle solution. But to get there, people have to stop shouting and do some serious listening. The blowhard megaphones of social media raise up exciting extremist hyperbole and suppress solution-finding but more-boring consensus. But that does not make consensus wrong. History will judge harshly those who lie and cheat to preserve and grow their power. Democracy is not perfect, but it is much better than any of the authoritarian alternatives. Democracy is fragile...we must all lift it up every day. Country before party. Vote against extremism wherever you see it! Vote!

In my work with the defendants (at the Nuremberg Trials 1945–1949) I was searching for the nature of evil and I now think I have come close to defining it. A lack of empathy. It's the one characteristic that connects all the defendants, a genuine incapacity to feel with their fellow men. Evil, I think, is the absence of empathy.

—Captain Gustave Mark Gilbert,
Nuremberg Diary

Chapter Takeaways and Reflection Questions for You

- What prejudice have you experienced?
- How did you deal with it?
- Be honest: When have you felt your own unconscious bias?
- How did you deal with this?
- How can we use empathy to fight hatred?
- What steps can an individual take to push back on hatred and ignorance?
- What is the best way to deal with a person spouting ignorance and hatred? Do you just sit there and listen? What can any one of us do? (Clue: Push back!)
- Do you read and consider opposing views to your own? Or are you far down the comforting rabbit hole of sameness?

CHAPTER 47

Are Humans Lost? A Story: Aliens, Viruses, and Planet Earth

The alien spacecraft swept low over the colorless moon of Earth and settled into its trajectory to make soft landing on the planet itself. Inside the craft, the alien was not so much an individual but more one of millions of components of the exogenous brain, the interconnected intelligence of their civilization that travelled throughout the universe, constantly communicating, multitudes of nodes thinking as one with all the others in real time. An anthill of sentient being, more knowing than we may ever know.

Only a very few civilizations survived their own fumbling attempts to kill themselves. The aliens knew that most but not all civilizations annihilated themselves for three reasons that fed on each other.

First, when science on any planet managed to split the atom, they invariably developed nuclear weapons, and the aliens knew that nowhere in the universe had any weapon ever been developed that was not eventually used. The awesome power of nuclear mass destruction, coupled with the other two driving forces of planetary annihilation, were oftentimes irresistible. In one famous case, so many nuclear

Are Humans Lost? A Story: Aliens, Viruses, and Planet Earth

devices were detonated that an entire planet was thrown off its axis and crashed off into the outer darkness, leaving its atmosphere behind and taking with it all of the dead protagonists. The aliens knew from radio broadcasts from Earth that the humans called their balance of nuclear power Mutually Assured Destruction, but without a trace of irony in the acronym, MAD.

The second cause of planetary self-immolation was exactly that. Once a civilization discovered fire, it was harnessed to serve three basic needs: light, heat, and power. But once the beings got busy-busy, they started wildly burning through the thin mantle of hydrocarbons on and just under the surface of the planet—the living beings of previous times that had taken millennia to accumulate: the remains of other animals, of plant life, and of their own ancestors. And through their carefree burning of fossil fuel, the species eventually raised global temperatures exponentially, melted their polar icecaps, raised sea levels, and lost most of the land mass on which they lived. Oh, and compromised the planet's atmosphere, on which their lives depended. Forced migration, a lack of potable water, great storms, forest fires, famine, pestilence, and plague resulted in wars for survival. It seemed odd that there were hundreds of eminent scientists among them pointing all this out, but not enough were paying attention to them, or perhaps the wrong ones: their leaders did little real leading and hardly ever showed long-term thinking amid the concerns of short-term election cycles. This year, seventy-three thousand fires were set in the Amazon rainforest in a single year for commercial gain. Truly it was most odd, and difficult to fathom if you were yourselves a rational species.

Both of these challenges were greatly worsened by the third syndrome that killed off most species of medium intelligence. The aliens had visited some one hundred thousand years earlier, during a time the humans would later call the Stone Age. Human life was run entirely on the basis of existential fear: fear of dying, fear of the dark, of hunger,

FINDING HAPPY

cold, wild animals, and most of all, of any other human who did not live in your cave. They surely must be after your food, your women, your cave itself, perhaps. And with brutal violence, you had better kill them before they killed you and yours. This was stirred to a high pitch by the cave leaders, who built their power by stoking the fear of outsiders: "They want what is yours. They want to kill you. Do what I say, and I will keep you safe." Life was cold, dark, hungry, and brutal. Average life expectancy in the Stone Age was twenty-seven years.

Of course, it did not feel good to reveal that you were scared stiff most of the time. Better to dress up all the fear as hatred, which gave the leader and you a sense of agency, of being a bit more in control. And in stoking the hatred it was helpful to come up with easy visual identifiers so you could keep track of whom the enemy were supposed to be this year: skin, hair, facial shape, body sizes, as well as suspiciously different clothing, the way they sounded, the gods they worshipped, and whom they loved. You didn't actually know or experience any of them—probably a good thing for your cave leader selling the hatred, because it was much easier to make you fear and hate others if you didn't get to know them. If you got to know them, you might realize that they were as scared as you, and just trying, like you, to raise their kids, feed them, and not die. They also yearned to be left alone.

And back then, of course, the prefrontal lobe of the human brain, the rational thinking part, had hardly begun to develop. Thinking about long-term consequences was not possible when you ran your life from the amygdala, the reptilian back of the brain that was binary in the options it presented: fight, flight, or freeze. And of course, especially in males younger than twenty-five, the prefrontal lobe was not fully developed even in 2025. Which was handy for leaders sending the young men off to die in wars. Strangely, the females generally get the front part working much earlier and see the whole picture. But the men do not tend to listen to them.

The aliens thought all this was perverse, irrational, and deeply fascinating. They knew from radio and television broadcasts that humans had analyzed their own DNA, the double helix of their ancestors that they carried throughout their own bodies. So the more educated of them knew full well that every single human being, all eight billion living on Earth, had descended from a single woman, their common ancestor who shared their DNA and who lived in East Africa around 120,000 years ago. The aliens wanted to know how humans could hate their cousins, other relatives, their own ancestors. Did they not realize that when the great migrations happened over tens of thousands of years, the humans who went north and south to parts of the planet with less sun lost some of the melanin in their skin...but still carried the same DNA? They were all relatives. An enigma for sure, thought the alien mind. Why demonize "other" by melanin in their skin? Why not height, or weight? Our alien had heard of Samuelson's Law: "You can take the humans out of the caves, but you cannot easily take the caves out of the humans." Our alien would have nodded, if they had a head.

Well might you ask why the aliens did not give up on humans, why did they not believe, on massive evidence, that they were well on the way to self-destruction? Well, because the radio and television broadcasts revealed that there were a precious few among them who spoke out heroically and attempted, with different degrees of success, to put the brakes on the runaway train of self-destruction. They were few, but impressive. The aliens wanted to know if other humans paid them any attention yet.

And in the end, the aliens knew they could reverse the rampant spiral to self-annihilation and force a planetary pivot by introducing a viral challenge that would force a reset, a reboot, for species of medium intelligence and their leaders, who had lost or had never developed the rational ability to think and act long term, nor the social structures and leadership to save themselves by thinking ahead, by facing facts. It was regrettable to have to do this, to intervene, to bring the Aliens' Burden to bear, and as the spacecraft moved towards touchdown, the commander still hoped to avoid the need for an intervention. But they would do whatever was needed to preserve the lifeform. They cared because caring was rational, and they had the means to force the pivot, painful though it would be.

As the alien observed curiously empty streets, everyone apparently confined to their homes, they wondered what exactly was going on. Could the humans have created their own pivot? *Fascinating*, they thought.

To be continued.

FINDING HAPPY

Chapter Takeaways and Reflection Questions for You

- Are humans capable of solving our own problems, or are we too disorganized, full of blame and hatred of "other?" Of course we are.
- Are you part of the problem or the solution?
- Is social media an asset or an obstacle to humanity? (Clue: It's both, like most technologies!)
- Does viral media rally the best or the worst of us?
- How can democracy survive if so many of those who vote display little critical thinking?
- "Education. Education. Education." Discuss.

Our country is like an old house. And the owner of an old house knows that whatever you were ignoring will never go away. Whatever's lurking will fester, whether you choose to look or not. Ignorance is no protection from the consequences of inaction. Many people might rightly say: "I had nothing to do with how this all started. I have nothing to do with the sense of the past. My ancestors never attacked Indigenous people and never owned slaves. Not one of us was here when this house was built."

Our immediate ancestors may have had nothing to do with it. But here we are the current occupants of a property with stress cracks and bowed walls and fissures built into the foundation. We are heirs to whatever is right or wrong with it. We did not erect these uneven pillars and joists and beams; we did not install the frayed wiring and the corroded pipes; but they are ours to deal with now, and any further deterioration is in fact on our hands.

Are Humans Lost? A Story: Aliens, Viruses, and Planet Earth

If we have learned anything from Covid, it is that an invisible organism without a brain managed to cause upheaval across the planet and overtake a presumably smarter species because it does not care about color. It does not care about nationality or immigrant status or gender or sexual orientation or national borders or passports. Covid sees all humans for what we actually are: one interconnected and interdependent species. It sees what we have in common if humans don't see it themselves. We are all in this together and it is time we started to act like it.

—**Isabel Wilkerson**, journalist and author,
Occidental College, 2023

CHAPTER 48

How Can We Walk in the Shoes of Others? First, Take Off the Mask

The wise old Greek proverb says, "If a man wears a mask long enough, his face will take on the shape of the mask." As many politicians have become increasingly bold in seeking to impose authoritarianism, and their outlying cultural, religious, and exclusionary ideas, on the rest of us, we witness the opposite of what the word "freedom" actually means. The Founding Fathers did not mean that it gave any minority the right to impose its will on everybody else. The whole point of democracy is to find a balance that respects the rights and the opinions of everybody, whether the 51 percent who voted for the political leaders or the 49 percent who did not.

The real meaning of freedom is the right to apply critical thinking to different versions of the truth, then to think it through and form a well-educated view of one's own. The purpose of education, in high school and college, is not to censor books and burn them as did the Nazis and various other authoritarian dictatorships because they found the opinions in the books unhelpful in imposing their will on everybody else. The role of educators is to teach critical thinking, to

How Can We Walk in the Shoes of Others? First, Take Off the Mask

provide a wide array of thoughtful opinion, and to help their students navigate to their own individual ever-evolving truths. You have to think for yourself, please!

"I don't know." It's a surprisingly difficult thing to say for someone who spends each day providing answers to millions of people on a lot of topics. It's hard to say, and especially in a society that seems to thrive on sharp opinion and absolutisms and shuns nuance.

Nobody wants to be the guy in the back of the room who feels like they are the only one who hasn't figured out the answer. But guess what? Chances are neither have the guys in the front rows. Until we can acknowledge what we don't know, we can't possibly be asking the right questions.

You don't have to be the smartest guy in the room. Your aim should be to be the one asking for more information. The one audacious enough to say: "I don't know."

—**Lester Holt**, Journalist, NBC Nightly News

An elected member of Congress was recently quoted as saying she would rather her adolescent child was dead than transgendered. A Florida charter school caused an uproar in showing Michelangelo's statue David: the school principal had to resign because a loud minority of parents felt that this iconic figure of Renaissance art was pornography. The United States bases its view of the relationship between children and adults on two thousand years of farming culture and common law. The belief quite often has biblical support: that children are chattel, the property of the grown-ups. Thus, they should do what they're told and wear the masks provided, top down, by the parents. In many parts of the United States, to be a gay or transgender adolescent, and to declare yourself to your church, synagogue, mosque, and family, results in you being immediately thrown out, ostracized, homeless, and indigent. In a matter of hours, you lose everything because you dare to assert who you really are inside. This is to me the opposite of freedom.

289

FINDING HAPPY

The governor of Arkansas recently signed a bill into law so that companies there can hire children under the age of sixteen. It will allow fourteen- and fifteen-year-olds to work in meatpacking plants and other dangerous jobs, and sixteen- and seventeen-year-olds to take construction jobs. This coincides with a rise in dangerous child-labor violations. The same hand that seeks to commercially exploit children—often their own children, as well as other people's—as cheap labor does not seem to understand that it takes a village to raise a child. That includes teachers, clergy, and other relatives. Some politicians are increasingly emboldened in believing that the free-lunch program in schools should be greatly cut back, because after all, children going hungry is someone else's problem and not that of the school district. To them, a child who is hungry in the most powerful economy in the world is no longer the responsibility of our joint village.

If parents own their children, they can do with the child whatever they want. They can deny them evidence-based medical care. They can overrule science and experts. They can make them work when they should be learning. They can wall them off from critical thinking and the other important abilities that adults need to learn as teenagers in school: basic skills for adult life. I don't agree. We all are the villagers.

What can you do about any of this? Well, first exert your own freedom to read, watch, meet, observe, and form your own views based on a diversity of input. Don't just read people who agree with you, or watch their videos. Reach out and watch the opposite. Read the reader comments on opposing websites to see the diversity of other opinions. It does not mean that you have to agree with them. Many will be obviously wrong-headed. But in a democracy, we need at least to understand what people with whom we disagree are actually advocating.

In my extensive work with children in foster care for the last twenty-five years, I know full well that in a significant proportion of cases, birth parents and foster parents of these children absolutely do not know what their children need or deserve. The prevalence of abuse or neglect, creating post-traumatic stress disorder (PTSD) in the children driven into foster care, is a national disgrace. Poor parenting goes beyond causing actual damage; it also includes a failure to allow children to thrive by depriving them of unconditional love and not helping

How Can We Walk in the Shoes of Others? First, Take Off the Mask

First Star with the Tottenham Hotspur Soccer Club.

them to achieve whatever is best for them on an individual basis. Parents commit 77 percent of substantiated abuse. In most of the country, the penalties for hitting a pet dog are more restrictive than for a parent hitting their child. "Spare the rod and spoil the child" has been refuted by a vast amount of research, and yet it is taught from the pulpit far too often and carried out by an authoritarian subset of our country that seeks to squash dissent, investigation, and curiosity, and to create rubber-stamp believers. A famous American football player, when arrested for whipping his small child, defended himself by saying, "My daddy whopped me, and it didn't harm me." Well, no sir, it did.

Some claim that a human fetus is a person from conception, and yet their logic is inconsistent: once born, the child's rights greatly diminish and become subjugated to those of the top-down political system. One bulwark of protection for children is our school system and individual caring teachers. But too often, authoritarian parents simply remove their children from school, and by homeschooling them, keep them shielded from any countervailing opinion on truth in the world. I believe that every child has innate rights, just by being born a human being.

Children are the only future that any community and country on the planet can possibly have. We should put our children in first

FINDING HAPPY

position, ensure that their minds are encouraged to grow, give them the fruits of our communal knowledge, of science, of technology, and as they become young adults, allow them to form their own views and to pursue them. Our future in a pluralistic nation of immigrants needs to be inclusive, not run for the benefit of a few old men by corrupt leaders who know they are lying to their base but do it anyway to take more money and keep hold of power. When the leading cable news company pays $800 million in a settlement, and reveals in its legal depositions and discovery that while lying to their viewers, they knew the actual truth on the matters at hand, they have lost the plot as far as the role of news in civilized society, and certainly in any ongoing democracy. Thank God there are other members of the press who are not self-serving and duplicitous. When powerful people lose their moral compass, that's a disaster for all of us. Read all sorts of views! Develop your own through questioning everything.

Chapter Takeaways and Reflection Questions for You

- As a child and young adult, when have you felt you were treated as having rights, and when as the property of someone else?
- If you grew up in a family and were then removed to foster care, did that make things better, or just different?
- Is it the case that beyond preventing abuse and neglect from recurring, the other purpose of the foster-care system ought to be encouragement and unconditional love, so that every young soul can find his or her path and thrive towards happiness?
- Is that what the system does?
- Is it OK to have strong political views? (Yes, so long as you research a wide range of views before locking yourself into one direction.) And please continue to read, talk to, and study those who don't agree with you. They can't all be completely wrong. Be open to changing your views. You are young!

CHAPTER 49

Why Care about Democracy?
Why Should We All Fight for It?

Freedom of speech and other true elements of democracy are being questioned and limited all over the world. Whether this means diminishing the truth with false balance or using our personal data to influence our democratic elections, the rule of law as well as freedom of expression and the media need active defending. The swollen amount of inequality and a lack of social mobility are challenging our ideas about everyone having the same possibilities and freedoms in life.

All of these questions are battles of values. And we all must take a side in that battle. There is no middle ground.

—**Sanna Marin**, Prime Minister of Finland, 2023

There is an old Chinese curse, "May you live in interesting times." You may have noticed that the country seems to be splitting itself in two. The valuable conservative right is moving further to the hard right, and into deep, dangerous, and uncharted waters. Not just because they lost so many elections. Not just because so many of their

FINDING HAPPY

elected officials and media personalities knowingly say the opposite of what they know to be the truth. No, the reason is that the hard right wing who now shout loudest among our conservatives have moved so far over the cliff of the extreme that you can no longer see them from the rest of the planet. And on top of that, they refuse to compromise at all. There is no shame: they are absolutely transparent, and say exactly what they want you to hear.

Look at some of the nutty ideas now becoming mainstream in a great American political party: the voices elected to power who repeatedly trumpet the existence of "legitimate rape" and the firm belief that God wants the victims of rape to bear its children. We now see these same forthright tall white men willing to raise taxes on 98 percent of the population, because they won't raise them by 4 percent on people who earn more than a million dollars a year. We should be grateful that they don't conceal how truly misguided they are to win votes. Theirs is double-talk dressed up in slick media that rivals the satire of George Orwell's novel *1984*.

We have to hope that the majority of Americans will grasp the full extent of myopia and self-serving wrong-headedness among those who now cow a previously grand old party. I for one believe strongly in the two-party system. I hope the moderates there survive and thrive. Democracy needs them to participate. With an electorate whose opinions are split and all over the opinion map, we need a legislature that conveys all of their views to government and which then rules from consensus in the center. Plus or minus, that's how grown-up democracies do it around the world, and it is how ours once did too, until entertainment "news" in our media, based on dead-end extremism and fear intended to sell more advertising, made compromise into a pejorative instead of the fundamental underpinning of any functional form of representative government.

And please be critical of the left too. Apply critical thinking there. Who are these people on college campuses marching and screaming against others because of their religion or race? Why do so many of those shouting not know the history and truth about their hated targets? This is dangerous territory. For example, how can half of Gen Z and Millennials know nothing about the Holocaust? What do you

Why Care about Democracy? Why Should We All Fight for It?

know about it? Remember George Santayana: "Those who cannot learn from history are doomed to repeat it. Those who do not remember their past are condemned to repeat their mistakes. Those who do not read history are doomed to repeat it. Those who fail to learn from the mistakes of their predecessors are destined to repeat them." Find out! Think! Don't just follow charismatic leaders offering easy solutions to complex problems.

We have the same loud finger-pointers on the selfsame day suggesting that we put more guns into our kindergartens, elementary schools, and every other kind of school in America—this, despite the fact that armed guards engage with, but mostly cannot stop, the teenage mass murderers before they kill. We hear their anti-immigration argument loud and clear, in all its strident illogic, from the same people who have forgotten they themselves are descended from immigrants: the British, the Irish, the Italians, and the rest who fled persecution and famine. They seriously believe immigrants steal American jobs and leech off society. They think immigrants don't pay taxes and that if we just rounded them all up and sent them home, or if we made things so tough and scary that they voluntarily left, our economy would benefit. The science says no. Farmers say no. High tech says no. Seek the truth before you blame others because they look or act different.

Look out of the window. As previously mentioned, immigrants not only made this nation, but they continue to make it function. Immigrants who are undocumented pay sales tax, property tax, excise tax, and if they work under someone else's Social Security number as is often the case, they pay into the system without any benefit in return. And more than the taxes they pay, they greatly uplift consumer demand for goods and services: these are people who live here, spending money to do so. For exactly the same reason economists pray for a healthy retail Christmas, we should want as many people as possible to contribute to the economy. These are among them. Furthermore, first generation undocumented aliens take the millions of menial jobs that Americans reject: ask the farmers how easy it is to get their crops harvested now that recent ICE crackdowns have scared away their traditional workers. The most powerful lobbyists in Washington, DC, argue for *more* immigration: they work for huge industrial agriculture companies.

FINDING HAPPY

I was invited to a conference at the Breakers Hotel in West Palm Beach. It was a gathering of some of America's wealthiest families, organized by their family offices, the folks hired to manage family fortunes of $50 to $100 million and up. Way up. This was a meeting of that top 1 percent everyone talks about. I had many meetings, and I had great admiration for many of those I met. Most of them had decided their legacy should be to lift up the world. One striking observation was that most of them were self-made—they or their parents had arrived in America with nothing, but a mere one or two generations later, here they were at the Breakers.

One principal challenge discussed was called The G3 Issue. This was not about how to share use of the family jet. It was precisely what to do about flaky grandchildren. The shared story I heard several times was like this: Grandpa and Grandma came over from the old country. By working incredibly hard, eighty hours a week for decades, they built one hardware store into a chain of stores, then sent their kids to college, where they qualified as lawyers, doctors, or MBA-clad businesspeople. Those kids saw firsthand the meaning of hard work, and they used it to build their own lives, often in the family business. These businesses and the families that owned them had acquired enormous wealth.

G3 refers to the third generation: the kids of the kids. Too often, I heard, they had major personality challenges, contributing little to family or society and often facing lives of substance abuse, failed relationships, and sometimes worse. Educated and privileged, they were too often squandering their birthrights, to the dismay of their parents and grandparents. What to do?

My own contribution was to suggest that the grandchildren be drawn into community service by taking meaningful roles in managing the family philanthropy and expanding it. If I was able to benefit thirty teenage foster children by taking them to serve lunch to the homeless on Skid Row, surely these families could expose their grandkids to the realities of life by demonstrating poverty and deprivation, creating a win-win both for society and their teenagers. It was gratifying, and I am still working happily in exactly this way with several of those families.

Why Care about Democracy? Why Should We All Fight for It?

First- and second-generation immigrants built this country, and they continue to fuel it now. Our world of mega-rewards has not yet swamped their work ethic and productivity. As one eye-opening example of this, look at the Patels. These families of devout, vegetarian, Gujarati Hindu farmers came to the US in the 1960s and 1970s. They worked at first in menial jobs, often cleaning rooms in our hotels and motels, but saved up and bought undervalued and dilapidated hotel properties, then turned them into thriving businesses. The people of Indian origin now own 60 percent of mid-sized motels and hotel properties, all over the nation. Of them, nearly one-third have the surname Patel. When we talk about the American Dream, ask the Patels: they have actually dreamed that dream, and built those lives. And yes, they, too, are now experiencing their share of the G3 problem. In the UK, it is the Gujarati Patels who own the corner stores, the ones that stay open until midnight and open again at 7 a.m., seven days a week.

The Census Bureau tells us that the US population has inched higher for the first time in years, now approaching 336,000,000. But this is not because there are more babies born than people dying. No, the natural growth rate had fallen to a level not seen since the 1930s. Our population this year only grew because of immigration. Without immigrants arriving, it actually would have shrunk. And a shrinking workforce and consumer base would have diminished GNP and led to further economic decline.

So, to those immigrants who arrived this year, I say, "Thank you for coming! We welcome and cherish your contributions to our economy. Please ignore the right-wing nut jobs who want to send you away. There are really not that many of them—they are just loud. Don't watch Fox News. It will upset you, as it upsets us. Happy Hanukkah, Kwanza, Christmas, and Diwali. Come one. Come all. Together we will build a better America."

Cleaning the statue of Japanese Consul-General Sugihara, who saved thousands of refugees from the Nazis, because his heart was moved. Look him up.

Chapter Takeaways and Reflection Questions for You

- What is critical thinking? Where did you get yours? Did you just inherit it?
- Don't take anything at face value. If your teacher is TikTok, the algorithm will only feed you stuff that repeats what you already think. That does not help critical thinking.
- What is the value of democracy? (Clue: The least bad solution to serve all our citizens.)
- Where are your ancestors from? How do you keep your ancestral culture alive?
- Can you be fully American as well as honoring where your people came from and what they brought with them?
- How important is it to vote? (Clue: Very, very, very important. Just. Do. It!)

Why Care about Democracy? Why Should We All Fight for It?

- How important is democracy? (Clue: The only system where the voters can change their minds!)
- How can you help keep democracy alive? (Clue: Volunteer for a campaign. Get out the vote!)
- Who should scare us the most if they get elected? (Clue: Those who despise free democracy and will abolish elections at their first opportunity. That's fascism and communism both. It's an evil ratchet.)

CHAPTER 50

How Can You Make a Difference?
The Meaning of Life, Part Two

"*Tikkun olam*" in Hebrew means "to heal the world." It is a philosophy of living that Jews are taught from the age of twelve and a half: you define the value of your life by whether you lift up your world, or whether you drag it down. The older I get, the more I realize that the greatest joy I've had, and what I really value in looking back, is through *tikkun olam*: quietly building a worthwhile legacy, trying to make a mark by helping others. These are the people you've raised, your children, your grandchildren, and all of the other people you have lifted up. And in creating worthwhile things that outlast you: for me, two and a half dozen films, some that mean something, a few of them at least good. These things endure. Is it enough? No, never. We push on.

The skills of a career film producer are intrinsically entrepreneurial. You're always doing new things and applying skills you've honed elsewhere. You apply pattern recognition to a whole new problem. You can take those skills and that toolkit sideways to address unmet needs in society and do something about them.

Think of how a film happens. You have to first judge the idea. Does this seem right? Is this going to work? Will people be open to this?

300

How Can You Make a Difference? The Meaning of Life, Part Two

Will they want to help? And then, if you think the idea is worth eighteen months of your life, you ask the planning questions: Where's the money coming from? Who's directing it? Where do we need an office? How do we do this? Whom do we go to for help and partnership? Who will distribute? And in the end: Was it any good? How do we measure success?

It's the same toolkit to dare to create a new social solution to an old social challenge. And that's the other thing about making films: you're always making a new film. So that's what I've done: "Starlight, starbright, first star I see tonight..."

Chaos Theory teaches us that all systems in the universe, if left unmanaged, eventually decay into random nothingness. If that is true, then the quest for civilization is a never-ending one: if we wish to bequeath something honorable, helpful, and loving to our children's children's children, we had better pay attention to the systems within our society that keep it afloat. Passive inactivity is a recipe for decay and atrophy. It really is not an option to sit on one's hands.

It seems to me that there are gigantic opportunities for people who thrive in business to apply the selfsame skills to righting some of the wrongs around us. Through a self-invented "entrepreneurial philanthropy," I have tried to focus on the grievous challenges of seriously ill children, of those kids who are abused and neglected, and of our urban homeless. It makes no sense to me that in this, the greatest civilization the world has ever put forth, we so often systematically marginalize our children and other people's children, even though they are our only future. The dark side of the "can do" of the American Dream is to try to fix things after they have broken rather than preventing them from breaking in the first place.

And if half of all foster children are homeless within two years of aging out of the system, wouldn't it be a lot less expensive to use college to get them into productive careers, rather than society paying for the rest of their lives? So why do only 9 percent of foster kids get a college education? Whose fault is that, and how do we fix it? First Star dares to suggest we can. Our alumni show it is true.

There is so much we can productively do by using our resources of intellect, entrepreneurship, and a sense that anything is possible if one

FINDING HAPPY

breaks it down into bite-sized chunks. And, yes, it often takes money, as well. Can we be more ambitious, please? Can we really not do better for homeless people sleeping rough amongst us than to give them the cardboard box our Sub-Zero refrigerator came in? Why?

Some of the most exciting things I have ever done have been through collaborations with like-minded people in philanthropy. An entrepreneur can helpfully exert his or her lateral thinking to serve the planet, not just to take from it. It's really no use to curse the gathering darkness—much better to light a few bright candles.

There is a poem by Percy Bysshe Shelley called "Ozymandias" about a gigantic crumbled statue in the desert. Erected by a long-forgotten emperor, only the legs still stand. "Look upon my works, ye Mighty, and despair!" reads the inscription carved on the base. That's all that's left! As Teilhard de Chardin wrote, "The task before us now, if we would not perish, is to build the Earth." If we want our lives to amount to anything worth remembering, should we not pay attention to the true and lasting value of our legacy—and have some wonderful excitement while doing so?

Early on Thursday morning, September 15, 2001, four days after an act of war on our country, I wrote this from my room at the Marriott in Tysons Corner, Washington, DC, as I watched in horror a huge black cloud of smoke rising from the Pentagon:

First Star, some thoughts...We will have our Board meeting this morning, and our three other meetings. And we will do so stubbornly, with resolve, with renewed dedication to what we hold dear and with absolute determination to push forward with our whole vital First Star agenda. Because these recent atrocities reaffirm our belief that the margin between evil and good is thin indeed. That the line between civilization and chaos is fragile. That we, every one of us, have to pick up our civilization and carry it forward on our backs if necessary. And clearly, it is necessary. We must each choose to be part of our social solutions, lest we add to our challenges and problems. We have no middle choice; we either nurture our civilization, or like every other natural system, by the immutable laws of physics it will decay into chaos.

We are privileged to work for all our children in First Star, children whose needs are the apex, the summit, the quintessence of all that we prize and seek to nurture. Because kids are our future. They are our aspiration and our motivation to improve this civilization. They represent hope itself. We shall not fail them.

I wrote that, then drove to the First Star board meeting at the Verner, Liipfert law firm. We began on time, focused, sad, stubbornly productive, in a meeting that was for each of us hugely moving. Then I drove across the country in an Avis rental car from Washington to Los Angeles...2,660 miles in 41 hours, sharing the driving with colleagues Richard Hull and Tyler Spring. Then I wrote this:

It has been a remarkable couple of days. Days of awe. I have seen hundreds of thousands of American flags, maybe millions, hanging from houses, tractors, truck stops, offices and a hayrick...between Roanoke, Knoxville, Little Rock, Oklahoma City, Amarillo, Albuquerque, Flagstaff, Barstow and San Bernardino. Every one of them at half-mast. I saw a young girl all on her own waving a tiny home-made flag from an overpass in Arizona and all the cars and trucks sounded their horns and we saluted her and us and this country and its terrible but awakening tragedy.

I spoke to friends, family and colleagues all around the world from my cell phone. I learned that on the set of our film 'The Gathering,' in the village of Northleach in Gloucestershire, England, cast and crew felt the shared grief and shock. There was a one minute silence across Europe. At the Changing of the Guard outside Buckingham Palace in London, the Queen personally ordered that the band replace God Save the Queen with The Star Spangled Banner. The French newspaper Le Monde had the headline on September 12th "Nous Sommes Tous Américains—We Are All Americans." Europeans thanked God their American cousins would now be part of the solution to a scourge they have lived with for years.

I spoke to a friend who cried when he told me he had lost friends in the Pentagon. I spoke to those dealing with expanding pools of grief from the New York murders...two degrees of separation; you either knew a victim or someone else who did. And I heard in my Washington calls already the Phoenix-like rising of that American genius, the resilience, the moral leadership, the stubborn fix-it-ness, the coming together of the world's greatest quarrelsome family yet again in face of common adversity. I found again over the cell-phone the absolute, stubborn American certainty that We Shall Overcome, the vital belief in our ability to change, to steer, to improve and to reach lofty goals that brought me to America twenty-six years earlier, because I loved it and needed to be a part of it.

And in the Avis car in the dead of night on Interstate 40, I realized that here—paradoxically amid carnage and devastation—there was dignity, resolve, power and determination. Barely two days after the attacks, we had sat with Representative Loretta Sanchez in her Congressional office to discuss policy that would better help abused and neglected children. The meeting was not cancelled. Our focus was on concrete ways to help kids, not on the devastation. And we hugged.

With that steely-eyed American resolve, those fighting to improve civilization do not flinch from the forces of chaos; they just push forward harder. And in a million ways like this, the outcomes of tragedy will be positive: out of the ashes will inevitably rise a better America and a better world. Hineini...Here I am.

Chapter Takeaways and Reflection Questions for You

- Do you know someone who remembers 9/11? Where were they? How did they experience it? Ask them what it meant to them.
- The saying goes, "It is always darkest before the dawn." Those days were very dark. We did not know if this was Pearl Harbor II...or was it the beginning of World War III? What have these two-plus decades since accomplished, for you and for America?
- What is good, and what is unfinished business, in the American Way?
- How can you help?
- How can you make your life count in the arc of humanity? What will be your role?
- How can you make a difference?
- No other question you can answer is more important.

CHAPTER 51

How Can You Bend the Arc of History?
How Can You Contribute?

There was a time, and it feels like decades ago, that the way Joe Public tried to influence the course of anything he cared about in the world around him was to write a letter to the editor, which usually wasn't published—or in the case of the very most active, to write the letter to his relevant member of Congress, where one assumes it was read, if at all, by a very junior person and became part of some dry tally.

But that was then, and this is now.

Something magical has happened to our smarter citizens, and it may well be the salvation of our democracy: they bought phones with digital video cameras in them and, not surprisingly, started pointing them at things that bothered them. And then they learned how to edit the videos, put them together with a piece of music, and then (shocking thought for those of previous generations) they got a very large number of strangers to pay a whole lot of attention to them online. The leverage is breathtaking, exciting, overall optimistic, and positive. The exogenous brain, the anthill of life! Would the Black Lives Matter movement have begun if one young woman had not lifted her phone to

306

capture the murder of George Floyd by a police officer while his colleagues failed to intervene?

Social media in the hands of you, our future leaders, is a rising tsunami that is changing America, changing the world, and making both a whole lot better. Our next generation is no longer shouting in a frustrating wilderness of press and social inertia. When Paddy Chayefsky and Sidney Lumet wanted to show angry citizens in their 1976 film *Network,* they had Peter Finch as the TV anchor urge them to open their windows and shout out, "I'm mad as hell and I'm not going to take it anymore." But nowadays, your window opens directly in and out of every other apartment and dorm room, and it's always ready, in your pocket.

These are much more than individual shout-outs; they are a whole new wave of assertion that is harnessing the internet to get into people's faces and change minds. What is democratic genius? How do you really change society? Take your phone out of your pocket and express your anger, your frustration—speak your truth. Blaze a shining path!

When I first sat decades ago on the Foundation Committee of the Academy of Motion Picture Arts and Sciences—the bit that gives grants to universities to fund internships in film—there was a common pattern in college admissions to study film: hardly anyone applying had actually *made* a film. They had written scripts; but the whole deal of making a short film with sound, a cast, equipment, Kodak film, editing, and whatnot was financially beyond anyone except those few who had families like Steven Spielberg's that would buy all those expensive necessities. But these days, there's hardly an eighteen-year-old arriving in college to study film who hasn't already made not one but several short films. They might be good, they might be bad, but the barriers to entry have gone down near what was once the cost of paper and a typewriter (remember them?).

Once upon a time, a person came to a village, stood on a rock, gathered a crowd, told them a story, or told them about the world. Then we invented moveable type and the printing press and started writing letters to the editor to express outrage. But forget all that, forget those old-people's megaphones. Wimpy, restricted, run top-down, and often-times with old-people gatekeepers restricting the flow of opinion. Our young adults have done a neat arabesque. They jumped straight over the top of that logjam. They are the future of self-expression, and the world will be better for their video citizenship. Use yours, please, to make a positive difference!

It's been truly amazing to see how your generation has rebelled against every bad habit of mine and every generation that came before me. Everything that we let calcify, you have kicked against and demolished. You've rejected that whole 24/7, no-days-off grind. You've rejected apathy. You've rejected ignoring your mental health because "you've gotta muscle through it no matter what." You've rejected alienation and cruelty. You've rejected not trying to include everyone. And you've rejected not looking out for each other.

And those are hard things to reject. Because accepting them sometimes makes life way easier. If you just shut off yourself from the world, life is way easier. It's also way less colorful, way less complicated, way less nourishing, and way less memorable.

—**Patton Oswalt**, actor and comedian,
William & Mary College

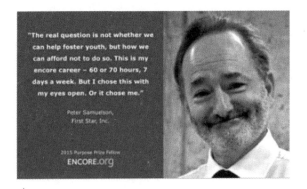

How Can You Bend the Arc of History? How Can You Contribute?

Chapter Takeaways and Reflection Questions for You

- What drives you crazy? How can you shine your light on it?
- How can you use social media to make real-world change?
- How do you win hearts and minds with media? (Clue: Move their hearts first. Empathy drives sympathy and a willingness to help move the obstacles.) Tell stories, well!

Senator Dianne Feinstein, RIP—September 29, 2023, age 90.

CHAPTER 52

What Will Be Your Place in the Universe?
The Meaning of Life, Part Three

Find your meaning and your own truth. This is the true joy in life, being used for a purpose recognized by yourself as a mighty one. Being a force of nature instead of a feverish, selfish little clod of ailments and grievances, complaining that the world will not devote itself to making you happy. I am of the opinion that my life belongs to the whole community and as long as I live, it is my privilege to do for it what I can. I want to be thoroughly used up when I die, for the harder I work, the more I live. I rejoice in life for its own sake. Life is no brief candle to me. It is a sort of splendid torch which I have got hold of for the moment and I want to make it burn as brightly as possible before handing it on to future generations.

—**George Bernard Shaw**

Chapter Takeaways and Reflection Questions for You

- What is your goal?
- What is your plan to get there?
- What are the steps on your path?
- Write it down. Rewrite it. Do it. Amazing how you can understand better when it is written down.
- Keep a daily journal.
- Wellness habits can help one deal with stress and support general resilience. Experiment with solutions!
- Meditation works best for people who are relatively mentally healthy, and can be problematic for people who are struggling with anxiety, depression, attentional issues (ADHD), or a thought disorder (psychosis). Meditation can be triggering or frustrating for those young people who struggle to meditate.
- Non-screen activities that help you relax are really important for general well-being. Mindfulness practices and breathing exercises can be easy to follow!
- Learn to swim! Great fun and perhaps it will save your life or that of someone else.
- Learn CPR. Learn how to help someone choking. Be a hero! The Red Cross and YMCA have courses.
- Volunteer! Where will you meet the Life Force and make the world a better place? Where will you make friends who care about the same things? Where will you make your mark and lift up your soul? Volunteering!

I wish you light, love, and happiness: Go For It!

—**Peter Samuelson**, Los Angeles, 2025.

Look up at the sky, the clouds, beyond the sun, the moon, the stars, when you need to recharge your spirit. Let the gravity of Earth give you a warm hug. Look up and remember what inspires you, what you were doing this for and why you cared in the first place.

—**Mae Jemison**, Astronaut, University of Delaware 2023

FINDING HAPPY

*And now here is my secret, a very simple secret:
It is only with the heart that one can see rightly;
what is essential is invisible to the eye.*

—**Antoine de Saint-Exupéry**, *The Little Prince*

Acknowledgments

Maimonides said that the upper level of the human soul is a membership club of those who feel strongly their obligation to lift up the world and to leave it better than they found it. My greatest gratitude is to have been allowed to bring my crazy ideas into the club, and to have so many other club members collaborate to pilot and deliver them. I could not have created new solutions to old problems without them pushing the boulder up the hill right next to me.

My agent, Jeff Silberman at Folio, kept me writing while I had no clue if the book would find a great publisher. We found several, and Regalo, distributed by Simon & Schuster, was the best one. Gretchen Young at Regalo is not only my publisher, but it is a huge honor that she personally has been my editor as well. Thank you. Madeline Sturgeon and Robert Bidinotto have contributed vast amounts of expert work in copyediting.

Shari Goldstein, my friend, colleague, and an eminent psychologist, was incredibly generous with her time in making sure I was fully sensitive to the vital young souls I dare to seek to help. She shared her profound knowledge regarding young adult mental health and its challenges. John Schimmel, previously story editor at Warner Brothers, then partner to Michael Douglas, now professor at the University of California, has been my dear friend for thirty years and leaned in with his considerable editing skills to prevent me from embarrassing myself. (I hope.) Robin Winston León, chief operating officer of First Star, has been my brilliant, steady hand in collaborating over so many exciting philanthropic adventures. Her input to this book has made it much better. Jennyann Gallo, who runs the First Star Alumni Program, has helped me immeasurably, to create the research framework needed for a book like this. The best executive I ever hired is the brilliant Lyndsey Collins Wilson, CEO of First Star USA. Her fingerprints are all over what is so successful in our high-achieving charity. Go team!

Desmond Douglas has brought his authentic voice of wisdom and personal experience to the chapter on staying alive as a young Black man in America. I am humbled and deeply grateful.

Reverend Kelly Brown Douglas, interim president of Episcopal Divinity School and canon theologian of Washington National Cathedral, gave me crucially important guidance on how to make helpful, and not on my part presumptuous, "The Talk," about which unfortunately she knows too much. And she told me the chapter was too important to omit. And then she introduced me to her son. No greater love. Thank you.

The vivid experience of hosting Sean and his mum, Brenda, in my Los Angeles apartment began because my cousin Emma Samms invited them when she met Sean in the hospital in London. And that trip inspired the charity Starlight. The process of Starlight's wish-granting was invented by the late, great Jacqueline Carlish in 1984. Howard Davine agreed to take over as president in 1997, which freed me up to launch First Star. My then girlfriend, now wife, Saryl, ran the accounts of Starlight, and when the lawyer asked what I wanted to call it, it was Saryl who replied, "You know that children's rhyme, 'Starlight, starbright, first star I see tonight...?' Why don't we call it the Starlight Children's Foundation?" Thus unleashing the naming of three charities. Richard Stellar, the Jewish Mountain Man, has loyally volunteered alongside me from Starlight to EDAR.

Henry Fields has been my friend, mentor, guru, and legal eagle from Starlight, through Starbright, First Star, EDAR, and all the way to PhilmCo. Diane Nabatoff encouraged me to review my text as though the young adults of First Star were constantly over my shoulder. Rachel Osborne must be the world's best copyeditor!

Acknowledgments

Dr. Debbie Heiser, founder of The Mentor Project, has herself mentored me artfully through the alien land of creating a book and aligning it with a publisher. Debbie has made me realize that lateral mentoring is a powerful uplift for any of us. I am a better mentor, writer, and friend because of her sage advice.

Starbright began as a mind-meld with Steven Spielberg, quite certainly the greatest creative thinker I've ever known. And the late, great General Norman Schwarzkopf did more than fundraise for Starbright.... I learned so much from him about leadership as an art and a science. David Haspel has been my great collaborator through so much heavy lifting in matters philanthropic. A wise owl always whenever I needed one, and a close friend.

First Star was a charity advocating for foster kids until Professor Kathleen Reardon wrote a book that asked the question, "If only 9 percent of foster kids go to college, what would happen if we housed, educated, and encouraged them on college campuses for the four years of high school? Wouldn't a lot more want to go to college, and be ready to do so?" Chancellor Gene Block at UCLA is the man in the room who said yes to the pilot of the First Star Academies. Vice Chancellor Janina Montero got me that meeting. And Suzanne Seplow got me the meeting with Janina! It takes a village.

An unhoused old lady living in a cardboard box off of Santa Monica Boulevard made me think that there had to be something better—leading to EDAR. President Richard Koshalek at the Pasadena Art Center College of Design took EDAR seriously and allowed me to sponsor the design competition.

Bob Relyea, the partner of Steve McQueen, gave me my shot to work on *Le Mans*. Tony Busching is the producer who invited me to come to Los Angeles, invited me to stay with his family, and lent me a car. Blake Edwards is the man who made me the production manager on *The Return of the Pink Panther*, a huge promotion. Jonathan Prince has been my friend and partner for eons in so many media projects. Yin to my yang. My brother Marc Samuelson was my partner for several years and on the fine films we made together. When we had a particularly good day, he would bring me back to earth by memorably saying, "Yes, it hasn't gone wrong yet."

FINDING HAPPY

Beyond anyone ever, my wife, Saryl, and my four children, David, Pamela, Jeffrey, and Rebecca, have provided me the unconditional love without which no entrepreneur could ever dare to do. Saryl has made many adventures possible with her pithy, wholehearted love, support, and encouragement. The fingerprints of her smart and unconditional collaboration are on most everything worthwhile I have ever done. And ah, my children, Becca, Jeff, Pamela, and David! Go Team Samuelson. Your ball. Sorry about the dancing and the puns.

These are my personal memories and recollections. All errors and mistakes are mine alone. This book expresses my personal views and opinions. They do not necessarily reflect those of any of the charities to which I have volunteered nor those of the companies and individuals with which I have worked or consulted.

About the Author

Co-founder and president of First Star (seventeen high school academies on college campuses for youth in foster care) and CEO of PhilmCo Media llc. (commercial films that use empathy to improve society), Peter Samuelson is a serial pro-social entrepreneur. In 1982, he co-founded the Starlight Children's Foundation (psychosocial services for seriously ill children). By 1990, the positive impact of Starlight seeded his next pro-social endeavor, Starbright World (the world's first avatar-based navigable social network for seriously ill teenagers), co-founded with Steven Spielberg. Following that, 1999 saw the formation of First Star; 2005 the founding of EDAR, the Everyone Deserves a Roof initiative (single-user mobile homeless shelters); and 2013 the launch of ASPIRE, the Academy for Social Purpose in Responsible Entertainment (media training for undergraduates not in film schools). In the midst of all this, Samuelson has produced twenty-seven films and raised four children. Educated at Cambridge and the Anderson School of Management at UCLA, he has been married to Saryl for thirty-five years, and continues to fight every day for those less fortunate, chief among them America's abused and neglected children.

First in his family to attend college, Samuelson graduated from Cambridge on a full scholarship with a Masters in English Literature. After serving as production manager on films such as *The Return of the Pink Panther*, he emigrated from England to Los Angeles and produced

FINDING HAPPY

Revenge of the Nerds, Tom & Viv, Wilde, Arlington Road, and twenty-three other films. Samuelson served on the three-person founding board of Participant Media, Jeff Skoll's pro-social media company, which produced *An Inconvenient Truth, The Help, Spotlight,* and *Green Book.* From 2012 to 2013, Samuelson was the founding managing director of the Media Institute for Social Change at the University of Southern California.

Samuelson divides his time between producing films and serving pro bono as cofounder of the Starlight Children's Foundation (www.starlight.org) with Steven Spielberg and founder and serving president of First Star (http://www.firststar.org/) and the Everyone Deserves a Roof initiative of Los Angeles (www.edar.org). He holds U.S. Patent No. 10,227,791 for a Single User Mobile Homeless Shelter. Samuelson lives in Los Angeles. Learn more at: www.samuelson.la.